I0824503

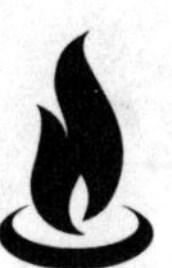

Opera Wars

Inside the World of Opera and the Battles for Its Future

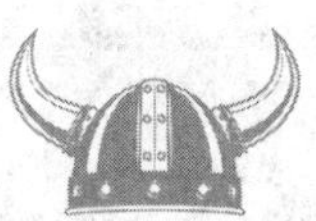

CAITLIN VINCENT

SCRIBNER

New York Amsterdam/Antwerp London
Toronto Sydney/Melbourne New Delhi

Scribner
An Imprint of Simon & Schuster, LLC
1230 Avenue of the Americas
New York, NY 10020

First Scribner hardcover edition January 2026

Interior design by Kyle Kabel

Manufactured in the United States of America

1 3 5 7 9 10 8 6 4 2

Library of Congress Cataloging-in-Publication Data is available.

ISBN 978-1-6680-8406-9
ISBN 978-1-6680-8408-3 (ebook)

For my mom, Sharon,
who helped me pursue singing but also made sure
I was prepared for what came after.

Contents

Note for the Reader

A glossary of opera terms appears at the back of this book. It can be a helpful resource for those who are just learning about the art form.

Introduction

Opera breeds fanatics.

People travel the world just to see different productions of Richard Wagner's four-opera *Ring Cycle*. They cosplay as operatic characters when attending performances. They own dozens of recordings of the same opera and can cite every single variation between them. There are opera groupies. Opera diehards. Opera obsessives.

I'm not one of them.

Don't get me wrong—I can rattle off the names of operas and their long-dead composers. I can talk snidely about stage directors, tout opinions about this or that production, and nod knowingly whenever I hear an excerpt from an opera in a pasta-sauce commercial. But I'm no fanatic. I'm not sure I'm even a fan.

I was once asked if I actually liked opera. It was an online comment, made in response to a short article I'd written about the opera industry for *The Conversation*. Opera companies face a major challenge in the twenty-first century, I wrote, because of disagreements about what to do with historical operas that are anachronistic to a fault, that are—let's be frank—a little racist.

From my perspective, the article was simply making an observation about the field, a kind of sympathetic *Sucks to be you* waved in the general vicinity of opera companies everywhere. But the article was unexpectedly controversial, and I found myself dodging lava flows of comments erupting across social media. Some commenters labeled me a snowflake, others the PC police, others a Nazi. One suggested I reread George Orwell until I understood him.

Then I came across a comment that gave me pause. *But does the author actually like opera?*

I decided to reply—trolls be damned—and outlined my credentials: a master's degree in vocal performance, a decade working as a professional opera singer, five years running a small opera company, an active career as an opera librettist and lyricist. I posted my response and sat back with a certain smugness. A few minutes later, there was another comment. *Fine, but it doesn't answer the question.* To my dismay, he was absolutely right.

I've dedicated most of my life to opera—singing it, producing it, writing it, researching it. For nearly two decades, the core of my identity was wholly wrapped up in the art form. My teenage years were spent taking voice lessons and listening to opera recordings. My college applications were aimed at the universities offering the best opera programs or boasting the best voice teachers. My twenties were spent performing in operas, auditioning for operas, and starting my own opera company. I was an opera singer. My friends were all opera singers. I even married an opera singer.

Fast-forward to the present, and I now firmly describe myself as a *former* singer—and only feel a slight twinge when I say it. But I still have a closet full of audition dresses, three boxes of opera scores gathering dust in the garage, and an absurdly large collection of scarves (the default singer accessory). I'm also still inescapably an opera insider: on a daily basis I work on writing new operas with composers, even as I research the intricacies of the opera industry in my academic day job.

But does the author actually like opera? Years later, I'm still not sure how to answer.

Opera offers so much to love, so much to inspire fierce devotion. There's the music, the way a singer's voice can soar above an orchestra and make the hairs on your arms lift up. There's the spectacle, the visual delight of extravagant costumes and over-the-top sets that magically materialize within the confines of a stage. There's the way the stories tap into the messy realities of human emotion, of words that were written three hundred years ago somehow prodding directly at the memory of your own first love or deeply felt trauma.

But opera also teems with issues. It's big and expensive. Old-fashioned. Exploitative. It's an art form saddled with centuries of artistic baggage and internal turmoil—a pursuit involving both navel-gazing and clinging to the past in ways that can exclude and alienate audiences and performers.

Weighing it all up, I'd have to say that I do like opera. I *love* opera. But I also hate it. Because I want opera to be an art form that belongs in the twenty-first century, and I continually see it falling short. I want to save opera. The question is, from what exactly? From its history? Its audiences? Its companies? All of the above? Or maybe, most of all, opera needs to be saved from itself. Because at its core, opera is a reflection of *us*, of our dysfunction and angsty development as a society over the past four centuries. Opera has traveled the same journey as we have, alternately shaping and being shaped by our culture since long before electricity or indoor plumbing. Even today, opera permeates our lives.

Think of the hundreds of commercials with operatic soundtracks—ads for cars, deodorants, beers, detergents, condoms—all drawing on a particular message about what opera means and who it's for. Think of Bugs Bunny wearing a horned helmet while Elmer Fudd sings "Kill the wabbit! Kill the wabbit!" Or the music pumping out of the helicopter speakers in *Apocalypse Now* (1979) as the squadron approaches its target in Vietnam. Think of the James Bond movie *Quantum of Solace* (2008), in which the villains plot via headsets during a performance of Puccini's opera *Tosca* until Bond smoothly interrupts with "I really think you people should find a better place to meet." Think of the first season of the Netflix series *Bridgerton* (2020), in which the rakish Anthony Bridgerton has an illicit affair with an opera singer. Think of socialites Paris Hilton and Nicole Richie deciding to write their own opera in the television special *Paris & Nicole: The Encore* (2024). Think of the classic wedding march "Here Comes the Bride," which was first heard in Wagner's opera *Lohengrin*.

Even if you think you don't know opera—have never been to an opera and have no interest in seeing an opera—you still know opera. At least one facet of it. But there's so much more to the story than the stereotypes of overweight women in metal breastplates or "rich people" audiences who may or may not be Bond villains. And if we take opera off the pedestal where it usually sits, we have a chance to see it for what it actually is: an art form of contradictions and complexities that is somehow just as fascinating as it is unmanageable. An art form whose death has repeatedly been predicted but that stubbornly refuses to die. An art form that shows us, as a society, exactly where we've come from—even when we don't care to look.

So, consider this book a quest—if not a rescue attempt—whose first step is kicking away the pedestal and shining a spotlight on the reality of opera as it exists today. From battles over tradition, to tensions over casting, to conflicts over funding, we'll scrape away all the clichés and presumptions, all the superficial glamour and seeming snobbery, until we can finally gaze at the true beating heart of this hot mess of an art form.

By the end of this book, we may face divisions that are just as deep and broad as when we started. We may still love opera, hate opera, or love-hate opera just as we always have. But at least we'll know it better. At least we'll have freed it, if only temporarily, from the constraints of its reputation. And maybe . . . just maybe, we'll have found a different path forward.

The orchestra tunes. The lights dim. Time to raise the curtain.

CHAPTER I

The History

— or —

Setting the Scene

And God said, let there be opera: and there was opera.

The year is 1600. A time of plague, codpieces, and poor dental hygiene. The Globe Theatre has just opened in London with a new play by William Shakespeare. The letter *J* is about to be added to the English alphabet. And twenty-five-year-old Marie de' Medici has just married King Henry IV of France in Florence, Italy.

It's Henry's second marriage—arranged primarily as a financial alliance—with Marie's dowry earmarked to cover the mountains of debt accrued during Henry's recent war against Spain. Awkwardly, the groom isn't at his own wedding, choosing instead to send the Duke of Bellegarde to marry Marie by proxy. Not a promising start. Regardless, it's the Florentine event of the season and will kick off weeks of lavish festivities for invited VIPs from across seventeenth-century Europe. There'll be parades, fireworks, dancing, overeating, and one highly anticipated *dramma per musica*, or "drama for music."

The work will be *Euridice*, with music by composer Jacopo Peri and a libretto by Ottavio Rinuccini. Based on the Greek myth of Orpheus and Eurydice, it will premiere on October 6, 1600, at the royal Palazzo Pitti for an audience of two hundred aristocrats. There will be five scenes. Approximately eleven characters. One audience member will describe the music as "tedious." And it will be one of the first operas. Ever.

* * *

Euridice provides an ideal origin story for Western opera, akin to the sudden bite of a radioactive spider. Before *Euridice*, there was nothing. After *Euridice*, your friendly neighborhood opera! But the truth is an entirely new art form didn't just emerge fully formed that day at the Palazzo Pitti. Opera's actual origin story is far less linear than that of a comic-book superhero, more a tangled web of overlapping artistic influences that long predated Marie and Henry's nuptials.

Throughout the 1500s, musicians, artists, and poets across Europe were experimenting with different ways of combining literature, music, and theater. One particularly active group was the Florentine Camerata, a collection of like-minded intellectuals and creatives who threw their weight behind the goal of reviving the theatrical forms of Greek antiquity. Key to their effort was the belief that the words in all those ancient Greek dramas were actually sung and not spoken. But even centuries earlier, other theatrical traditions were dipping their toes in operatic waters. Take intermedi, the spectacle-driven musical interludes staged between scenes of spoken theater starting in the late 1400s. Or the liturgical plays performed throughout the Middle Ages that integrated music and sung chants into stagings of biblical scenes.

If we want to get more pedantic, *Euridice* isn't even technically the first opera that Jacopo Peri and Ottavio Rinuccini wrote—just the first that survived the ravages of time. Two years earlier, they penned the actual "first" opera for the Carnival of 1598—this one inspired by the Greek myth of Daphne and Apollo. Alas, all traces of the music for *Dafne* are long gone, but we know members of the Medici family attended the performance and apparently were impressed . . . at least enough to hire Peri and Rinuccini for *Euridice.*

So, *Euridice* wasn't really the first—and certainly not the best, at least according to that one audience report. But it's still a significant milestone in opera because of the way it consolidated centuries of discussion and practice. For one of the first times in Western history, a theatrical work intentionally combined text with different styles of singing, all with the aim of creating a compelling dramatic experience for an audience.

Seven years later, composer Claudio Monteverdi made an even bigger operatic splash with his own take on the Orpheus myth, a *favola in musica* (that is, "fable in music") entitled *L'Orfeo*. Written with poet Alessandro Striggio, *L'Orfeo* was similarly funded and staged within the confines of an Italian court—this time in Mantua, thanks to the patronage of Duke Vincenzo Gonzaga (also a guest at Marie de' Medici's wedding, by the way). However, Monteverdi's work was significantly larger in scope and sophistication than *Euridice*, requiring an orchestra of nearly forty instruments and incorporating a broader range of singing styles. There were solo arias, or extended melodies sung by a single singer. There were duets, or melodies sung by two singers together. There were ensembles with large groups of performers singing together in harmony. There were even recitatives, or sung dialogue: the operatic version of conversation between characters. All driven by Striggio's text and inspired by the tenets of classical Greek drama. Bad luck for *Euridice*, which would soon be relegated to the historical equivalent of a Trivial Pursuit question.

I have a particular soft spot for *L'Orfeo* because it was the first opera I studied in college. Every Tuesday and Thursday at 10:00 a.m. (or more accurately 10:15 a.m., since I was chronically late), I'd cram into a wood-paneled lecture theater with four hundred other undergraduates and listen to Professor Thomas F. Kelly talk about Monteverdi and *L'Orfeo*. There were jokes. There were musical performances. And for the first time I started to think about opera as more than just the pages of printed music scattered around my dorm room. I began to think of it as an event, as something meant to be performed and experienced—and perhaps discussed in a lecture hall four hundred years later.

For a few decades after the premiere of *L'Orfeo* in 1607, opera remained a private form of entertainment exclusive to Italian nobility—all the rage behind closed gilded doors but not something meant to be enjoyed by the masses. That is, until the 1630s. In 1636, Francesco and Ettore Tron, two entrepreneurial brothers from the Venetian aristocracy, were granted permission to rebrand their old family theater in Venice as a *teatro de musica*, or "theater of music." Their venture, the Teatro San Cassiano, was officially inaugurated a year later with a performance of the opera *L'Andromeda* by composer Francesco Manelli and librettist Benedetto Ferrari. And, in a move that would send shock waves throughout Italy, the performance of *L'Andromeda* was open for anyone to attend, noble or otherwise—for a price. The cost of a single ticket was four lire, then roughly a day's wage for a master builder in Venice.

A year later, the Tron brothers did it again, presenting another new opera by Manelli and Ferrari, again open to anyone who could pay for the privilege. This time, it caught on. Over the next three years, three new opera houses opened in Venice, and another four new operas were staged for paying audiences. Within ten years, thirty-three new operas were staged. Within forty years, more than two hundred. All open to the public. All charging for admission.

As the market for opera grew, so did the competition between different opera houses. Opera producers, or impresarios as they were called, incorporated increasingly spectacular visual effects into their productions in the hope of persuading audiences to attend their theaters over those of competitors. Think lavish painted sets, flying stage machinery, and seemingly magical set transformations. A production of the opera *La Calisto* staged in 1651, for example, featured an onstage working fountain, a giant serpent eating its own tail, and flying rainbows that carried Greek gods descending from the heavens.

For generations that have come of age in the time of *Avatar* and the Marvel Cinematic Universe, the idea of mechanical rainbows and papier-mâché snakes may seem uninspired. But to the Venetian tourists and townies who flocked to opera houses in the seventeenth century, the effects were mind-boggling. And this new audience wanted more. More new operas. More scenic marvels. No matter what it cost behind the scenes.

Thus opera as we more or less know it was born: an art form that combines text and music but is also fundamentally defined by spectacle. And expense.

It wasn't long before the new model of commercial opera stretched beyond the borders of Italy. By the 1670s, the premise of a paying audience had officially arrived in France and Germany, among other countries. As the art form snaked and spread throughout Europe, it also began to change. Each country added its own nationalistic flavor, even as different impresarios, composers, and librettists made their own tweaks to the Italian export.

The effects-driven opera of the seventeenth century was soon overthrown by *opera seria*, or "serious opera," a form that emphasized historical events and royal figures over all those Greek myths and legends. True to its name, *opera seria* exhibited more than a little disdain for the scenic razzle-dazzle of its artistic predecessor. Another god descending from the clouds? Another volcano transforming into a forest glade? Can you *be* more unserious?

But *opera seria* didn't stay on top for long. Other emerging opera genres were soon grappling for attention in the early eighteenth century, including Italy's *opera buffa*, France's *opéra comique*, Spain's *zarzuela*, and Germany's *Singspiel*, each of which rejected the sober, noble tone of *opera seria.* Instead, comic operas by the likes of composers Alessandro Scarlatti and W. A. Mozart layered on the shtick, incorporating stock comedic characters, farcical plots, and a healthy smattering of spoken dialogue.

Fast-forward a few decades and along came the *bel canto* form of opera spearheaded by Italian composers such as Gioachino Rossini and Vincenzo Bellini in the early 1800s. Literally translated as "beautiful singing," *bel canto* operas were characterized by expressive arias and simple accompaniment. Then there was *grand opéra*, a large-scale form popularized by the Paris Opéra in the 1820s. With its five-act structure, exotic historical settings, and extravagant stagings, *grand opéra* is where composers such as Giacomo Meyerbeer and Giuseppe Verdi cut their teeth—and set a benchmark for the later epic "music dramas" written by composer Richard Wagner starting in the 1850s.

The second half of the nineteenth century also saw *opéra lyrique*, a hybrid version of *opéra comique* and *grand opéra* (less comedic than the former, less spectacular than the latter). As well, there was the frothy *operetta* form mastered by French composer Jacques Offenbach and British dream team W. S. Gilbert and Arthur Sullivan, and after that, the *opera verismo* style, driven by composers Giacomo Puccini and Pietro Mascagni, who wanted to bring more realism into the opera house. The twentieth century saw even more variations emerge, from the short-lived jazz-infused *Zeitoper* of the 1920s to the radio operas of the 1930s and 1940s to the avant-garde minimalist operas of the 1970s.

And that's just the highlights reel. There are dozens upon dozens of different operatic forms peppering the history of the art form—enough to make any college music major blanch at the thought of a pop quiz. Some are French, some are Italian, some are German, some are Spanish. Some are irritatingly niche, such as *opéra féerie*, which refers exclusively to French operas about fairy tales. Others err on the side of finicky, such as *opera semiseria*: serious, but not *too* serious. Still others are likely to lead to an awkward misunderstanding. Take it from me: *opera eroica* means heroic, *not* erotic.

With so many evolving and overlapping forms over the centuries, it's no surprise that the boundaries between different genres of opera are sometimes blurry. The lines between opera, operetta, and musical theater are even more opaque. So what *is* opera anyway?

Here's the best definition I can muster. Opera is a work of theater, usually presented onstage. And most of the performers sing. Most of the time.

Now, if you're about to throw this book out the nearest window, I understand. After all, the declared topic here is opera . . . shouldn't I be able to provide a clear-cut definition of what the hell we're even talking about? Don't blame me. Blame the art form. Opera is notoriously nebulous and difficult to define. Try to add any additional requirements or restrictions to the vague definition outlined above—try to home in more closely on what exactly opera is or isn't—and you'll face inevitable stumbling blocks.

Let's start with the classic: it's *only* opera if the performers sing the entire time. A clean and simple definition. Until you remember W. A. Mozart's opera *The Magic Flute*, which is crammed with spoken dialogue. As is Ludwig van Beethoven's opera *Fidèlio.* And Georges Bizet's opera *Carmen*. Plus the entire catalog of operas from the *opéra comique*, *zarzuela*, and *Singspiel* traditions, in which most of the characters quite simply never shut up.

Let's try again. It's *only* opera if the singers don't use microphones. Another clear and practical definition, especially since we know opera singers are trained to sing without amplification. Except sometimes they don't. Sometimes they can't. Sometimes an opera is staged in a massive outdoor venue such as a park or baseball stadium, where it's physically impossible to be heard without a microphone. Sometimes theaters are so poorly designed that so-called sound enhancement is needed to counteract bad acoustics. That doesn't even scratch the surface of the many contemporary operas that use amplification for artistic, dramatic, or musical effect, not to mention the radio operas of the 1930s, which were literally written to be sung into microphones.

Last try. It's *only* opera if the singers sound "operatic"—if their vocal technique produces a powerful and resonant tone with abundant vibrato (that's the oscillation you hear whenever they hold a long note). Correct! Unless you consider operas that don't require that kind of vibrato-heavy singing, such as Monteverdi's *L'Orfeo*, Jean-Philippe Rameau's *Les Indes galantes*, and all the other operas written before 1750 or so. Not to mention all the avant-garde operas that also use nonoperatic vocal techniques. Does that mean none are technically operas? And what happens when singers sound "operatic" when performing musical theater such as Richard Rodgers and Oscar Hammerstein's *Carousel* or Stephen Sondheim's *Sweeney Todd*? Does that suddenly make *them* operas? Or were they already operas the whole time?

As I said, don't blame me—blame the art form. While we're at it, let's also take pity on the dictionary editors who have long struggled to write their own definitions. The *Collins Dictionary* defines opera as "a play with music in which all the words are sung"? Close, but no cigar.

The pithiest definition of opera I've heard came from Beth Morrison, founder of Beth Morrison Projects, a New York–based opera company founded in 2006. "Opera," Morrison told me in 2024, "is sung theater." I immediately gasped and nodded vigorously. Opera is sung theater, of course! It's short, snappy, and fits perfectly on a bumper sticker. But within a few hours of our interview, my brow was already furrowing: What exactly does that *mean*? Dig a little deeper into Morrison's definition, and it ends up looking almost as open-ended as my own attempt. Which is perhaps the point. Opera assumes many different forms and meanings. It's ambiguous, dynamic, even volatile—none of which reconciles easily with the clear-cut expectations or word-count limits of a dictionary entry.

But then how can we wrap our heads around this beast of an art form?

The only way to make sense of opera is to deconstruct it, to examine each of the elements that collectively form the whole. There's the text. The music. And the stage.

In an ideal scenario, these three elements merge seamlessly, creating what composer Richard Wagner called *Gesamtkunstwerk*, or the "total work of art." It's the equivalent of the perfect grilled-cheese sandwich, with each ingredient transforming and transcending into something more than the sum of its parts. But how exactly this transformation occurs—not to mention whether a total work of art is even possible—is more than a little murky. Because opera is also *nothing* like a grilled-cheese sandwich. Unless you're spreading on a layer of plutonium.

* * *

Let's start with opera's first building block: the text, or the libretto. Literally translated from the Italian as "booklet," the libretto is written by a librettist or poet (or nowadays, often a screenwriter, playwright, or novelist) and includes everything sung or said in an opera. Those romantic words comparing the soprano's eyes to the moon? Written by the librettist. The villain's curse-filled rant in the second act? Written by the librettist.

The stereotype of opera generally defaults to Italian—*Mamma mia! Carbonara!*—but the text of a libretto can be in any language, usually depending on the native tongue of the writer. Nineteenth-century French librettist Eugène Scribe only ever wrote in French. The operas of Richard Wagner were all written in German. But that doesn't mean audiences need to riffle through a German-English dictionary to understand a Wagner opera. At least not anymore. Since the early 1980s, standard practice has been for opera companies to translate the libretto into English (or whatever language is spoken by the majority of the audience) and project the translation above the stage during the performance. They're called supertitles or surtitles because of their placement above the stage (as opposed to the *sub*titles that sit at the bottom of your television screen when you're watching that Korean drama). Note to the unwary: never snag opera tickets in the front row, or you may develop neck spasms from staring at the supertitles directly above your head.

A libretto does more, however, than simply set down the basic words to be uttered onstage. The libretto is responsible for establishing an opera's overarching narrative, including the characters (Who's who?), the setting (Where are they?), and the plot (Who dies? Who falls in love? Who falls in love and *then* dies?). The libretto also includes basic written instructions for how scenes should be staged, known as stage directions (e.g., "tenor enters and stabs mezzo-soprano"), as well as how certain lines of text should be delivered (e.g., "passive aggressively"). The libretto is essentially the skeleton upon which the entire opera hangs. So, whenever an opera fails miserably—at least in a dramatic sense—we can usually blame the librettist.

Our next building block is the music, which falls squarely in the realm of the composer. The music encompasses every musical note and rhythm sung by the performers in the opera, as well as the notes and rhythms played by the orchestra. For the composer, this means setting each word of the libretto to a specific note or combination of notes, ideally in a way that conveys the emotions of a given character without impeding the singer's vocal technique. Those high notes when the tenor compares the soprano's eyes to the moon? Written by the composer. Those rage-filled low notes during the villain's rant? Written by the composer.

The composer is similarly tasked with marking *how* each note should be sung or played. This includes the dynamics (Is it loud? Is it soft? Getting louder? Getting softer?), the tempo (Is it slow? Is it fast? Speeding up? Slowing down?), and the musical expression, or, for lack of a better word, the vibe. Above all, the music is responsible for transforming the skeletal narrative of the libretto into something fully formed, adding layers of depth to the bare bones of character and story.

This marriage of text and music comes with significant hurdles, not least of which is the sheer logistical challenge of taking two distinct art forms—and two distinct creative authors—and squashing them together. In most cases, the libretto comes first. The librettist will take an idea or concept for an opera (sometimes provided by the composer, sometimes not) and write it up in practical terms, building a dramatic structure out of scenes and lines of text in the same way a playwright crafts a spoken play. Once the draft of the libretto is finalized, the composer then begins *their* work, setting each scene and line of text to music.

Over subsequent working drafts, the music will evolve from initial sketches to a complete piano-vocal score—that is, a version of the opera for singers and piano accompaniment—and then finally to a complete orchestral score, or a version that has individual lines of music for every player in the orchestra. Throughout the process of composition, there will be continued rewrites, negotiations, arguments, and compromises as text and music are combined. Scenes will be added and deleted, arias rewritten and expanded, phrases tweaked and massaged. It's the creative equivalent of nuclear fusion, except with bigger egos.

It should therefore come as no surprise that many operatic marriages are characterized more by dysfunction than wedded bliss. As opera composer John Adams told *The Paris Review* in 2024, "The two most painful things two human beings can do together are a double ax murder or an artistic collaboration." While I can't speak to ax murders, I can certainly attest to the ugly operatic divorces that mark my own career as a librettist. Once a composer disappeared for months, only to reemerge a few weeks before the final deadline without having written a single note of music. Instead, they'd spent the entire time rewriting my libretto—badly. Another time, I was commissioned to write a libretto on a rush job with the promise of immediate payment. Years later, I'm still waiting for that check. Going back centuries, we can catch glimpses of similar dramas behind the scenes.

In a 1783 letter to his father, composer W. A. Mozart complained repeatedly about librettist Giambattista Varesco, with whom Mozart was writing a new comic opera. He threatened to drop Varesco from the project entirely, grumbling, "He must change and remold things for me as much and as often as I wish, and not follow his head, which lacks even the least knowledge of practice and the theater." Mozart eventually followed up on his threat, abandoning both the in-progress opera and its librettist.

The fights between nineteenth-century composer Giacomo Puccini and his many librettists were allegedly so heated that Puccini's publisher frequently had to intervene. In 1889, Puccini even declared his intention to write the libretto for the opera *Manon Lescaut* himself, just to ensure "no idiotic librettist" could "ruin the story." In the end, Puccini elected to stick with the music, but he still chewed through six different librettists before finally completing the project.

In true operatic fashion, the battle between composers and librettists has even been depicted onstage. In 1786, composer Antonio Salieri and librettist Giovanni Battista Casti premiered a one-act opera, *Prima la musica e poi le parole* ("First the music and then the words") about a librettist and composer hired to write a new opera in just four days. Cue two dueling sopranos, a crippling case of writer's block, and extended arguments about text versus music. Composer Richard Strauss and librettist Clemens Krauss employed a similar idea for their 1942 opera, *Capriccio*, which follows a countess trying to choose between two lovers, one a poet, one a composer. (Spoiler: the opera ends with the countess still undecided.)

In addition to the practical negotiations and occasional personal disasters of merging text and music, there's a deeper philosophical debate at work here. Which element actually matters more in opera, the text or the music? And to that end, *who* matters more? The librettist or the composer?

For the first century or so of opera's history, it was unquestionably the librettist. Recognized as practitioners of the high arts of poetry and literature, librettists were widely extolled for their work. Some were so famous that a single libretto would be set multiple times by different composers. For example, Pietro Metastasio, one of the preeminent librettists of the eighteenth century, wrote sixty librettos, which were, in turn, set a jaw-dropping eight hundred times by more than three hundred different composers. In comparison, composers were lucky if a copy of their music was even published. For the 1637 premiere of *L'Andromeda* in Venice—four lire a ticket, if you recall—composer Francesco Manelli wasn't even listed on the title page of the printed libretto. Ouch.

The golden age for librettists didn't last, however, and their star power began to flicker with the rise of *opera seria* in the eighteenth century. As visual effects fell out of favor, impresarios needed another way to lure operagoers to their theaters. They quickly zeroed in on singers as the new headline act, capable of wowing audiences with their vocal skill and musical pyrotechnics. Suddenly, the libretto was no longer paramount to the operatic experience. Even the basics of character and storyline were largely beside the point. Instead, opera now served primarily as a musical vehicle for star singers—something meant to be embellished with extra high notes and then paused for copious applause.

The nineteenth century only leaned further into prioritizing music over text. Thanks to the Romantic movement, music was increasingly recognized as its own form of artistic expression, capable of being emotive and transformative regardless of any accompanying text. And, as the music became opera's primary attraction, composers found themselves in a position of unparalleled artistic power. Nineteenth-century composer Giuseppe Verdi began choosing the topics for his operas entirely on his own, essentially relegating his librettists to the equivalent of subcontractors. Composer Richard Wagner eliminated the role completely, choosing to write both the text and music for his operas himself. Librettists were now secondary figures, functioning solely in service of the music.

The twentieth century saw further shifts to this artistic dynamic. As celebrated writers such as E. M. Forster, W. H. Auden, Alice Goodman, and Gertrude Stein added the title of librettist to their list of literary accolades, composers lost some of their artistic dominance. With this change also came a growing recognition from both composers and opera companies that an opera needs a good libretto (and a good librettist) to succeed. Nowadays, most new operas are developed with the premise of an equal (or equal-ish) partnership between the two creators. But as a symptom of the way these roles developed over time, many operas are still credited solely to the composer in marketing materials and performance reviews—thus, the recent push by the Dramatists Guild of America to give librettists equal billing via the social media hashtag #CreditTheLibrettist.

But back to our building blocks. Let's say we've somehow managed to resolve the conflict between text and music. There were tears, profanities, and numerous angry letters, emails, and text messages between our composer and librettist. Both have privately vowed never to write another opera as long as they live. But the libretto is done! The music is written! And together, these two components merge to form the musical score of an opera. Heartiest congratulations, popping corks, and handshakes all around.

Now we add the third element of opera: the stage. This is where the trouble really begins.

* * *

An opera is only technically complete—only technically an opera—when it's been staged. This added element introduces an entirely new set of stakeholders (and artistic egos), including stage directors, conductors, designers, and performers. Staging is inextricably informed and shaped by the score, which functions as both inspiration and foundation for what's presented in the theater. But how does the transition from score to stage even happen? How does one take something that's fundamentally two-dimensional—text and music printed on a piece of paper—and transform it into something decidedly *three*-dimensional? More important, where can it all go wrong?

For the first few centuries of opera's development, the relationship between the score and the stage was amicable—harmonious even. For one thing, composers and librettists were usually directly involved in the performances of their work. The librettist would typically oversee and manage staging rehearsals—duties we'd now associate with a stage director—as well as coordinate the practical aspects of a show: for example, instructing stagehands when to pull a certain pulley or drop a certain set piece. The composer was then responsible for the musical aspects of the work and would usually rehearse the singers and lead the orchestra from the keyboard during the performance.

Meanwhile, the staging itself was fairly straightforward. Sure, it was logistically complex—remember all those lavish sets, floating rainbows, and magical transformations from seventeenth-century Venice?—but it was also highly literal. The forest glade that was described in the score was the same forest glade that was represented onstage (more or less): the only creative interpretation was in which green paint to use. The movement of the singers onstage was similarly presentational, involving a series of preset gestures and stances that were well known to audiences at the time.

Come the eighteenth century, and this status quo largely stayed in place. Sets were getting bigger and more expensive, but staging was still mostly a matter of coordinating entrances and exits. The star singer would pick a spot in front of the painted background scenery and simply stand in place until their aria was over—a practice now lovingly ridiculed as "park and bark." An eighteenth-century singer who was feeling creative might throw in a few gestures, perhaps a gentle swoop of the arm in time with the music. (Here the goal wasn't so much theatrical as to create a sense of visual unity with all those vocal acrobatics, a kind of smugly unspoken "Oh, *these* high notes?")

The slow pace of advancing technology at the time meant that staging inevitably fell short of what the composer and librettist envisioned, particularly in special effects. But even when the reality of the stage didn't quite align with the ideal of the score, the composer and librettist still usually retained oversight over what was happening. And, in the majority of cases, it was also only happening once or twice. Throughout the seventeenth and eighteenth centuries, opera was characterized by novelty. New works were written and staged for immediate consumption and then dumped in favor of the next new thing. There were few second chances for staging, let alone third ones. So, if the staging of an opera didn't quite work, the composer and librettist simply shrugged—they were already working on the next one.

But this operatic utopia was short-lived. Tensions with staging began to intensify in the early nineteenth century due to the rise of music publishers such as Giovanni Ricordi. For the first time in opera's history, publishers began printing official versions of musical scores for widespread dissemination—fantastic for the composer's and librettist's bank accounts but also a shift that posed new complications. How could a composer and librettist still have direct oversight over their work when their operas were now being produced by companies all over Europe? How could they be in multiple places at once?

The solution posed by publishers was elegant: staging manuals. These were stand-alone booklets printed alongside the score that contained detailed instructions for sets, costumes, and the movement of the singers onstage. The idea was to exert artistic control from a distance, not only keeping a viselike grip on an opera's text and music but also on how it was performed. And these "how-to" guides weren't framed as optional. "It is absolutely necessary that artists take full notice of the staging . . . and conform to it," warned the front page of a Ricordi staging manual published in 1877.

Composers such as Giuseppe Verdi and Richard Wagner quickly seized on the opportunity to control staging from afar. After first encountering staging manuals at the Paris Opéra in 1855, Verdi enthusiastically constructed or commissioned a manual for every new opera he wrote until his death in 1901. Wagner was equally compulsive in documenting his staging preferences for posterity. Leading up to the premiere of his *Ring Cycle* in 1876, Wagner hired writer Heinrich Porges to attend staging rehearsals and record exactly how things were done.

What was happening on the stage itself was also evolving. New technologies were driving innovations, including panoramic backdrops, three-dimensional set pieces, and even projected imagery. The question of what to do with singers onstage was similarly changing. For the premiere of his *Ring Cycle*, Wagner explicitly prohibited his singers from using the cookie-cutter gestures of earlier forms of opera. The singers should never look directly at the audience, Wagner declared, and absolutely *never* break character: they should act as though they belonged to the world onstage.

Wagner wasn't alone in his aspiration to transform staging into something new, something more dramatic and immersive. From the 1890s, there was a growing recognition that performance was an art form in itself, something independent of script and score. The stage was suddenly a third contender in opera, vying equally with text and music for artistic control. With this change also came the emergence of the stage director as a new kind of artistic authority, one not only distinct from the composer and the librettist but with the power to decide how an opera would be interpreted onstage (more on this in a moment).

Now, if you thought the relationship between the text and the music was dysfunctional, take a minute to prepare yourself. The dynamic between the text, the music, and the stage would become even more violent, even more prone to artistic fissures and fractures. And the reason is simple. At the same time the stage—and the stage director—was coming to the fore, opera was undergoing a seminal shift in its development, one with long-standing repercussions into the present day.

Enter the Canon.

* * *

When I think of the Canon, I picture a darkened room with a vaulted ceiling, dripping wax candles, and a group of mysterious cloaked figures. One holds a parchment scroll listing the name of every composer who has ever dared to flirt with the operatic form. Solemnly—and perhaps accompanied by a dramatic organ interlude—the lead figure intones each name, and the group delivers their collective verdict.

Giacomo Puccini? In.

Ethel Smyth? Out.

Giuseppe Verdi? In.

Luciano Berio? Out.

A single bell chimes. A boy soprano holds an extended high note. And thus, the Canon is magically inscribed in golden letters at every opera house in the world.

Of course, there's not actually a darkened room or secret society that unilaterally decides the fate of every opera. But the Canon *is* real—and an unavoidable source of both angst and outrage in Opera Land.

In the twenty-first century, we can think of the Canon as a collection of roughly fifty or so operas, all written by white European men in the eighteenth, nineteenth, and early twentieth centuries. Bizet's *Carmen.* Puccini's *La bohème.* Mozart's *Don Giovanni.* Verdi's *La traviata.* To name a few. These are the operas that are universally recognized as masterpieces of the genre, that enjoy enduring popularity with audiences, and are programmed ad nauseam by opera companies.

Here artistic quality goes hand in hand with commercial concerns. Canonical operas are programmed regularly not just because they're good but because they sell tickets. They're what stage director Kasper Holten once called the "core canon of safe bets." Or alternatively, the kind of work that nineteenth-century critic Filippo Filippi described as a "piece of driftwood that could come to the rescue of all drowning impresarios." The Canon, in other words, is good business—even if it does leave us with an unresolved question à la the chicken or the egg. Are canonical operas programmed because they're popular? Or are they popular because they're programmed?

Poultry aside, the specifics of the Canon are more fluid than you might imagine. There's not so much a single list of canonical operas as there are many slightly different lists, usually depending on where you are and whom you're talking to. Any number of French operas are undoubtedly canonical, but only if you happen to be in France. The same goes for operas by English composer Benjamin Britten: canonical in the United Kingdom but not quite meeting the mark for the rest of Europe. I have my list of canonical operas, which won't be quite the same as your list, despite a few obvious overlaps (cough, cough, *La bohème*). And opera scholars Philippe Agid and Jean-Claude Tarondeau have *their* list. In their case, it's exactly thirty-seven operas, ranging from Verdi's *La traviata* to Wagner's *Lohengrin*. With their benchmark in place—subjective or otherwise—we can get a sense of just how pervasive the Canon is.

Consider the eleven largest opera companies in the United States, the companies with the biggest budgets and the biggest audiences: the recognized leaders of the field. More than half of the operas staged by these companies between 2005 and 2020 were from Agid and Tarondeau's list.* That's more than half of fifteen

* I counted.

hundred different opera productions over fifteen years, all from that list of thirty-seven works. And that doesn't even include all the other operas from the nineteenth century or earlier that are just a smidge less popular and might even have made the canonical cut if Agid and Tarondeau were in a different mood when drafting their top picks. Operas such as Donizetti's *Don Pasquale* or Wagner's *The Flying Dutchman.* Add these kinds of canonical-ish operas to our core list of thirty-seven, and the stats become overwhelming. Nearly 75 percent of all operas staged by the largest American companies between 2005 and 2020 were either canonical or canonical-ish.

Not that this is breaking news. While the precise figure might be a surprise, it's no secret the Canon has dominated opera stages since the turn of the twentieth century. It's the main reason why the field is so often accused of being out of touch, if not downright Jurassic. Most of the operas being staged today are the exact same operas that were being staged more than a century ago—around the same time the *Titanic* was headed toward that iceberg.

As a singer, I was never explicitly told about the Canon, but it still insidiously crept into my consciousness. There was the opera CD I was given by my first voice teacher—ostentatiously titled *The World's Greatest Opera Album* and featuring very famous arias sung by very famous singers. There were the complete recordings of Puccini's operas *La bohème* and *Madama Butterfly* presented to me by my first tenor boyfriend in college. (Given that both Puccini's heroines die tragically, I should have taken the hint and, from that point on, sworn off tenors.) There were also the works covered in my college music-theory and music-history classes, all focused on the usual operatic suspects: Mozart, Rossini, Puccini, Verdi, Wagner. And then the operas staged by my graduate school—again, a steady diet of the Canon, with a few contemporary operas shoved into the black box theater on the side. No one needed to tell me about the Canon. It was inescapable.

Like the art form itself, there's no radioactive spider to blame. The Canon crystallized over centuries, shaped by different social upheavals and shifts in how opera was perceived and consumed. That said, the nineteenth century did its fair share of heavy lifting. Take the nineteenth-century view that musical works were Works with a capital *W*, something to be idealized and set in stone. Or the same century's growing recognition of opera as a marker of prestige and social standing. Or the simultaneous influx of music publishers distributing "official" copies of select scores and staging manuals throughout Europe.

Amid everything, opera companies were paying attention—and saw an obvious commercial opportunity. All those published Works with a capital *W* weren't just being purchased by opera companies, they were also being bought by audiences, by people who enjoyed playing and singing catchy operatic tunes at their pianos at home and were increasingly interested in seeing the same opera more than once. And why should a company bother with the expense of commissioning a new opera when audiences now had *favorites*—favorites that were already written, already proven, and already certain to draw a crowd?

Companies gradually began to orbit around a shrinking number of works. Between 1760 and 1770, roughly 75 percent of operas staged in London came straight off the assembly line of brand-new works. Within fifty years, this had dropped to roughly 30 percent. By the 1850s, major opera houses across Europe were staging just a few new operas each year. The rest were all existing ones.

For composers and librettists, the stakes changed. There'd be no more shrugging off a single performance and moving on to the next project. The success of an opera was now cumulative, measured in the number of stagings it received across Europe. The new goal was legacy over novelty.

And so, bit by bit, the works that defined opera began to age—first ten years, then twenty, then thirty—until by the turn of the twentieth century, the eyes of both opera audiences and companies were fixed on an increasingly distant past. This is where the simmering tensions between the text, the music, and the stage would finally boil over and sear the countertop.

While some operas were now timeless, their creators weren't. By 1901, nearly all the purported masters of the art form were dead, including Mozart, Verdi, Wagner, and Rossini. (Puccini would hang on for a few more years, but then he'd be gone as well.) The vacuum they left behind was fated to be filled by two operatic heirs. First, the conductor, considered the heir apparent of the composer and given authority over the musical aspects of an opera. Second, the stage director, framed as the heir to the librettist and tasked with overseeing an opera's performance, just as the librettist had once been.

But inheritance is a tricky thing, especially depending on what's been bequeathed. The conductor was given the musical score, that printed foundation of text and music. The director, however? A handful of stage directions and a few dusty staging manuals. Because, of course, a performance isn't something that can physically be passed down. It's not tangible. Not replicable. Even all those detailed staging manuals would prove to be of limited value. Take the manuals written by Giuseppe Verdi, which are endlessly, even obsessively, comprehensive. Too bad Verdi wrote them before the introduction of electric stage lighting, an innovation that transformed all those painstakingly written instructions into little more than a historical snapshot of a long-outdated stage.

So, what happens when a dubious, wispy-at-best inheritance is given to the stage director at roughly the same time the role is being recognized as an independent artistic force in the theater? *And* at roughly the same time opera is being defined by an endlessly repeating list of Greatest Hits? Boom goes the dynamite. Because when an opera such as Verdi's *La traviata* has already been staged thousands of times since it first premiered in 1853, how many more times can it be staged the exact same way before someone is desperate to try something new?

One of the first gauntlets was thrown down by the Kroll Opera in Germany in the 1920s. The company had a history of staging operas that were canonical or canonical-ish and soon became known for its unusual and avant-garde interpretations. Bare walls, sparse sets, stylized movements—this was opera staged in a way most audiences hadn't seen before. In the 1940s, stage director Walter Felsenstein followed in the Kroll Opera's footsteps with his own company, the Komische Oper Berlin. Felsenstein's stagings continued to elevate the role of the stage director while also leaning into the idea of singing actors as opposed to the park-and-bark divas of previous generations.

At the Bayreuth Festspielhaus in the 1950s and 1960s, Richard Wagner's grandsons Wieland and Wolfgang further shifted precedent with their radical stagings of Wagner's operas (no doubt prompting Grandpa to spit out a few German curses from beyond the grave). Here their aim was artistic but also strategic. Wagner's operas were in desperate need of a rebrand after Adolf Hitler's very public infatuation with them. And what better way to create some distance from Wagner's not-so-coincidentally blond and blue-eyed Aryan heroes than with some avant-garde staging that completely recontextualized the operas? This departure from tradition catalyzed a host of other reinterpretations, driving a new approach to opera staging that would become known as *Regietheater*, a term that translates from the German as "director's theater."

By the 1980s, very new stagings of very old operas were the norm. Mozart's *The Marriage of Figaro* set in New York's Trump Tower. Wagner's *Ring Cycle* set during the steampunk Industrial Revolution. Verdi's *Rigoletto* with the Duke of Mantua wearing a gorilla costume. Stage directors played with different settings, different time periods, different characters, different plots—all with the conceit that the stage was a blank canvas, something that couldn't (and shouldn't) be dictated by long-dead composers and librettists. But the instant directors began to exercise their artistic power in this way—the instant it became clear that staging couldn't be posthumously controlled—the first battlegrounds of the Opera Wars emerged.

On one side were the opera traditionalists—those who trumpeted strict fidelity to the musical score and its one "true" meaning onstage. See German critic Paul Schwers, who described a modernist staging of Wagner's *The Flying Dutchman* in 1929 as "a total destruction of Wagner's work, a basic falsification of his creative intentions." On the other side were the opera progressives—those who supported modern and abstract stagings of canonical operas, as well as more nuanced understandings of their meanings. These freethinkers could mete out scorn with equal vigor. Consider French conductor and composer Pierre Boulez, who, in 1967, accused the Paris Opéra of being a museum "full of dust and crap."

The battles over the score and the stage have prompted so much artillery fire that we'll spend the next two chapters just sifting through all the shrapnel. And as we'll see, the animosity reverberates far beyond the spotlights of the stage, seeping into rehearsal rooms, boardrooms, and even the very culture of the industry itself. But perhaps that's only to be expected: the baggage, the hang-ups. Why *wouldn't* the world of opera be rife with discord and hostility when the very nature of the art form is built on a battleground?

Pack your gear. We're off to the front.

CHAPTER 2

The Score

— or —

That Belongs in a Museum!

A massive grassy plain. In the distance, an irregular blur of gray along the horizon, clouds of dust coming ever nearer. The enemy.

Just ahead, thousands of mounted knights wait in orderly rows, their armored horses stomping in anticipation. Banners flap wildly in the rising wind: a golden background emblazoned with the image of . . . the musical score for the opera *Carmen*?

The lead knight gallops past the front lines on a noble white stallion. "Illustrious knights!" he shouts. "Defenders of the score! Today we live or die to protect the Canon!"

The army emits a rousing cheer of "Fidelity! Fidelity!"

The horns of battle sound.

Cue our first battleground: the score.

* * *

When it comes to the war of the score, it's hard to avoid religious metaphors. Of all the battles in Opera Land, this one reaches the highest pitch of moralistic fervor, akin to the Crusades or the Spanish Inquisition.

The issue stems from opera's two dueling identities. One identity takes the form of the musical score, a physical object containing the pages of music and text notated by the composer and the librettist. Through the act of its authors setting pen (or quill) to the page, the score achieves a corporeal form. It can be put on a bookshelf. It can be held in your hand. Opera's second identity can be found in the performance. Unlike the score, a performance is anything *but* fixed. It's ephemeral, a transient event that only exists at a particular moment in time. It's impossible to hold on to a performance or precisely replicate it.

Of the two identities, the score has long been considered definitive. Performances are too unpredictable, too slippery to control, not to mention too susceptible to the interference of wayward stage directors. But the score of an opera—the notes, the text, the story—*that's* an unequivocal, conclusive record of the intentions of the composer and the librettist.

Musicologist David Littlejohn goes so far as to describe the score as the "Scripture" of an opera. And for many, the score is seen as something to be enshrined and protected, even worshipped. For opera traditionalists, it's the source of all answers and all meanings, and a truly pious operatic knight need only crack it open to understand the truth of an opera such as *Carmen* or *La bohème*. And so, whenever critics or audiences don't agree with how an opera is presented onstage, they inevitably refer to the score. Therein lies the proof that a director or conductor has betrayed the composer and the librettist. Therein lies the proof that the staging, to be blunt, is wrong.

Take the 2009 review of the Metropolitan Opera's production of *Tosca* in *The New Yorker*, pointedly titled "The Case of the Missing Candlesticks." The issue? Stage director Luc Bondy deviated from the tenets of the score. At a certain moment in the opera's second act, the character Tosca is "supposed" to place candlesticks around Scarpia's body (that's the baritone who's just tried to rape Tosca and whom she subsequently stabs to death). It's a moment explicitly outlined in the score and even given an extended musical interlude by composer Giacomo Puccini. But Bondy cut the candles—and promptly found himself raked over the artistic coals. Responding to the outcry, Bondy quipped, "I didn't know that *Tosca* was like the Bible in New York."

And it's not just *Tosca* that's gospel. The score for every canonical opera is seemingly sacred. Dare to change the music, text, story, or even stage directions, and a director risks accusations of sacrilege and desecration. Meanwhile, those who stand against such debasements are framed (at least by themselves) as opera's protectors, devout custodians who safeguard the score from villainous external forces. Cut one of Mozart's arias? Change one of Puccini's stage directions? "Never!" they shout, raising their banner over the grassy plain. "Fidelity! Fidelity!"

The primacy of the score is especially drilled into opera singers. If the score is Scripture, singers are its most devoted disciples. The majority of vocalists even start their training using the exact same musical score: Schirmer's *Twenty-Four Italian Songs and Arias*. Known as The Yellow Book, it's the creed of classical singing, roughly one hundred pages that lay out the basics of vocal technique, including how to sing legato (smoothly), how to sing loudly versus softly, and how to sing in Italian, among other foundational skills.

Now for a quick crash course in operatic singing. The four primary components are the voice, the breath, the music, and the text. The first component, the voice—or the sound that's produced when air moves from the lungs through the vocal folds in the larynx—is something singers are born with and cultivate over time. Breath, the second component, is mastered through training, with singers learning how to regulate the flow of air through their vocal folds. Next comes the music, which includes the pitch (how high or low a note is), the rhythm (how long or short a note is), and the combination of multiple notes and rhythms to make longer phrases of music. Finally, there's the text. Singers must master singing in Italian, French, German, and English—each a standard operatic language and each with its own set of rules for pronouncing vowels and consonants.

Both the music and the text are inextricably tied to the score. It's the end-all authority, the benchmark that determines whether a singer is on the right or wrong note, whether they're dragging behind the correct rhythm, or whether they're garbling the printed Italian text. But regardless of how closely a singer clings to the score, no flick of a switch enables them to successfully combine all four elements of singing at once. It's more like trying to bake a cake in the dark—without knowing where the ingredients are or if you're even in a kitchen—a mixture of physical coordination, can't-quite-put-your-finger-on-it sensations, and the use of mental imagery designed to achieve particular physiological outcomes. Nebulous imagery like "Think down instead of up" for high notes or "Imagine you're having a bowel movement." Really. The latter is a common prompt to help singers activate their pelvic floors for better breath control. Admittedly, I always struggled to apply it in my own singing, primarily because of the persistent rumor that a famous American baritone soiled himself every performance.

Even with a dedicated voice teacher, opera singing requires decades of training to master. And there's no end point, no formal graduation date when a singer can officially bid adieu to voice lessons. Not only are voices constantly shifting and developing, but every musical score involves a different combination of notes, rhythms, and text. Every score requires some degree of reinventing the wheel.

So, let's say you're a professional singer. You've just been hired to sing the role of Carmen in Bizet's opera (celebration!), a role you've never learned before (panic!). Where do you start? With the score, of course.

First, you write the literal translation of the libretto into your copy of the score, going word by word with the help of your handy French-English dictionary. Above that, you write the precise pronunciation of every French word using the International Phonetic Alphabet (known as IPA). Because it's not enough to know what you're singing about—you also must pronounce every word with flawless Parisian diction. Then, you start learning the actual musical notes printed in the score, including the pitches and rhythms, as well as the exact spots where you'll pause to take a breath. Meanwhile, you're taking voice lessons to ensure your technique is sound, that not only are you singing the correct notes but you aren't going to injure yourself vocally. You're also working with a vocal coach to refine your musical interpretation and master those annoyingly nasal French vowels.

Learning an operatic role can take four to six months. And throughout this period of intense labor and dedication, the score remains a singer's ever-constant companion until the moment the stage lights go up.

I have boxes full of lovingly notated scores, many of which have been with me since my earliest days as a singer. As I look at the markings now, it's a nostalgic glimpse into once-used vocal imagery and notes to self, not to mention the cramped phonetic transcriptions and literal translations written into every piece of music I ever sang. But always in pencil, always easily erased and replaced. Only the notations of the composer and the librettist were worthy of true permanence.

But the so-called Scripture of the score isn't as clear-cut as it seems to a singer who's obsessively immersed in its pages, let alone to an audience member who takes issue with a pair of missing candlesticks.

"Fidelity! Fidelity!" the knights shout. But fidelity to *what* exactly?

* * *

Holding a musical score gives one a sense of holding a historical artifact, the kind of leather-bound tome that inspires Indiana Jones to go on an archaeological quest and is perhaps occasionally bathed in a beam of celestial light. This score, you think solemnly, is a direct link to the composer and the librettist from two hundred years ago—a museum-worthy manifestation of an opera in material form.

Except it's not. At least, not really.

When it comes to historical operas, the reality of the score isn't that of a carefully preserved antiquity that's been handed down to generations of devoted acolytes. A closer analogy is a centuries-long game of Telephone, with phrases of gossip being warped and misheard almost from the very start.

At its most fundamental level, a score reflects a series of choices made by the composer and the librettist when creating the opera. Decisions about notes, rhythms, and text are captured, compiled, and formally notated in manuscript form. In the olden days, this would have been done by hand, resulting in what's known as an autograph score, or a score written in the actual hand of the original creators. Et voilà, one opera, one score, and we're done, right? Wrong.

Like all artists, composers and librettists tend to fiddle. They edit, revise, and reconsider, particularly once an opera moves from the compositional stage into rehearsals. It's not even unusual for a composer or librettist to pull out a previously written work, scoff at the decisions made by their past selves, and start slashing and burning with a metaphorical red pen. This means that throughout the eighteenth and nineteenth centuries, opera composers rarely produced a single definitive score for their operas. Instead, almost every canonical work is orbited by an asteroid field of sketches, drafts, rehearsal versions, performance versions, vocal scores, and orchestral scores, not to mention letters, journals, staging manuals, and other potentially relevant documents.

Take the score for the opera *Carmen*, which has been handed down to posterity in nine competing versions. There are five different "final" versions and four different preliminary ones, all created between 1874 and 1877. Three of the five final scores were finalized before composer Georges Bizet died in 1875, including the orchestral score he used for the opera's first performance (in which he added a number of new stage directions and revisions); his autograph score, which he further revised before his death; and the piano-vocal score, which he personally approved for publication with French publisher Choudens Père et Fils. Two more final scores were created after Bizet's death—including one that replaced the opera's original spoken dialogue with recitative (that is, sung dialogue) written by Bizet's friend Ernest Guiraud. Suddenly, we're facing an "I am Spartacus" situation. Will the real *Carmen* please stand up?

And *Carmen* isn't an outlier here. Ludwig van Beethoven wrote three different versions of his opera *Fidelio* between 1805 and 1814, along with four different versions of the overture alone. Giacomo Puccini similarly wrote multiple versions of the opera *Madama Butterfly*, as well as his operas *Edgar* and *Tosca*. All fantastic for archival historians but more than a little problematic when trying to select The One Score to Rule Them All.

"Version control" is particularly challenging when composers such as Georges Bizet die before anointing The One. But the situation can be just as tricky—if not trickier—when composers *don't* die and then keep tinkering with operas after they've been premiered.

Consider W. A. Mozart, who unhelpfully oversaw the premieres of multiple versions of some of his most beloved operas. The opera *Don Giovanni*, for example, exists in two distinct forms, each of which was formally premiered—one in Prague, one in Vienna. It's a similar story with Mozart's opera *The Marriage of Figaro*, which first premiered in 1786 and was performed again three years later with two new arias for the character Susanna. Which score is Scripture? Don't ask me. Both are stamped with Mozart's official seal of approval.

But when the legacy of a canonical opera is at stake, the choice of which score will be crowned king is a weighty one. Faced with three or four potential heirs to the throne—all blessed equally by their dying father—there has to be a way to weed out the pretenders. The most common strategy is to frame certain scores as being somehow inferior. Maybe they were early versions or mediocre works in progress. Maybe they were later versions but were still somehow corrupted. (This is often where rationalization can take on an air of desperation.) Maybe the composer was going senile when they made those changes! Maybe the composer was bullied into making those cuts!

Nearly any version of a score can theoretically be framed as The One depending on which primary sources are deployed and which ones are ignored. Like the act of composition itself, it comes down to a series of choices—between this version and that one, between this aria and that one. The more insurmountable challenge is trying to get everyone to agree.

Remember those two competing versions of Mozart's *The Marriage of Figaro*? In 1998, Italian mezzo-soprano Cecilia Bartoli bucked standard practice by performing the two arias from the opera's second version for a production at the Metropolitan Opera. Audiences were horrified. Critics were aghast. Even the production's stage director, Jonathan Miller, publicly distanced himself, telling *Opera News* that he'd agreed to the substitution "rather in the way that France had agreed in 1939." But was Bartoli actually in the wrong? For all we know, Mozart preferred the second pair of arias to the first.

These swirling issues of version control become even more complex when we add music publishers to the mix, because you can't sell a score to opera companies or singers without first making some copies.

A music publisher will print a score for mass consumption in exchange for a share of any revenue. But in the eighteenth and nineteenth centuries, this wasn't a simple matter of making a Xerox copy of the original—especially since xerographic copies wouldn't be invented until 1938. Instead, the publisher would task an in-house or freelance music editor with manually transforming the autograph score into the consistent black and white of a published version: grappling with the composer's illegible handwriting, squinting at hard-to-read musical notes, and generally proofreading and double-checking every single notation. Once this work was done and the scores were officially printed, the composer, librettist, publisher, and music editor could then sit back and wait for their cut of the profits.

But time passes. Composers and librettists inevitably die. Copyrights inevitably lapse (if they even existed in the first place). Another music publisher eventually emerges, and another music editor. Then another. And another. Perhaps one who's anxious to publish a new print run or a new edition. Perhaps one who's interested in printing the score in a different language. Perhaps one who just wants to compete with the original publisher.

And so, the process begins anew. Every published edition of a score involves a different set of eyes, a new look at the original handwritten score, and the inevitable discovery of things that were missed in previous editions: wrong notes, typos, perhaps a squished insect once mistaken for a musical chord. The result is a swarm of different published editions of any given canonical opera from the likes of publishers Choudens Père et Fils, Könemann, C. F. Peters, Schott, G. Schirmer, Dover, and Bärenreiter, among others.

But how different can these scores actually be, you might ask. They're different editions, but it's still the same opera, right? Isn't it the same scenario as the publication history of a novel such as F. Scott Fitzgerald's *The Great Gatsby*: dozens of different editions and different covers but always the same text?

Not quite. Consider: The text for *Gatsby* exists in a single approved version that was directly authorized by Fitzgerald himself, as well as his descendants and publisher. The opera *Carmen*, remember, exists in nine. This means all those different published editions of *Carmen*—all those scores printed and sold over the past century and a half—are also vastly different depending on the music editor, the publisher, and whichever version (or versions) of *Carmen* they deemed most authoritative.

Take the edition of *Carmen* published by Schott. This version combines the notes and rhythms from Bizet's piano-vocal score with the musical markings from his orchestral score—then adds the dialogue from the first libretto, just to make things confusing. Compare that with the version printed by C. F. Peters, which cuts and pastes the vocal lines from the piano-vocal score with the instrumental lines from the orchestral score. Or, for a real Frankenstein's monster of a mess, look at the 1964 edition published by Bärenreiter, which was scathingly described as "an arbitrary selection from almost every stage of Bizet's work" and "perhaps the most corrupt score of any major masterpiece published in modern times." Yikes.

Across these ambiguities, it's clear the musical score is far from a reliable primary source, let alone the museum antiquity imagined by opera traditionalists. "Fidelity . . . fidelity," our knights mutter, their golden banner looking a little worse for wear.

But this uncertainty also presents further complications. The instability of the score means opera's Greatest Hits are wide-open for operatic infidels to revise, reinterpret, and deconstruct—a seeming license to "ignore the basic mandates" of the composer and the librettist, as conservative writer Heather Mac Donald lamented in 2007. Meanwhile, our knights aren't abandoning their defense of the Scripture, even if that Scripture doesn't hold up to actual scrutiny. If anything, the uncertainties surrounding the score only make the battleground more brutal.

This poses a significant challenge for opera companies, which are trapped in the middle of two charging armies and trying to get each side to buy tickets. No artistic work exists in a vacuum, and presenting an eighteenth- or nineteenth-century opera for a twenty-first-century audience may necessitate adjustments to the score. The question of *which* adjustments, however, lies at the heart of the matter.

* * *

With any score, four categories of content can potentially be tweaked, revised, or, dare I say, ignored. There are the stage directions, which focus on the actions of the characters and are generally notated in superscript above the musical lines. There's the text of the libretto, or what the characters say. There's the music, or the specific notes, pitches, and rhythms. Lastly, there's the overarching story.

Up through the nineteenth century, changes to all four categories were commonplace. Companies would gleefully rearrange and reorder music, drop in excerpts from other operas, add new characters, and even rewrite entire storylines. See, for example, the 1887 production of *Carmen* staged at Spain's Teatro de la Zarzuela, in which principal characters were renamed, key scenes were rewritten, and the entire libretto was revised and then translated into Spanish. By the turn of the twentieth century, however, the idea of an opera as a fixed musical work was cemented in consciousness. And that Work with a capital *W* was embodied by the musical score.

So, where's the line between fidelity and desecration? And who gets to decide?

To unpack the rules of engagement, I spoke to Jonathan Dean, the long-standing supertitlist and in-house dramaturg for Seattle Opera. As a supertitlist—the person responsible for translating and projecting the text of an opera for a performance—Dean is always knee-deep in the libretto. But as a dramaturg, he's also intimately involved with the intricacies of the score as a whole. Dramaturgs essentially function as artistic advisers for opera productions. They know every in and out of a given work and provide feedback on the most accurate staging approach or, alternatively, the best way to manage problematic elements.

According to Dean, there's a clear hierarchy for fidelity to the score. And stage directions are the first to go. "Nobody pays attention to the old stage directions. That went away a hundred years ago," he said.

The rationale is that stage directions are already the most tenuous of notations. Many were inserted by editors and publishers rather than by the composer or the librettist, while others are simply a historical record of how things were done at the first performance (for better or worse). Still others are just downright impractical. Take the stage directions for Richard Wagner's opera *Siegfried*, in which he specifies the dragon Fafner should "spit from his nostrils" during a battle with the titular hero. Easier said than staged.

But if stage directions are at the bottom of the pecking order, the music of the score, Dean told me, is at the very top. Music is still largely perceived as being untouchable, the last bastion in preserving an opera as it was originally envisioned. Some conductors and companies will refuse to change a single note if it's printed in the score. Others are less rigid but still operate under the premise that tampering with the music isn't the "done" thing. "The game is, you try to do the notes pretty much as they are in whatever printed version has some kind of authority," Dean explained.

This doesn't mean music isn't regularly trimmed, moved around, or even cut. Changes are frequently made for financial reasons—shortening the length of an opera can mean paying less overtime to stagehands and instrumentalists. Changes are also made to help singers combat vocal fatigue, including judicious trims or even shifting an entire aria slightly higher or lower. Perhaps most often, music is cut out of consideration for audience attention spans. An eighteenth-century opera such as G. F. Handel's *Tamerlano* can politely be described as a slog, with a total running time of 240 minutes. Several well-placed musical cuts might enrage a Handel aficionado, but the rest of the audience will likely thank the company for it—if they even notice. Because here, it often comes down to appearances. Many companies are willing to change the music of the score, but only if the changes aren't explicit (or outrageous) enough to attract negative attention from traditionalists.

Now, what about the third component of the score . . . the text?

According to Dean, the libretto of a canonical opera often needs to be edited or revised, especially if a production is set in a different time period. Changes might be as minor as replacing a single word in the supertitles to avoid incongruity with the staging: swapping out *carriage* for *sedan* in a production set in the 1930s, for example. Editorial tweaks are also frequently made to address outdated or offensive language. Dean cited a 1999 production of Mozart's *The Magic Flute* at Seattle Opera for which the company removed racist elements from the text sung by the Moorish character Monostatos. This included a specific line in one of his arias, in which he says, "Must I avoid love because a Black man is ugly?!" Luckily, Monostatos was costumed in a green spandex fat suit for the production, so it was an easy fix: the text was changed from the German *schwarzer* (black) to *grüner* (green).

This script doctoring, as Dean calls it, is increasingly common for companies that want to present historical operas without appearing to support problematic ideologies in their texts. But Dean also made clear it's not a matter of mere censorship. Decisions about which changes are made—and how—involve careful consideration by the director, designers, and company leadership. One approach, he said, is to change the text to "protect the audience from the message," as with the change to Monostatos's skin color in *The Magic Flute*. It was "a G-rated, fun kids show," Dean explained. "We didn't want people to have to think too hard about it." The other approach is *not* to protect the audience but rather to intentionally confront them. This involves making revisions that heighten racist or sexist language and therefore remove any ambiguity about its offensiveness.

There's clearly a code of conduct when navigating a musical score, even as there's clearly precedent for making changes to the stage directions, music, and text—as long as those changes are made as surreptitiously as possible. But there's also no official rule book, no Committee of Operatic Fidelity that sends a cease-and-desist letter when a seeming line is crossed. As long as a score is in the public domain, there's nothing to stop a director, conductor, or company from taking a more extreme approach.

In 2022, director Yuval Sharon staged a production of Puccini's *La bohème* for Detroit Opera, in which the opera was presented in reverse order. In his version, consumptive heroine Mimì dies at the beginning of the opera instead of the end, coming back to life over the course of the work and eventually walking into the Parisian sunset with her lover. Sharon also cut the opera's intermission, trimmed Puccini's music down to a zippy two hours, and added a new character to introduce each act. It's not hard to imagine traditionalist knights looking at one another in abject horror from their seats in the theater: "But he can't do that! Is he *allowed* to do that?!"

Technically, yes. But there's always a risk in breaking from the seeming Scripture, particularly when it comes to the expectations of the audience. And nowhere are audience expectations more firmly entrenched than in the final component of the score: the story.

The story of an opera, or its plot, is established and sustained through the combination of stage directions, text, and music. But the story can also exist as much in the minds of the audience as in the pages of the actual score. Many in the Western world know the plot for *Romeo and Juliet* without looking at a copy of Shakespeare's play. In the same way, many audiences are already familiar with certain operatic storylines, particularly canonical ones. This means changes to the story can constitute a far more visible, invasive, and even offensive intervention.

Which brings us back to *Carmen.*

* * *

In 2018, Italian opera festival Maggio Musicale Fiorentino prompted an uproar when it changed the ending to Bizet's opera. *Carmen* usually ends with the sexually liberated Carmen being stabbed to death by her ex-lover Don José. Standing outside the bullfighting arena where her new toreador boy toy is performing, Carmen defiantly tells Don José to either kill her or let her pass. Not one for good choices, Don José opts for the former: he stabs Carmen, she falls, she dies. Cue the applause.

But in the Maggio Musicale production, Carmen *didn't* die. Instead, during her final confrontation with Don José, she snatched his gun and shot him in self-defense. The curtain fell with Don José dying and Carmen, for once, alive and well.

Festival superintendent Cristiano Chiarot cited Italy's high rates of violence against women as the primary motivator for the change. With one woman killed every three days in Italy, Chiarot argued the company had a moral responsibility to take a stand on the issue. "It was just the last thirty seconds and we wanted to draw attention to one of the plagues of our society," he said, defending himself in an interview with the *Financial Times*.

But the tweak was not well received—to put it lightly. During the final scene enraged audience members screamed, "Kill her! Kill her!" Stage director Leo Muscato was voraciously booed and subjected to threats of violence through his website contact form. The story was picked up by dozens of media outlets and swiftly hurtled across social media platforms. "Bizarre Bizet: A #MeToo Carmen Doesn't Die, and the Audience Shouts 'Kill Her!'" exclaimed a headline in the *Daily Beast*. "What's next? Should we change *Romeo and Juliet* to address suicide, or *Othello* to combat racism?" scoffed journalist Pietrangelo Buttafuoco in Italian newspaper *Il Foglio.*

In this instance, the festival company was caught in a perfect storm of political polarization and public attention. It wasn't all bad from a business standpoint: all six performances quickly sold out. But both the festival staff and the production's creative team were taken aback by the reaction. "It has caused an excessive, exaggerated fuss," said the stage director in a 2018 interview with *El País.* "I was not seeking to shock. . . . They can't burn me at the stake without seeing the whole opera."

Of all the sacred cows in the Canon, *Carmen* is perhaps the most holy. With a libretto by Henri Meilhac and Ludovic Halévy, the work is one of the most successful Western operas of all time, with hundreds of thousands of productions since its 1875 premiere. The story of Carmen and her doomed relationship with Don José has achieved an almost mythological status, with dozens of adaptations across film, television, and Broadway stages. And always with the same narrative arc. Boy meets girl. Boy loses girl. Boy kills girl.

So, we can't be all that surprised by the reaction to the Maggio Musicale's revision. Though to be fair, this wasn't the first—let alone only—production to deviate from Bizet's score in such a way. In a 2018 production directed by Barrie Kosky at the Royal Ballet and Opera at Covent Garden, Carmen is stabbed by Don José but then stands back up and shrugs at the audience in an added coda. The version staged by the Emma Abbott Grand English Opera Company in the 1880s added a pantomime in which Carmen tries to stab Don José first. (Suddenly, Don José's theoretical lawyer is preparing a plea of self-defense instead of voluntary manslaughter.) I even heard of a production at New York City Opera where Carmen committed suicide—though this wasn't planned in advance. Apparently, the tenor playing Don José had a temper tantrum during the final scene and stormed offstage, leaving Carmen to take matters into her own hands.

Carmen was actually the first opera I ever saw. I was ten years old, and my parents took me to a production directed by Keith Warner at Seattle Opera. Now, an opera about a woman getting stabbed to death may not seem the most intuitive choice for a child's first opera. But my mother anticipated the show would have colorful costumes and dancing, ideal for a kid raised on a steady diet of Rodgers and Hammerstein—hopefully the licentious stuff would go over my head. If this had been a traditional production of *Carmen*, my mother would have been spot-on with her assessment. Unfortunately, Keith Warner's production was far from traditional.

Set in Francoist Spain in the 1950s, Warner's version of *Carmen* was sparse, abstract, and featured gratuitous sex and violence. Described in a review by critic Melinda Bargreen: "The cigarette girls writhe around on the ground with their skirts and bodices hiked up. Characters are slapped and beaten and thrown to the ground so often that the cast should be getting hazard pay. Believe the warnings." The production was so controversial *The Seattle Times* set aside two consecutive weekends of print space to accommodate all the angry letters to the editor. "Did you happen to hear that terrible rumbling sound the other night at about 8 p.m.? It was Bizet turning over in his grave!!!" wrote one outraged reader.

If my mother was hoping for some bright scenic designs to distract my ten-year-old eyes from all the onstage violence, she was also disappointed. There were no lush Old World re-creations of a Sevillian cigarette factory . . . just a few wooden chairs and an asymmetrical white wall.

We watched dozens of audience members walk out during the performance. But my mother was torn: Do the same, or try to teach me an important lesson about never walking out of a show? As a professional dancer herself, the ethics of respecting the performers won out. We stayed until the bitter end.

I don't remember much about the production, except for the final scene. Dressed in a tea-length white gown, Carmen leaned against the asymmetrical white wall and challenged Don José to kill her. Don José brandished a knife and brutally stabbed her in the stomach. Carmen turned, pressed her body against the white wall, and slowly staggered from one end of the stage to the other, leaving a massive streak of blood on the wall behind her. Finally, and to the relief of many in the audience, she fell to the floor and died.

I'm not saying I was traumatized by this moment, but I vividly remember it thirty years later. The white dress. The slow stagger. The red streak of blood extending the full length of the set. Somehow since then I've managed to avoid attending any other staged production of *Carmen*. Must be a coincidence.

But blood spatter aside, just how unequivocal *is* Carmen's death? Who says Carmen has to die at the end of the opera and can't, say, die of lung cancer forty years later?

I asked this of mezzo-soprano Denyce Graves, who famously played Carmen at nearly every major opera house in the 1990s and 2000s. A production photo of Graves in the role was even on the cover of my opera-history textbook in college. As you might imagine, I tried to play it cool during our interview and failed miserably.

For Graves, Carmen absolutely has to die. "One of the things that's important about her is she's completely uncompromising," she told me. "She sees life as a series of experiences to be savored, which often leads to conflict with traditional values and ultimately to her tragic demise. Death is an inevitable consequence of her refusal to conform, yet even in death, she maintains a sense of defiance and independence."

It's not hard to be persuaded, especially when you're starstruck. But what does the score say?

First, the stage directions. Across the varying published editions of *Carmen*, all are unequivocally consistent, if not in precise wording, then certainly in meaning. In the G. Schirmer edition: "He stabs her; she falls and dies." In Choudens Père et Fils: "He strikes her, she falls and dies." In C. F. Peters: "He stabs her. Carmen falls and dies." You get the idea.

Next, the text. The libretto includes several references that make the case for Carmen's death. For starters, after Don José stabs her, he literally confesses to the crime: "*C'est moi qui l'ai tué!*" (It was I who killed her!) Or look earlier in the opera, when Carmen foresees her own death while reading tarot cards. Strike two.

What about the music? Many argue that Carmen's death is mandated by Bizet's notes and rhythms. A key point of evidence is the recurring "fate motif" that pops up at dramatic moments, functioning as a kind of musical portent of doom until the very moment Carmen dies.

If we take the score as Scripture, the stage directions, text, and music seem to support the argument for Carmen's death. But as we know, there's precedent for changing all three elements. That stage direction? Thrown out. Those passages of text? Easily tweaked or reinterpreted. As for the music . . . there's certainly a motif and it certainly means something. But who's to say what exactly?

That still leaves us with the story, the public face of the opera outlined in the score but equally fixed in the minds of the audience. The story of Carmen and Don José has transcended the opera house. People who've never seen—who *will* never see—Bizet's opera still know the plot. This means changing the story of *Carmen* means changing its identity—and that's a modification that will inevitably discomfort nearly everyone in the audience, from opera novices to die-hard traditionalists. In most minds, the sequence is fated. Boy meets girl. Boy loses girl. Boy always kills girl.

* * *

Ultimately, you *can* change the music, text, stage directions, and even story of an opera—as long as you're willing to face the potential consequences. But there's still one final piece of ammunition in the battle over the score, one last-ditch effort by our traditionalist knights, now partially hoarse from all those shouts of "Fidelity! Fidelity!" Just because you can, they gasp, doesn't mean you should. Because what matters most of all—more than even the black and white of a printed musical score—is what the composer and the librettist intended.

"Intention"—or what the original creators wanted for their work—is frequently invoked to defend operas from seeming interlopers and to imbue performances with a je ne sais quoi of artistic legitimacy. This isn't just any staging of *Carmen*, it's a faithful reconstruction of what Bizet and his librettists wanted!

It's a recurring theme in opera marketing campaigns and critical reviews. "Faithful to the intentions of composers and librettists," promised the Opéra Royal de Wallonie-Liège in its 2019–20 season announcement. It's "what Wagner actually wanted to see onstage," confirmed General Manager Peter Gelb of the Metropolitan Opera's 2010–12 production of the *Ring Cycle*. "Our artistic mission is to be faithful to the composer's intentions," noted Victor DeRenzi, then artistic director of Sarasota Opera, in a 2014 interview.

Intention has even cropped up in funding bequests. In 1987, the Metropolitan Opera received a $27 million donation, with a portion of the funds earmarked to support a new production each season. But not just any new production, mind you—only a production that, according to the agreement, was "staged and performed in a traditional manner that is generally faithful to the intentions of the composer and the librettist." When the Metropolitan Opera elected to use some of the cash for a 2001 production of Wagner's *Tristan und Isolde* that *wasn't* generally faithful—or at least, wasn't faithful enough—the donor's estate sued the company and demanded the funds be returned. The case was eventually settled out of court.

Given how often the intentions of the composer and the librettist are touted, cited, and declaimed, one might assume they're explicit in the score. But once again, it's not that simple.

Some intentions can be gleaned from basic notations. We might even know the precise musical moment when the soprano is supposed to die onstage, her hand dropping to the ground amid a tragic sounding of brass. But many of the more nuanced intentions associated with certain characters, certain lines of text, and certain passages of music are inevitably ambiguous. Most of the time, they aren't even notated one way or the other. Maybe they were verbally communicated during rehearsal. Maybe the composer and the librettist assumed they were obvious and didn't bother writing them down. Maybe they were intentionally left open for interpretation. Or maybe they were never considered in the first place.

As a librettist, I'm often approached by singers who compliment me on a particular meaning or theme in one of my texts. I'm always happy to take credit. But I'd be lying if I didn't admit that, on more than one occasion, the deeper meaning so gallantly attributed to me was something I'd never before considered, let alone explicitly intended.

The truth is we can never be absolutely sure about intentions. In 1988, famed American musicologist Richard Taruskin described the very premise of intention as a "red herring." "Composers do not always express them. If they do express them, they may do so disingenuously. Or they may be honestly mistaken," he wrote. "If anyone doubts this, let him listen to the five recordings Stravinsky made of *The Rite of Spring*, and try to decide how the composer intended it to go." There will always be gaps in the facts, Taruskin argued. And intentions, even those notated in the score, are inevitably more gap than fact.

When it comes to *Carmen*, we do know with certainty that Bizet wanted Carmen to die. The two codirectors of Paris's Opéra-Comique (that's the theater that hosted the opera's premiere in 1875), along with librettist Henri Meilhac, actively lobbied Bizet *not* to kill her. An arbitrator was even brought in to try to force Bizet's hand. But he dug in his heels: he wanted her to die. Our traditionalist knights nod smugly.

But this brings up a deeper existential question beneath the turmoil of this battleground. Does it actually matter what Bizet wanted? Especially when he's spent the last century and a half crumbling to dust in a tomb in the Cimetière du Père-Lachaise? Once an opera has surpassed the lifespan of its original creators—once a score is being considered by a new audience in a new time and social context—does the principle of fidelity still apply?

I asked opera librettist and educator Mark Campbell how he'd feel if his creative intentions were posthumously ignored by an opera company or stage director—if the score for one of his operas was liberally tweaked and edited. One of the world's most successful living librettists, Campbell has written the librettos for more than forty operas, including the Pulitzer Prize–winning *Silent Night* (2011), which he created with composer Kevin Puts.

"Of course I'd hate it," Campbell said. "Intentions matter. They don't realize how much effort we put into this work, how much thought. But I also won't be around. I can only ask that directors wait until I'm dead to revise my work."

Campbell understands the impetus to revise certain scores, particularly the ones that flirt with racist or sexist themes. But he also posed a pointed question to the opera companies that are scrambling to change these operas: "Why are you even trying to save this racist story? Why are you trying to save this sexist story? There are so many operas out there that could be just as popular if you program them. But you continue to program these works because that's what you think your audience wants to see. And then you have to update them, you have to rewrite them, you have to apologize for them. Why not produce a different opera? Why not produce a new one?"

For many, the score belongs in a museum. But the reality of this battleground isn't about fidelity to some idealized physical artifact. It's actually about fidelity to us. To the audience. To subjective ideas of what a score says and what an opera means—and whether that can change after its creators are dead.

No matter how carefully a score is preserved, worshipped, or protected, it will also never be more than a fragment of the whole, never more than one of the two interrelated identities that make opera what it is: both a tangible score and an ephemeral performance. And so, the score is only our first battleground, one that sows the seeds of discord that will take root and blossom when the score is interpreted and realized . . . onstage.

CHAPTER 3

The Stage

— or —

(Yellow)Facing the Music

In 2017, another production of a canonical opera was met with rabid booing and teeth gnashing. Not because the lead character didn't die when she was supposed to. Not even because the company messed with the score. In this case, the problem was the staging. The opera was *La bohème*. The company was the Paris Opéra. The stage director was Claus Guth. And the setting? Wait for it . . . Outer space.

La bohème is a classic tale of love, starving artists, and tuberculosis set against a backdrop of 1830s Paris. With music by Giacomo Puccini and a libretto by Luigi Illica and Giuseppe Giacosa, it's one of the world's most frequently performed operas, ranking a close second to *Carmen* in popularity. In 2024, nearly four thousand different productions of *La bohème* were staged worldwide, with the total number of performances since the opera's 1896 premiere extending into the millions. (That's not even counting the 525,600 different productions of *Rent*, the 1994 rock musical inspired by *La bohème.*)

The setup for the opera is almost sitcom-esque. Four handsomely disheveled roommates—a poet, a musician, a painter, and a philosopher—are shivering in a frigid apartment on Christmas Eve when their neighbor Mimì knocks on the door and asks for a light for her candle. The poet Rodolfo (a tenor, naturally) immediately falls in love and then immediately regrets his financial life choices when Mimì starts coughing up blood and he can't afford a doctor. Cue a lingering demise for the soprano, a devastated tenor singing "Mimì!" very loudly, and curtains. Both for Mimì and the opera.

Traditional stagings of *La bohème* lean heavily into a nineteenth-century Parisian aesthetic. Think trousers and grimy cravats for the men, corsets and puffy-sleeved gowns for the women, and a set that evokes a dingy French garret overlooking the Seine. But for his staging in 2017, director Claus Guth decided to take a different approach.

Guth's version is set on a spaceship, with the audience joining the action on day 126 of a mission gone terribly wrong. An ominous report is projected via the supertitles: "Expedition in danger—off course—engines inoperative—life-support resources almost exhausted." Our four roommates (now astronauts) begin to hallucinate from the lack of oxygen, prompting Rodolfo to recall his long-lost love Mimì as a kind of sci-fi apparition. And in case anyone's expecting an Apollo 13–type turnaround, no such luck for these bohemians. The spaceship is forced to land on a distant planet, and Rodolfo's hallucinations grow increasingly intense until he finally succumbs to oxygen deprivation. RIP.

Critical response to Guth's staging was, shall we say, mixed. "Claus Guth's spaceship production crashes and burns," said a 2017 review in the *Financial Times*. "Bizarre to the point that it's incomprehensible," said another in the *Twin Cities Arts Reader*. Or take this burn from an opera blogger: "This is my candidate, not only for the worst opera production ever, but for the worst production ever on a theater stage." Tell us how you really feel.

Then there was the audience. Sound might not travel in space, but it certainly traveled in the auditorium of the Opéra Bastille. Boos, heckling, shouts of "Give us back Puccini!"—the noise was so deafening that conductor Gustavo Dudamel had to stop the orchestra multiple times. Guth told me he was even physically attacked during the performance: "People were pushing me. It was crazy."

Guth admitted he expected some resistance to the staging, but not quite that much. He even warned Stèphane Lissner, then *intendant* (general manager) of the Paris Opéra: "I told Lissner I love this music, but I'm not interested in continuing the clichés of the story," Guth told me in 2024. "What I *am* interested in is what if Paris doesn't exist anymore and we've ruined the whole planet, and then we're in a space capsule and we're running out of oxygen. What do we do? We remember the most human and warm and exciting stories of our life." In this, Guth was intentionally drawing from the 1851 novel that inspired the opera, Henri Murger's *La Vie de Bohème*, in which two old men idealize their misspent youth in Paris. "Your intellect can say that it's wrong. That it's not *La bohème*," Guth continued. "But your body will respond that it's amazing and spectacular and in connection with the music in some way. And that will make your intellectual resistance smaller, step by step."

For Guth, *La bohème* doesn't exist by itself. "It's like a poem, something that has to be interpreted," he told me. "It has to be rediscovered every time. The notes exist. The text exists. But it's only through the performers that it comes to life. The rest is just paper."

Welcome to our next battleground.

* * *

Some opera lovers experience opera without the fuss of staging. They settle into a comfortable armchair, drop a needle on their favorite record, and imbibe the art form as an audio-only phenomenon. Who needs the distraction of sets and costumes, they scoff, when one can simply ride the sonic wave of a thrilling high note?

Maybe. But most fans of the art form also understand that opera isn't technically opera *without* the staging—that it's counterfeit without those pesky sets and costumes, those singers walking around in character, and that audience watching everything unfold in real time. For those well-dressed audience members the battle of the stage is impossible to ignore.

The term *staging* encompasses everything an audience sees when the curtain goes up. This includes sets, backdrops, lighting, projections, and props (short for "properties" or any movable object used onstage), which collectively establish the setting in which the story takes place. See, for example, the *Star Trek*–esque interior of the spaceship in the first act of Guth's *La bohème*, which features clinical white walls, flickering electronics, and a large viewscreen that shows the swiftly approaching planet in the distance. Staging also includes the way the performers are integrated with the physical setting, from their costumes, wigs, and makeup to their physical movements.

Both components—the setting and the performers—are linked by the overarching stage concept, or the particular interpretation of the opera that's being presented. The concept is the *how* and *why* that drives everything, informing the sets, costumes, lighting, and props, even as it shapes the way the characters look and behave. In Guth's *La bohème*, the concept wasn't just that the opera was set in space. It was also that the entire storyline was a figment of Rodolfo's oxygen-starved imagination.

When it comes to staging, the concept is king. And the king of the concept is the stage director. While the conductor is in charge of everything the audience hears—the music, the orchestra, the singing—the director is responsible for everything the audience *sees.* The director decides how exactly an opera will be presented and assumes authority over each of the visual elements. But not alone. Every opera production has a team of designers, each of whom works with—and for—the director.

First, there's the set designer, who essentially functions as the director's second-in-command from the earliest stages of the production's development. *Herr Direktor* wants the first act to be set in a postnuclear dystopian world and the second act set in a Russian ballroom? No problem! The set designer rolls up their sleeves, pulls out a pencil and/or 3D design software, and carves out the physical world of the stage, from the sets and backdrops to the furniture and props. Everything except for the lights and costumes.

The lights fall under the purview of the lighting designer, who wields floodlights, spotlights, and color gels (among other technical equipment) to evoke certain moods and environments—an appropriately starry night for Romeo and Juliet's balcony canoodling, for example. The lighting designer is also tasked with directing the gaze of the audience wherever the director wants it (and when) to make sure the audience understands the story and concept. Most of all, the lighting designer uses their toolbox of light to connect the different visual components onstage.

Next is the costume designer, who's responsible for deciding what the characters will look like, from their apparel and hair to their shoes and accessories. What will Mimì wear for her initial hallucinatory meet-cute with Rodolfo? The costume designer designs and then either sews, rents, or buys Mimì's gown, then works with a wig and makeup designer on the finishing touches. Here, it's not only a question of appearance but also practicality. Which costume will evoke a particular character and align with the director's concept, while also ensuring the singer can successfully negotiate a pile of space rocks?

Depending on the production, there might be even more designers attached. Video and projection designers are an increasingly common addition to creative teams, since many productions now incorporate animations or projections into their staging. That distant planet growing ever closer in Guth's *La bohème*? The tenor's wild hallucinations projected onto the walls of the set? All the handiwork of video designer Arian Andiel.

Every designer on the creative team holds a key piece of the staging puzzle. But when it comes to the concept—the how and the why—it always comes back to the pointiest point of our artistic pyramid: the director. And aside from budgetary constraints and potential outrage from audiences, there's no limit to how far a director can boldly go when staging a canonical opera. There are no blueprints, no copyright restrictions, and certainly no staging manuals powerful enough to bend a director to their will. A director can stage *La bohème* in 1830s Paris as per tradition. Or in outer space. Or in 1930s Berlin, a modern-day New York tenement, or the cancer ward of a hospital. (All actual productions, by the way.)

This brings us to the burning question that ignites the skirmishes of this particular battleground. How are operas *meant* to be staged?

Enter our two warring factions, which emerged alongside the crystallization of the Canon and the rise of the director in the early twentieth century.

First, the progressives, aka the *Regietheater* crowd. The premise of *Regietheater*, or "director's theater," is that a director has total freedom when it comes to staging, regardless of what's printed in the score or the intentions of the composer and the librettist. A director can elect to change an opera's setting, add secondary storylines or subtext, transform a plot into an abstract allegory, or even subvert the work entirely. Consider, for example, Doris Dörrie's 2005 production of Verdi's opera *Rigoletto*, which wasn't set in sixteenth-century Italy as noted in the score but rather on the Planet of the Apes.

The broader goal of the *Regietheater* approach isn't to stage an opera exactly as it was staged when it first premiered. Instead, the aim is to add new layers of meaning and commentary that will resonate with modern-day audiences. "It is not our responsibility to stage these works as the authors originally intended; how could that even happen?" said stage director Peter Konwitschny in a 2005 interview. "Our job is to ask specific, important questions in such a way that they stimulate discussion. The operas themselves are the material; they are no end in themselves."

Thanks to the efforts of mid-twentieth-century German practitioners such as Richard Wagner's grandsons Wieland and Wolfgang, Germany is the recognized epicenter of *Regietheater*, with public appreciation for director's theater seeming to decrease exponentially the farther away from Germany you get. And it's deep in the heart of enemy territory that we find the headquarters of our opposing faction: the opera traditionalists, or the *Werktreue* crowd.

Translated from the German as "faithfulness to the work" or "true work," *Werktreue* refers to the belief that staging should be faithful to an opera's "true" meaning—that there's one right way to stage *La bohème* and it's definitely not in space. The score plays a critical role in establishing the benchmark of right versus wrong: Puccini says *La bohème* takes place in 1830s Paris, therefore all productions should be set in 1830s Paris. But the bigger line in the sand is the tradition that's associated with certain operas, or the way they were staged at their premiere and then subsequently staged over following decades.

Now, on paper, this dispute might sound fairly reasonable. Here we have two thoughtful if opposing perspectives on staging that presumably agree to disagree and then perhaps go out for a light lunch together. In practice? It's a bloodbath.

Depending on which article or review you read, you'll encounter accusations that *Regietheater* stagings are "psychotic nightmares," a "sick, unenlightened distortion of reality," and "the ruination of opera." There's an entire Facebook group, called Against Modern Opera Productions, that's exclusively dedicated to derailing the *Regietheater* movement. Boasting nearly sixty thousand followers, the page posts frequent diatribes against nontraditional stagings, often accompanied by a bevy of vomit emojis. "Opera Friends! Is this the opera you want? If not, fight!" reads a post from April 2024.

There's even a precedent of legal challenges. After attending a *Regietheater* staging of Johann Strauss II's operetta *Die Fledermaus* at the Salzburg Festival in 2001, an audience member took the company to court, claiming they'd substituted a different opera from the one he paid for. The audience member may have had a point—director Hans Neuenfels reimagined the operetta's traditional nineteenth-century ball as a cocaine-fueled disco—but the Austrian court ultimately ruled against the plaintiff, citing the festival's artistic freedom.

The heirs of composer Francis Poulenc and writer Georges Bernanos similarly sued the Bavarian State Opera and director Dmitri Tcherniakov over a 2010 production of Poulenc and Bernanos's opera *Dialogues of the Carmelites*, which modified the opera's ending through its staging. While the Carmelite nuns are traditionally guillotined, Tcherniakov's version arranged for them to be rescued before getting the chop (all save one, who's blown up). After the lawsuit worked its way through the French court system, it was deemed Tcherniakov's staging misrepresented "the spirit of the work," and DVD sales of the offending production were banned. (The decision was later overturned.)

To be fair, many *Regietheater* productions are designed for shock value, with some directors seeming to revel in the indignation they inspire. Take the 2004 production of Mozart's opera *The Abduction from the Seraglio* staged by director Calixto Bieito for Germany's Komische Oper Berlin. Normally a lighthearted comedy about a group of Europeans who end up in a Turkish harem, Bieito's staging included depictions of sex, blow jobs, rape, suicide, and torture, not to mention nipples being cut off, forced urine-drinking, and real-life prostitutes. Audience members shouted "Fire the director!," sponsors threatened to pull their funding, and all seven performances sold out, with Bieito no doubt chuckling as he deposited his hefty paycheck.

But even less extreme stagings can prompt equal vitriol from *Werktreue* devotees, including productions that only change an opera's time period or setting and nothing else. Consider this proclamation from Olivier Keegel, former editor in chief of the *Opera Gazet* and avowed *Werktreue* advocate: "No director has the right to perform an opera in a way that is alien to or contrary to the historical setting and/or the specific set descriptions of the composer or librettist," he wrote in 2022. "But good Lord, the barbarians do it anyway."

It's common for traditionalists to use *Regietheater* (or, as it's frequently dubbed, Eurotrash) as a slur for any and all stagings that even hint at the nontraditional. But a production of *La bohème* isn't necessarily *Regietheater* just because it's set in space instead of 1830s Paris, even if outraged audiences bandy the term around. If the arc of the story remains the same, if the characters still function and interact in the same way as in the original, then the production is still arguably "true" to the work, still arguably *Werktreue* (albeit with light sabers and/or tricorders).

The actual authenticator of *Regietheater* is whether it aims to deviate from the original arc of the story or rethink the characters as a way of adding that additional layer of commentary and interpretation. With his *La bohème*, Guth wasn't simply copying and pasting Puccini's opera into a sci-fi setting. He was intentionally reframing it, reconceiving both the story and the relationships between its characters. A tenor tripping out of his mind, Mimì as a long-dead ghost, a crash landing, and everyone dying at the end? Ding ding ding—that's *Regietheater.*

At a fundamental level, the conflict between *Regietheater* and *Werktreue*—and the various gradations between the two extremes—is a disagreement about what a staged opera actually *is*. Is it a reenactment? A reconstruction? An attempt to re-create the original as closely as possible? (Nods in *Werktreue*.) Or is it an adaptation? A kind of artistic offspring that's based on the original but also something new? (Winks in *Regietheater*.)

Outside the opera house, we're all well familiar with the concept of adaptation. My formative teen years were spent watching the 1995 BBC adaptation of Jane Austen's *Pride and Prejudice* (Colin Firth as Mr. Darcy!), plus every other film and television adaptation of Austen I could lay my hands on. Every adaptation was rife with changes, cuts, and tweaks to the original, all made with the goal of reframing a well-known story for a contemporary audience. And did I care that Mr. Darcy took a swim in the lake at Pemberley in the BBC adaptation but not in the original novel? Definitely not.

But the notion of adaptation also presumes an existing familiarity with the original. This is one reason why *Regietheater* and *Regietheater*-adjacent productions often rub audiences the wrong way. A conceptual staging or "adaptation" of *La bohème* only works if the audience has already seen a gazillion different productions of *La bohème*—if they actually know the original and can recognize what's commentary and what's not. For many audiences, especially in countries that don't have a strong culture of opera attendance, that level of familiarity isn't always present.

An even bigger catalyst for this conflict, however, is an emotional one. For many proponents of *Werktreue*, traditional stagings are the equivalent of comfort food, evoking nostalgic memories of childhood and benevolent grandparents taking them to the opera for the first time. These audiences don't want new insights or commentary, thank you very much. They want their *La bohème* like their grandmother's apple pie, forever fixed in time and made with the original recipe.

Here's where things on the battlefield take a darker turn. Because when audiences defend traditional stagings of canonical operas—the way they've *always* been done—they aren't just defending nineteenth-century corsets, grimy cravats, and Parisian garrets. They're also defending more insidious staging traditions that have long lingered in opera, traditions that few outside the opera house are still defending. Traditions such as blackface and yellowface.

* * *

As an art form, opera developed against a background of colonial expansion: new (to Europe) worlds, new (to Europe) cultures, and a European public that was ravenously curious about all of it. The so-called Orient—vaguely everything from North Africa to East Asia—was as mysterious and intriguing as the people who lived there. So, it's no wonder that a huge number of operas written in the eighteenth and nineteenth centuries actively dabbled in the exotic. Why bother setting an opera in humdrum Germany or France when audiences would much rather be transported to a faraway land with jewels, spices, and hot-blooded women?

Amid the swirling interest in the Orient came the emergence of several operatic character tropes. One was the Turk (aka Muslim), who cropped up in hundreds of operas from roughly the 1680s to the

1820s. Then there were Moors—also dark-skinned Muslims—such as Monostatos in Mozart's *The Magic Flute* and Otello in Verdi's *Otello* (that's *Othello* if you're speaking Shakespeare). Then there were Ethiopians and generic "Africans," such as the princess Aida in Verdi's *Aida* and Sélika in Meyerbeer's *L'Africaine*; "Gypsies"* such as Carmen in Bizet's *Carmen* and Azucena in Verdi's *Il trovatore*; and various iterations of "Oriental" women from Asia and Southeast Asia, including the man-hating Turandot in Puccini's *Turandot*, the Sri Lankan priestess Leïla in Bizet's *The Pearl Fishers*, and the submissive geisha Cio-Cio-San in Puccini's *Madama Butterfly*.

Alongside these new characters came a plethora of recurring storylines. One cookie-cutter plot was the abduction scenario, in which a European woman is kidnapped by a licentious Turk or Moor, only to be returned safely by the end of the opera, purity intact (phew). Another boilerplate plot was the colonial love affair, in which a European (or European-ish) man becomes involved with a foreign woman, always with tragic results.

The challenge with all of this was that your average eighteenth- and nineteenth-century European composer and librettist knew bupkes about the exotic locations they were writing about, not to mention the people who lived there. Instead, as a default, most simply drew on the cultural stereotypes circulating at the time, clichés that were already familiar to Orient-obsessed European audiences. Want to set an opera in China? Just add a pagoda. Constantinople? Slip on those harem pants. Japan? Better round up some geishas.

---

* This term was a common ethnic identifier used in opera in the eighteenth and nineteenth centuries and is now widely considered to be offensive. Accordingly, I only use the term where necessary, as well as embedded within quotation marks.

Not that we can blame composers or librettists for their scanty research practices. Source material about such places as Africa and Asia was incredibly sparse. In many cases, composers and librettists had little to work with besides imported goods (think porcelain vases), plus written reports from travelers who'd made it "there" and back. When setting his opera *Turandot* in ancient China, for example, Giacomo Puccini relied on a Chinese music box and a book written by a Belgian customs officer. Not exactly a recipe for a fleshed-out portrayal.

These operas are artifacts of their time, glimpses of a particular (and outdated) worldview. So, are many of their plots and characters racist when viewed through twenty-first-century eyes? Duh. This doesn't take away their value as historical works. But remember that opera is only actually opera when it's *staged*. And this is where we run into trouble: when the cringeworthy plots and characters of these operas are linked to their staging traditions.

Throughout the eighteenth and nineteenth centuries, white performers playing Moors or African characters would rub their skin with burnt cork, red iron oxide, or lard to attain darker skin tones. For the European premiere of *Aida* at the Teatro alla Scala in 1872, Verdi's staging manual specified the singer playing the titular Ethiopian princess should use makeup to create "olive, dark reddish skin." For the premiere of *Otello* in 1887, tenor Francesco Tamagno also darkened his skin and wore a curled black wig to play Otello.

White performers playing Asian characters used similar techniques to change their appearance. For her premiere as the Japanese character Cio-Cio-San in *Madama Butterfly* in 1904, Italian soprano Rosina Storchio sported a full kimono and geisha-style wig. For his turn as the Japanese marriage broker Goro in the same production, tenor Gaetano Pini-Corsi wore eye makeup to evoke an "Oriental" eye, plus a kimono and a wig with a black topknot.

In such cases, costumes, makeup, and wigs were used in concert with sets, backdrops, and lighting as an integral part of an opera's staging. While the elements of the physical set created the exotic world of the setting—the Egypt of *Aida* and the Japan of *Madama Butterfly*—the specific costume and makeup choices helped to "people" that world, creating the requisite Egyptians, Ethiopians, and Japanese to transport the audience into the story. And because performers of color were largely excluded from opera (more on this in the next chapter), this meant white performers were inevitably the ones assuming different ethnicities.

Today, we can identify these practices through the contemporary lingo of *blackface* and *yellowface*. Onstage, blackface and yellowface can include the use of makeup, wigs, and costumes, as well as physical movements or mannerisms—anything that helps a performer assume the guise of a different ethnic identity.

The use of blackface in this sense can be traced back to theatrical performances in Europe as early as the 1500s. The practice was later imported to the United States, where it became closely associated with minstrel shows. Starting in the 1820s, white performers would "black up" for the entertainment of white audiences, not only using makeup to exaggerate Black facial features but also incorporating buffoonery, slapstick physical comedy, and caricatured speech. The American form of blackface was eventually exported back to Europe by touring minstrel troupes.

Yellowface showed up on theatrical stages soon after minstrel shows did, thanks to Japan's opening up to European trade in 1853, plus rolling waves of Chinese migration in the nineteenth century.

Unlike the blackface of minstrel shows, however, yellowface was never closely associated with a single genre of performance, at least in the United States. Instead, it was associated with *all* of them, with Asian character tropes such as the cruel Dragon Lady, innocent China Doll, groveling servant, and Fu Manchu–esque villain becoming popular conceits across theater, ballet, vaudeville, and opera.

Two specific varieties of yellowface emerged in practice, both of which traded in racial stereotypes through a combination of makeup, posture, and costumes. One was used by male performers and involved greasepaint (No. 16, "Chinese," was the shade of choice—no, really), taped or prosthetically altered eyes, and hackneyed gestures such as shuffling and bowing. The other, described as "cosmetic yellowface" by scholar Esther Kim Lee, was reserved for female performers and evoked geisha-style aesthetics: ivory-skin makeup, small painted mouths, winged eyeliner, elaborate costumes, and dainty or coy gestures (e.g., tittering behind a fan).

Both blackface and yellowface can be recognized as historical forms of propaganda. But here's the rub. Flash forward to the present day, and these practices remain commonplace at many opera companies worldwide. Attend a traditional staging of *Madama Butterfly* and you'll inevitably encounter a sea of kimonos, black wigs, and winged eyeliner. Traditional productions of *Lakmé* or *The Pearl Fishers* frequently go hand in hand with saris, bindis, and bronzer liberally applied. Even productions with African or Moorish characters often still rely on singers "blacking up" for their roles, particularly in Europe. Incredibly, in 2014, the UK's English National Opera was hailed as the first major opera company to have a white tenor play the role of Otello *without* darkening his skin.

But these traditions are no longer flying under the radar. In recent years, a wave of controversies has rocked the opera industry, with numerous companies accused of using blackface or yellowface in their staging. Take the 2022 production of Verdi's *Aida* at Italy's Arena di Verona Festival, which found itself at the center of a media firestorm when production photos showed white soprano Anna Netrebko playing the role of Aida wearing a dreadlocked wig and dark skin makeup. "Everywhere in the world used to have what you call blackface," the company defended itself in a public statement. "So as long as we have a historical production, it is very hard to change them. . . . We must respect the historical truth."

When it comes to blackface and yellowface, there's an assumption that—to borrow from US Supreme Court Justice Potter Stewart—it's like pornography: you know it when you see it. But in Opera Land, it's significantly more nuanced than Mickey Rooney wearing fake buckteeth and prosthetically slanted eyes in the 1961 film *Breakfast at Tiffany's*. Many aspects of opera staging can exoticize or caricaturize in ways that are off-putting or even offensive to some audiences. The most obvious players are makeup and altered eye shape—but there's also potentially wigs, costumes, physical mannerisms, and even how the performers are directed to act onstage. All are subtle but very real aspects of how blackface and yellowface can manifest—and can also be completely independent of who's underneath all that eyeliner and foundation.

The question is, when is it a caricature, and when is it just a costume?

* * *

According to mezzo-soprano Nina Yoshida Nelsen, there's uncertainty in the opera industry over where to draw the line with yellowface. A fourth-generation Japanese American, Yoshida Nelsen cofounded the Asian Opera Alliance in 2021, an advocacy group that promotes Asian singers and works with companies that are staging Orientalist works—that is, historical operas that take a stereotypical and often derogatory view of the "Orient." In 2024, Yoshida Nelsen added a new administrative hat, becoming the artistic director of Boston Lyric Opera.

"Some people consider yellowface to be any non-Asian wearing a kimono onstage," she told me in 2023. "For other people, it's about changing facial features or what type of wig they're putting on. There's also potentially a difference between what yellowface might look like in opera compared to what it might look like in television and film." In other words, there isn't a set definition—at least one that everyone acknowledges.

Stage director Aria Umezawa, whose mother is white and father is Japanese, defines yellowface as "anything that would allow a person not of Asian descent to portray an Asian character." Speaking as part of a webinar hosted by Opera Colorado in 2023, Umezawa shared her belief that yellowface includes makeup and costumes, as well as how performers are directed.

Oliver Mears, director of opera at the UK's Royal Ballet and Opera, is one who resists at least part of that definition. In an interview leading up to the company's 2022 production of Puccini's *Madama Butterfly*, Mears said, "No responsible opera house—including Covent Garden—would now dream of attempting to change ethnicity with makeup." True to Mears's word, the white soprano who played Cio-Cio-San in the production didn't wear geisha-style makeup. She did, however, still wear a kimono and a black wig, as did all the women in the chorus. Was that yellowface? Mears would say no. Umezawa would presumably say yes.

The question of whether a production is using blackface is similarly subject to debate. For some Black opera singers, a white person wearing dark makeup to perform a role such as Otello or Aida is distinct from the blackface of minstrel shows. In a 2019 interview with the Associated Press, soprano Latonia Moore noted she didn't have objections to using dark skin makeup for certain roles. "The only issue I've had is the Al Jolson look," she said, referring to the shoe-polish black makeup and exaggerated pink lips worn by Jolson in the 1927 film *The Jazz Singer.* Bass-baritone Eric Owens agreed: "That's blackface when you're disparaging the person. When you look at Otello and Aida, someone aspiring to be the leader or the princess of Ethiopia, I've never had a problem with it. If they were trying to make fun of black people, that's different." Both Moore and Owens zero in on the question of intent and whether the staging is meant to demean and stereotype. And if it's not? Then, maybe makeup's just makeup.

But here's where it becomes clear that operatic blackface and operatic yellowface also come with different kinds of historical baggage. All of opera's exotic characters, from Turks and Moors to Ethiopians and "Africans," are the product of European Orientalist fantasies. But the Asian ones—Cio-Cio-San in *Madama Butterfly*, Turandot and her advisers Ping, Pang, and Pong* in *Turandot*, among many others—are explicit racial stereotypes in a way that characters such as Aida and Otello aren't. Cio-Cio-San evokes the

* Yes, those are really their names.

submissive yet sexually available China Doll; Turandot is a master class in the ice-cold Dragon Lady; Ping, Pang, and Pong are part groveling servant and part Fu Manchu villain. The staging that's traditionally associated with these characters—geisha makeup, Fu Manchu mustaches, elaborate silk costumes, copious bowing and shuffling—is also the same kind of "yellowface" that audiences were seeing on stages in the 1850s. Meanwhile, characters such as Aida and Otello, while described as being respectively Ethiopian and Moorish, remain a far cry from the offensive stereotypes portrayed in American minstrel shows. And of course, neither *Aida* nor *Otello* was ever traditionally staged using that particular brand of minstrel-show blackface.

Phil Chan is the cofounder of Final Bow for Yellowface, an advocacy group that works with ballet and opera companies to address how Asian characters are presented in canonical works. "Imagine if every time we told a story about German people, or every time there was a German character onstage, they looked like German people the way German people historically looked in, say, 1940," he told me in 2023. "Imagine if every depiction in all of our media—in every story and every narrative—had the Germans as Nazis, even in 2023, when most Germans today are not Nazis. Imagine that it continues to be the main narrative about what is at the heart of Germanness, and who the German people are. Then it becomes more than just a costume." For Chan, intent is irrelevant. What matters is the *impact* of the staging, both on the performers and the audience.

"It's rarely from bad intentions that people do something offensive, like wear yellowface and shuffle around onstage," said Nina Yoshida Nelsen. "It's from a lack of education and understanding of how what we do onstage and in the rehearsal space directly affects people in our communities. We must think about how it makes Asian audience members—and singers—feel seeing what oftentimes comes across as a 'mockery' of their culture."

For Japanese American mezzo-soprano Jane Monari, the sight of white singers being made up to look Asian is always jarring. "I have seen countless productions in which it is literally like going to a Halloween party where everyone has gotten dressed up in a bad racist costume," the singer said in an interview published by San Francisco Opera and the Asian Opera Alliance. "When I see this, it hurts me because, well, I look like what I look like, and I can't take it off when I leave the theater."

The effect on some audience members can be equally traumatic. After attending a production of Puccini's *Turandot* at Opera Australia in 2022, Vietnamese Australian writer and lawyer Cat-Thao Nguyen expressed her dismay in an opinion piece for the *Sydney Morning Herald*. Originally directed by Graeme Murphy in 1990, the production trades in more than a few exotic visuals, most notably the staging of Ping, Pang, and Pong wearing Fu Manchu mustaches and white makeup with black Kabuki accents. "As I sat in the theatre, the horrible caricatures kept coming like a tidal assault. Ping, Pong and Pang pranced around the stage with their Fu Manchu–style moustaches and fake ponytails. . . . I felt utterly sick," Nguyen wrote. "As the scenes unfolded, I felt a violent wilting of dignity for myself and my Chinese husband."

Still, many opera audiences, particularly among the traditionalist set, don't understand this reaction. They see traditional staging as being a historical artifact in the same way the operas themselves are historical artifacts. How can makeup and costumes be offensive when they're just tradition?

Here's where we're also seeing a further generational divide. Older audiences often watch traditional stagings of *Madama Butterfly*, *Turandot*, *Lakmé*, and *The Pearl Fishers* without any semblance of discomfort. But millennials? Generation Z? We've grown up in a vastly different landscape, in which debates about cultural appropriation have taken a front seat in public discourse. That discourse not only comes with us into the opera house but shapes the way we see all that winged eyeliner.

This leaves opera companies in a quandary over what exactly to do with opera's more exotic-minded repertoire. Millennials and Gen Z may be the audience of the future, but the Boomers and Gen X are still alive and kicking—and generally have more disposable income to spend on opera tickets. So, what are the options? Uphold the staging traditions so beloved by the *Werktreue* crowd, even when they err on the side of cringeworthy and lead to public backlash? Or try to somehow reimagine these operas to dodge their racism? *Regietheater* presents the perfect opportunity to reframe and recontextualize operas such as *Madama Butterfly* and *Turandot*. After all, if a stage director has free artistic reign, they can potentially eliminate, or at least tame, all that awkward exoticism. But beyond the *how* and *why* of staging, this also means taking a closer look at the *who*. Who's directing? Who's designing? And does it matter?

*   *   *

For many companies, the creative team offers the best solution for these staging woes. The director and designers are the ones that ultimately decide whether Ping, Pang, and Pong will sport Fu Manchu mustaches and heavy eye makeup in *Turandot*. They choose whether to embrace an opera's staging tradition or reject it. This is where we run into what some call the identity politics of creative teams.

Mary Birnbaum boasts a decades-long career as a stage director in opera and theater and has been on the Juilliard School faculty since 2010. Currently the general and artistic director of Opera Saratoga in New York, Birnbaum also holds the dubious honor of being one of just two women stage directors hired by the Santa Fe Opera (one of America's most prestigious festival companies) between 2005 and 2020.

For Birnbaum, there are two underlying issues to unpack when it comes to creative teams. The first relates to the kinds of operas that have outdated cultural stereotypes. "There's the issue of who should curate or care for that work. And *should* it be cared for," she told me in 2024. "Then on the other hand there's the issue of who needs to be in the room to sanction a kind of storytelling. I think it can be very different depending on the work."

Debates over who's "in the room" have become increasingly heated, with both sides of the staging battleground weighing in. Traditionalists declare that anyone should be free to direct and design any opera, regardless of its setting or characters. What matters is talent and artistic vision, not ethnicity or cultural background. The opposing argument is that lived experience *is* necessary to stage certain operas, that some cultural understandings are simply beyond the grasp of certain directors and designers. As a final knockout blow, the argument goes, the historical exclusion of women and people of color from creative teams demands a pendulum swing in the other direction.

I admit I fall more on the progressive side here. In my day job as a researcher, I've pored over thousands of data points that confirm exactly who's directing and designing operas at the biggest companies in the world. Spoiler: it's mostly white dudes. But if we set aside the ideal of equity for equity's sake, does it actually matter who's staging what, when, and how? When it comes to operas such as *Madama Butterfly* and *Turandot*—the ones with enough staging baggage for a troupe of bellhops—does it not only matter who's directing and designing . . . does it somehow matter *more*?

Beginning in the early twentieth century, there was an understanding in Opera Land that certain operas were better—more real—when staged by directors and designers with, ahem, "relevant" backgrounds. The rationale was that some practitioners had an intrinsic affinity for certain works, particularly ones depicting non-Western cultures. By hiring these directors and designers—so it was thought—companies ensured an authentic interpretation. In other words, staging an opera set in Japan? You need someone Japanese. Case in point: the 1958 production of *Madama Butterfly* staged at the Metropolitan Opera by Japanese director Yoshio Aoyama and Japanese designer Motohiro Nagasaka. Commenting on the production in 1972, then General Director Rudolf Bing gushed, "The Japanese and American characters moved and looked authentic."

As a benchmark, the goal of authenticity in staging seems to ring true. No audience wants to pay hundreds of dollars to see an opera that *isn't* authentic. And what better way to ensure a production is, indeed, authentic—or at the very least, free from glaring errors—than to hire someone with firsthand cultural experience? Consider the alternative, such as Icelandic Opera's 2023 production of *Madama Butterfly*, which allegedly used Chinese written characters on its set instead of Japanese ones. Whoops.

Not surprisingly, "authenticity" has become a popular marketing buzzword whenever companies are staging operas steeped in historical stereotypes. Take the Royal Ballet and Opera's 2022 production of *Madama Butterfly*, for which Japanese experts were invited to "make discreet changes in the name of greater authenticity." The resulting staging is "a *Butterfly* both true to the spirit of the original, and authentic in its representation of Japan," wrote Director of Opera Oliver Mears in an opinion piece for the *Guardian*. By way of beating a dead horse, the company's website included a media feature titled "A Revival with Authenticity." We get it, Royal Opera, it's "authentic."

The issue with this approach is that most canonical operas aren't actually authentic to begin with. Operas such as *Turandot*, *Lakmé*, *The Pearl Fishers*, and *Madama Butterfly* are the product of white Europeans trying to write something neither white nor European—with varying degrees of success. "What do these works have to do with the cultures they're representing?" Phil Chan asked me. "The Orientalist works are Europeans' fantasies about Asians. They have nothing to do with our story or our heritage or our culture. By bringing Asianness into an Orientalist production, you might as well add a German clog dance or an Argentinean tango. It's just as authentic."

In that case, what does it even mean to claim a production is authentic? Or that a certain director or designer adds authenticity by nature of their background? Can we honestly say the outlandish version of ancient China depicted in Puccini's *Turandot* aligns with the lived experience of a modern-day Chinese person?

Here's where notions of authenticity and affinity—not to mention rules for who can and can't stage certain operas—assume an undeniable air of ick. Identity is a messy construct. None of us checks a single box—none of us is just one thing. And even if we were somehow one-dimensional, we'd still be unique, each shaped by our individual experiences, upbringings, and environments. But that doesn't stop assumptions from being made, assumptions that broad categories of identity have a universality that crosses countries and generations.

Director Mary Birnbaum has noticed clear trends in the kind of work she's asked to direct, both because she's a woman and because of her Jewish last name. "The amount of pieces about Jewish identity that have come across my desk . . . it's at least fifty percent of what I get offered to direct," Birnbaum said. "It's beautiful to be chosen by a community. But I was raised Quaker. I've never been to temple in a religious way. And so, this brings up some tensions for me. To what degree do you feel like you're assuming a different identity while you're doing this work? And can I really tell this story?"

Phil Chan sees similar issues for practitioners of color, both in the kinds of opportunities they're given and in the perspective they're expected to bring. "There is an expectation that what sets you apart as an artist is your lived experience as a member of a non-White racial or cultural group," Chan said in his 2023 book, *Banishing Orientalism: Dancing Between Exotic and Familiar*. "Unlike European-descended artists, who don't need to make a point of it, artists like me often want to or are expected to include elements of our own cultural experience into our work. . . . Yet this serves to pigeonhole us as 'ethnic' artists—White artists don't face these expectations."

It doesn't take much to see how these expectations have played out in hiring practices. Out of the fifteen hundred productions staged by the largest opera companies in the United States between 2005 and 2020, just twelve credited a stage director who publicly identified as Black or African American. Eleven of the twelve productions they were hired to direct were specifically about Black historical figures or some aspect of Black lived experience. I found similar stats for other practitioners of color. Out of the same fifteen hundred productions, just sixteen credited a director who publicly identified as having Asian heritage. More than half of the operas they were hired to direct were similarly Asian-specific. "I'm almost exclusively offered *Butterfly*s and *Turandot*s," confirmed director Aria Umezawa in 2023.

Assumptions about who's allowed to stage certain operas comes with obvious artistic limitations. Even worse, it tasks a small cohort of practitioners with "fixing" operas that are increasingly difficult to fix. But then, where does that leave us? Given the fallacy of authenticity—plus the ick factor of pigeonholing by identity—who *should* be directing and designing all those Orientalist operas? Does representation "in the room" even make a difference onstage?

* * *

Puccini's *Madama Butterfly* has become the opera industry's most obvious problem child for these questions around staging and creative teams. With a libretto by Luigi Illica and Giuseppe Giacosa (the same fellows who wrote Puccini's *La bohème*), *Madama Butterfly* premiered in 1904 and is a textbook example of the colonial love story trope. While stationed in Japan, an American naval officer named Pinkerton pays for an arranged marriage with a fifteen-year-old geisha, Cio-Cio-San, aka Madame Butterfly.

Shortly after their "marriage," Pinkerton returns home, leaving the lovelorn Cio-Cio-San behind to wait faithfully and have his baby, whom she somewhat dramatically names Dolore (translated from Italian as "sorrow" or "trouble"). When Pinkerton finally returns to Nagasaki three years later, he brings along his new American wife. They decide to adopt Dolore, now the spitting image of dear old Dad, and Cio-Cio-San kills herself. So much for a happy ending.

Is the music of *Madama Butterfly* stunningly beautiful? Yes. Is the story an absolute tearjerker? Yes. Is the opera very much a product of its time? Oh yes. There's cultural appropriation and stereotypes galore, from the representation of the Japanese characters to the libretto's gratuitous use of pidgin English and invented Japanese words. That doesn't even scratch the surface of the opera's traditional staging practices: a cornucopia of kimonos, geisha wigs, and winged eye makeup.

Because of these varying issues, *Madama Butterfly* is now seen as a high-risk venture by many opera companies. For those in countries such as the United States, England, and Canada where tensions around representation and diversity are particularly front of mind, the odds are high that *any* staging—traditional or otherwise—will potentially lead to a backlash. And that's something companies are desperate to avoid. After all, all publicity is good publicity . . . until you're accused of being racist. But *Madama Butterfly* also remains a mainstay of the Canon—ever popular with traditionalist audiences and a reliable ticket seller—not the kind of work that companies can afford to send gently into that good night. So, it's no wonder that creative teams are increasingly considered the best—if not only—way to salvage the opera and its ticket revenue.

In 2023, four different productions of *Madama Butterfly* were staged by major American opera companies, all featuring stage directors and designers (and in some cases, conductors) of Asian heritage.

San Francisco Opera's production, directed by Amon Miyamoto and conducted by Eun Sun Kim, presented the story of *Madama Butterfly* through the eyes of Cio-Cio-San's son. "In our staging," wrote Miyamoto in a company press release, "we see Cio-Cio-San's son, Trouble, now an adult in his early 30s who has grown up experiencing discrimination as a biracial person in 1920s America."

New Orleans Opera's production, directed by Aria Umezawa and conducted by Judith Yan, framed the opera as a meta theatrical production, adding the character of a white stage director who observes the narrative action. According to Umezawa's program notes, at the end of the opera, Cio-Cio-San "begins to see the theatrical world she is inhabiting for what it is: a fabrication of her culture created by people who had no real understanding of those they were fantasizing about." Rather than killing herself, Cio-Cio-San throws down the knife and walks offstage.

At Cincinnati Opera, director Matthew Ozawa, conductor Keitaro Harada, and designers Kimie Nishikawa, Maiko Matsushima, and Yuki Nakase Link reconceived *Madama Butterfly* as a virtual reality game. At the beginning of the staging, the player—a twentysomething white man with something of an Asian fetish—enters the world of the "game" and assumes the role of Lieutenant Pinkerton. "We decided we're going to honor the fact that this is a white man's fantasy—a fantasy of a culture and a fantasy of a woman," Ozawa told the *New York Times* in 2023.

At Boston Lyric Opera, director Phil Chan worked with dramaturg Nina Yoshida Nelsen and designers Yu Shibagaki, Sara Ryung Clement, and Jeanette Oi-Suk Yew to set *Madama Butterfly* in San Francisco's Chinatown in the 1940s. Cio-Cio-San is reimagined as a nightclub singer who spends the second act of the opera incarcerated in a Japanese concentration camp.* She survives at the end of the opera but experiences a different kind of death: her son dies of tuberculosis.

All four productions clearly fall in the realm of *Regietheater*. They're intentionally conceptual, intentionally designed to add new layers of meaning and commentary to Puccini's original opera—even to the point of reconceiving it entirely.

At Boston Lyric Opera, Phil Chan's production stemmed from a yearlong series of public conversations about the complexities of Puccini's work. Chan was initially invited to lead the series due to his expertise on yellowface and was then offered the opportunity to direct the opera. Chan told me the experience was unique because everyone on the creative team was Asian American except for conductor David Angus. "Everyone already had a level of awareness about the experience of being Asian American at the start of every creative conversation. We didn't have to explain in order to tell our story."

This level of representation, Chan said, had a tangible impact on the kinds of staging decisions that were made. "I didn't have to tell our costume designer why there wouldn't be a single kimono in this

* The Japanese American community prefers the term *concentration camp*, as the term *internment* implies Japanese Americans weren't American citizens when they were incarcerated.

production," Chan said. "She knew, and I didn't have to say, that we were trying to avoid oversexualizing the Asian women in the cast. Because our female Asian American costume designer knows what it looks like to wear something that's a little bit revealing and go out in public as an Asian woman living in 2023. She knows what that lived experience is, so was thoughtful about it."

With Chan's production, the nuances of the staging were clearly shaped by who was in the room: it *did* make a difference to have an Asian American creative team. But Chan is explicit that his interpretation of *Madama Butterfly* isn't an "Asian" take. It's *his* take—Phil Chan's take—just as the productions staged at San Francisco Opera, New Orleans Opera, and Cincinnati Opera are the takes of their respective directors. "They're all radically different *Butterfly*s," Chan said. "You can't say there's an Asian perspective for *Butterfly*. But what we do share is being able to not just see, but also feel, the problems of the piece, which drove our desire to reimagine it."

This deeper understanding did, however, come with a cost. Chan told me he felt a palpable pressure not only to fix the underlying issues in *Madama Butterfly* but also to represent the larger Asian community. "The stakes were different. Because if we messed up, we had to bear the burden of the repercussions of doing something that didn't work."

Chan is also aware that his Asian heritage may have been a factor in his being hired by Boston Lyric Opera—and that having an Asian or Asian American director provides potential political cover for companies. "*Madama Butterfly* is a title you want to do. And these days, more and more, you want to have an Asian person direct it," he said. "Because even if it flops, even if it's bad, even if it's problematic, it will sell tickets and also will absolve the organization. They'll be able to say, 'Well, we put resources behind this person of color. We did exactly what you wanted us to do.'" This is a dynamic white directors don't have to consider, he pointed out. "They never have to think, 'Why did I get this opportunity?' To them, it's clear. 'It's because I'm talented.' They never have to wonder if it's because of something else."

* * *

Traditional stagings of operas such as *Madama Butterfly*, *Turandot*, and *Aida* may one day be a thing of the past. Even now, it's clear that productions that rely on kimonos, geisha wigs, and eyeliner—or alternatively saris and bindis, or dreadlocks and dark skin makeup—are increasingly a dying breed. So, perhaps we can understand—even empathize with—the frenzied teeth gnashing of traditionalist audiences. They feel they're facing the loss of something precious, something irreplaceable, both to them and to the art form.

But traditions change, evolve over time. Unlike Grandma's apple pie, traditional stagings of *Madama Butterfly* have been well preserved—I count at least a dozen DVDs of different kimono-heavy productions available to buy on Amazon. Video recordings of traditional stagings of *Turandot*, *Aida*, *Otello*, *The Pearl Fishers*, and others are similarly commonplace. One also has to consider the risk-benefit ratio of perpetually digging in one's heels for the sake of tradition, despite its leading to backlash and alienated audiences. At what point are you holding on to an opera so tightly that you inadvertently crush it to death?

There's a further variable to consider in the question of staging, however—an element that's central to our next battleground. The concept, the sets, the costumes, the props, the lights—all of it creates the world that exists on the stage, but who actually *lives* there? Who's wearing all those costumes and all that makeup?

Who was cast?

CHAPTER 4

The Singers

— or —

She's Got the Look

It was the casting controversy to end all casting controversies, at least in the years before Facebook, Instagram, and the twenty-four-hour news cycle. It was (dramatic pause) the Case of the Little Black Dress.

The facts, dear Watson, are these. The year was 2003. Soprano Deborah Voigt was booked to perform the lead role of Ariadne in Richard Strauss's opera *Ariadne auf Naxos* for the Royal Ballet and Opera at Covent Garden. At the time, forty-two-year-old Voigt was considered one of the best sopranos of her generation and was particularly acclaimed for her portrayals of Ariadne—a role she'd performed so many times she jokingly referred to herself as "Ariadne, Inc."

But then Voigt was summarily and unexpectedly fired. The alleged sticking point was a little black dress. Stage director Christof Loy apparently envisioned a sleek cocktail number for Ariadne's costume. And Voigt—who weighed nearly 350 pounds—didn't fit, literally or figuratively.

"Get this: the management of Covent Garden just released me from my contract for *Ariadne auf Naxos*. They simply said I was too fat!" Voigt said in a 2003 interview. The soprano laid the blame squarely on company casting director Peter Katona, who "made it clear that I won't be singing in his house as long as he's around." Voigt said, "I have big hips and Covent Garden has a problem with them. If I was running an opera house, I'd want the best singer for the role, whether they had hips or not."

The drama rapidly devolved into a public airing of dirty laundry. Michael Benchetrit, Voigt's manager in England, harrumphed, "The producer said that the black dress had to stay and that the woman had to go." But a company spokesperson disagreed: "It was a question of the whole style and look of the production. It was just felt that Deborah Voigt was not right for it." Added casting director Peter Katona, "We wanted to present it in elegant, modern evening dress. We had to make it theatrically convincing." (Translation: a woman who wears a size 30 can't possibly be "theatrically convincing" in a cocktail dress.)

So, Voigt was out and a different (slimmer) soprano was in. But the controversy didn't end there. A few months later, Voigt underwent gastric bypass surgery and lost nearly two hundred pounds. In 2006, the Royal Ballet and Opera announced it was reviving Christof Loy's production for the 2008 season and had reengaged Voigt to sing Ariadne. While Voigt denied her surgery was related to her firing, the company similarly denied any wrongdoing in releasing her from her original contract. "When you hire anybody to sing a role, you do need to take into consideration what they look like, how they act," declared Antonio Pappano, music director of the Royal Ballet and Opera in 2007. "We have the right and prerogative to cast how we want."

Enter our next battleground.

* * *

More than twenty years after the showdown between Deborah Voigt and the Royal Ballet and Opera, mezzo-soprano Jamie Barton remembers it vividly. The dress. The drama. And the crystal-clear lesson behind it: if you want to be an opera singer, how you *look* matters.

Barton is currently one of the world's most famous opera singers and roughly the same age as Voigt when Covent Garden gave her the boot. But at the time, Barton was still early in her career, trying to make her way up the ladder of the opera industry. And that little black dress was like a punch to the gut. "I remember thinking, 'If Debbie Voigt is getting fired because of a costume choice, then what chance do I have in this?'" Barton told me in 2024. Because, in addition to her nose ring and occasionally colorfully dyed hair, Barton is plus-size.

Even now, with numerous awards and accolades under her belt, Barton is aware her body type has played a role in her casting. "I've never been offered a Carmen in a staged production," she told me with some chagrin. "Because you think of Carmen, and you automatically think of a petite woman with long curly hair and luscious boobs. For productions that are out there right now, I just wouldn't be a fit. We're not at a place where everyone is ready for a curvy Carmen."

One of the great myths about opera is that it's only about the Voice, that the physical standards of size and beauty that pervade other fields of entertainment are somehow absent. Think of the classic stereotype of an opera singer. Blond braids, horned helmet, multiple chins . . . the archetypal "fat lady" from Yogi Berra's famous line "It ain't over till the fat lady sings." Like many stereotypes, this one has a certain grounding in truth. The fat lady in question refers to the character Brünnhilde from Richard Wagner's *Ring Cycle*: a Valkyrie (aka badass female warrior) who heralds the downfall of the gods with an eighteen-minute aria. (Get it? It ain't over . . . till she sings?)

Throughout its history, the industry has had its share of hefty singers. Take famed tenor Luciano Pavarotti (1935–2007), who once tipped the scales at 350 pounds. Or Italian soprano Luisa Tetrazzini (1871–1940), whose legendary appetite purportedly inspired the cream-based pasta casserole. Or the so-called Three Tonners, the punny but cruel moniker given to sopranos Jane Eaglen, Sharon Sweet, and a pre-gastric-bypass Deborah Voigt by writer Manuela Hoelterhoff in 1998.

Nearly as ubiquitous as the plus-size singers themselves have been the small-minded responses from audiences, critics, and even company administrators about their weight. The 1853 premiere of Verdi's opera *La traviata* was deemed a disaster specifically because of the size of lead soprano Fanny Salvini-Donatelli, who was apparently too plump to be convincing as a courtesan wasting away from tuberculosis. According to reports, the audience burst into laughter every time she feigned a cough.

In the early 1950s, soprano Maria Callas was described as "monstrously fat" by opera impresario Rudolf Bing, who declined to hire her at the Metropolitan Opera. Only after Callas dropped eighty pounds did Bing change his mind, and Callas finally made her Met debut in 1956. (Callas publicly attributed her weight loss to a diet of chicken and salad. The more convincing urban legend, at least during my conservatory years, was that she intentionally gave herself a tapeworm.)

Still, the focus on appearance in opera has intensified in recent years, and for one decidedly cinematic reason. In 2006, just a few years after the brouhaha of the Little Black Dress, the Metropolitan Opera became the first company to broadcast opera productions into movie theaters. These broadcasts didn't rely on a single, wide-angled shot of the stage from a distance like the one you'd get from the cheap seats in the theater. Instead, they put the audience in the middle of the action, with shifting camera angles, surround sound, high definition, and a focus on the close-up . . . close enough to see sweat streaming down the tenor's face and the gush of spittle during the soprano's high note. Other opera companies soon followed suit, including the UK's Royal Ballet and Opera, San Francisco Opera, and Paris Opéra. With this shift came the emergence of a new industry term that struck fear into the heart of every singer: *HD ready*. Forget about your voice and technique, your diction and your acting . . . what about your face? Your body? Are you ready to be seen by audiences in high definition?

Even without the pressure of an HD close-up, opera is ultimately just like every other theatrical art form that involves acting and the illusion of an onstage world. Audiences come to the theater expecting to see blurred lines between fantasy and reality. They want to believe, and they want the singers to be believable—at least until the curtain call. And so, questions of believability have always been intrinsically tied to casting, the deciding of which singers will be hired to sing which characters in an opera. This includes the main characters or principal roles (aka the stars), the supporting characters or secondary roles (aka the sidekicks and wingmen), and the nameless characters that mill around in the background (aka the chorus and supernumeraries).

Casting isn't only a matter of choosing singers to play individual characters but also considering how different singers will interact with one another and how the entire picture of the stage will look. Will the soprano be believable as the romantic ingenue? Will she *still* be believable if she's cast opposite that tenor? Or alongside that baritone? An added variable is the production design, or the choices made by the director and designers for the concept, sets, and costumes. Singers not only need to fit into the character they're playing but also into the onstage world that's being created around them.

As the daughter of a performer, I never had any illusions about the importance of appearance in casting. From the time I began auditioning for musicals in middle school, my mother reiterated the lesson she'd learned during her own career as a professional dancer in the Martha Graham Dance Company. Even if my audition was impeccable—even if I sang better than everyone else—the deciding factor would be whether or not I "looked" the part. If I did, I'd probably be cast. If I didn't, I wouldn't.

When I arrived at the Peabody Conservatory for graduate training in vocal performance, I heard similar warnings from voice teachers and coaches. Having a voice, they told us, was the bare minimum, but it wasn't enough on its own. Casting would also be determined by how we moved. How we acted. How we looked.

When it came to the specific "look," the benchmark was set by our *Fach*, that is, the German classification for operatic voices based on their range, size, and quality. For women, the basic options are soprano (the highest voice), mezzo-soprano (the middle voice), and contralto (the lowest voice). For men, it's tenor (the highest voice), baritone (the middle voice), and bass (the lowest voice)—or the rarer breed of countertenor, a man who sings in the female range. Each category of *Fach* has further variations and subcategories depending on particular vocal traits—a "coloratura soprano," for example, is a soprano who can sing high and fast, while a "dramatic coloratura soprano" is a soprano who can sing high, fast, *and* loud.

On the surface, it's a highly efficient system for categorizing voices. In practice, it can be gallingly subjective and restrictive, particularly for a singer whose voice doesn't naturally fit into one of those little boxes. (Don't worry, there's a *Fach* for that, too: *Zwischenfach*, literally "between *Fach*s.") But regardless of its limitations, the *Fach* system plays a key role in determining what exactly an opera singer will sing. Every subcategory of voice types is aligned with a particular batch of characters from the Canon. So, if you know your *Fach*, you already know the roles you'll be expected to learn and sing—and, in turn, how you'll be expected to look.

If you're the kind of mezzo-soprano whose *Fach* says you'll sing the femme-fatale role of Carmen, then you need to look like a Carmen. If you're a soprano whose *Fach* says you'll sing queens and noble priestesses, then you need to look regal and refined—and ideally act that way as well. One soprano I interviewed told me she was explicitly advised "not to be herself" in auditions because her bubbly personality didn't match her queenlike vocal profile.

My *Fach* sat between soubrette and light lyric soprano, two vocal categories with characters mostly consisting of maids and ingenues. So, of course, my look needed to scream "maid" and "ingenue," at least for auditions. This meant long hair, always worn down. Wrap dresses in a jewel tone with three-quarter-length sleeves and a hint of décolletage. Classy makeup. Minimal jewelry. Definitely no piercings, tattoos, or, heaven forbid, a visible wedding ring. By the time I graduated from Peabody, I'd mastered my look to perfection, from the exact shade of nude stockings to the precise heft of false eyelashes. My look was likewise reflected in my professional headshot, a close-in portrait of my face that I used promotionally and for auditions. Long hair. Check. Winsome smile. Check.

But I still had a problem, or so I was told. I was too tall. At five foot eight—five foot eleven in heels—I wouldn't be hired by opera companies, they said. A soprano who was taller than the tenor simply wouldn't be believable.

I was actually luckier than many of my classmates, some of whom were repeatedly told to lose weight. Ten pounds, twenty pounds—whatever it took to better portray a Parisian courtesan or consumptive heroine. And it wasn't just the women. The visual bar for men was lower, but there were still clear expectations. Tenors who aspired to play romantic leads were told to hit the gym until they could objectively be described as hunky. Baritones were encouraged to grow strategic goatees and Baritone Hair (lustrous locks just shy of a mullet) to achieve the proper look of a villain or father figure. The advice was always accompanied by the same rationale: you need to be believable.

If this all sounds a bit toxic, it was. But it also reflected the reality of the industry we hoped to enter, a field characterized by overwhelming competition for a small number of professional jobs. In some ways, I was grateful for the brutal honesty of our coaches and teachers. They already knew what most of us would soon realize: that when there are seventy sopranos, all equally talented and competing for the same role, casting is determined by the smallest margin. By an almost arbitrary knife edge. By whoever most *looks* the part. And that decision would be made in an unavoidable rite of passage known as an audition. Or as I like to call it, the tenth circle of hell.

* * *

The alarm blares: 4:30 a.m. I drag myself out of bed and step straight into a shower that never seems to warm up. I dress with bleary eyes, then blow-dry my hair into romantic waves. My stomach's too unsettled to eat, so I grab a Clif Bar and thermos of tea for the road. I already packed my bag last night, so at least I don't have to worry about forgetting something crucial. It's all there—double- and triple-checked—dress, stockings, heels, makeup, hairbrush, water bottle, cough drops, tea bags . . . plus a handful of safety pins and bobby pins in case of wardrobe or hair malfunction. I've also thrown in a book I won't read and two bananas. Most important, the bag contains the black binder with the sheet music for my audition—each page carefully printed, labeled, and hole punched.

The Greyhound bus is scheduled for 5:45 a.m., and I make it to the park and ride in Baltimore with fifteen minutes to spare, just enough time to get thoroughly chilled in the early-morning freeze of mid-November. The bus arrives, and I pile in with the rest of the passengers, each of us competing to avoid the seat closest to the toilet and the one next to the guy who's nursing a bottle of malt liquor. Only three and a half hours to go.

I should have eaten more breakfast, I think. And warmed up my voice. But what's the point of singing vocal scales at five in the morning just to sit on a cold bus for the next three hours? I rest my nose against the window and try to stave off the rising nausea. Forty-five minutes out from New York City, I start putting on my audition makeup—foundation, blush, eye shadow, fake eyelashes. Thanks to the bus driver's unsteady foot on the brake pedal, my liquid eyeliner looks more like an EKG than an elegant cat eye. Hopefully the panel won't notice.

The bus pulls into Port Authority station at Eighth Avenue just as I'm about to be carsick. I disembark unsteadily, breathing in the city's faint perfume of garbage, hot-dog water, and spilt coffee. The audition venue is a few blocks away, much closer than the one last week, which was a thirty-block trek uptown. I hum quietly as I walk, dodging pedestrian commuters and again wishing I'd been able to reserve a practice room to warm up my voice before they were all booked. A few vocal exercises in the bathroom will have to do.

I step into the elevator on the ground floor of the building and push the button for the seventh floor. As the elevator doors ding open, I plaster on a bright smile and stride to the front desk to check in: "Caitlin Vincent. I have an audition at ten thirty."

I'm directed to wait in a narrow hallway, just outside a door labeled AUDITIONS IN PROGRESS. All the chairs are full of waiting singers, none of whom makes eye contact. Nothing like a glimpse of the not-so-friendly competition to make your stomach clench. *You're prepared,* I tell myself. *You're ready. You're exactly what they're looking for.* I strut to the bathroom, all poise and confidence, and only heave a shaky breath when I'm safely locked inside a cubicle. I start to sing a scale, just to make sure everything's still in there, and then see the sign taped to the cubicle door, vehement in all caps: NO WARMING UP IN THE BATHROOM. Shit.

I pull out my dress from my bag and smooth out the wrinkles. Now's the tricky part of trying to put on Spanx, stockings, dress, and high heels without touching the discolored linoleum with my bare feet or accidentally falling into the toilet. Luckily, it's my fifth audition this month, and I've become a master at the one-legged wobble. I put the finishing touches on the armor of my turquoise wrap dress, pull up my Spanx as high as they'll go, and defiantly sing a few scales under my breath while simultaneously flushing the toilet. Then I stride back out the door and into the hallway to wait.

The clench in my stomach is now a near-constant lurching. I have an overwhelming urge to sprint for the elevator. *You're prepared. You're ready. You're exactly what they're looking for.* I glance surreptitiously at the other singers. How many are also sopranos? Definitely the one who just name-dropped her famous voice teacher. Definitely the one who's looking at me with narrowed eyes, trying to use X-ray vision to take a peek at my aria binder. I peel one of my bananas and force myself to take small, calm bites. Twenty minutes to go.

Straining my ears, I can just hear the singer inside the audition room: a baritone singing the Figaro aria from Rossini's *The Barber of Seville.* Nice voice, but—oh, dear—he didn't quite make that final high A. The door opens, and the baritone walks out, looking slightly greenish. The soprano with the narrowed eyes is called in next. I wish I had a legitimate reason to hold a glass to the door.

Definitely a soprano, I confirm as she starts singing. And she's good. *Really* good. They ask for a second aria.

The narrow-eyed soprano finally comes out, giving me a smug look before collecting her bag. That means I'm next. *Oh, God, I'm next. I'm next I'm next I'm next I'm next.* My heart is pounding. My binder is streaked with sweat from my hands. "Caitlin Vincent?" they call. I take a breath. *You're prepared. You're ready. You're exactly what they're looking for*. I smile and walk into the room with a cheerful "Good morning!"

The panel is seated at a folding trestle table at one end of the room—three of them—each with their own pile of headshots and CVs. One panelist smiles at me. The other two look bored. I cross to the piano at the far end of the room and give the pianist my binder, already open to the first page of my starting aria. I take a few seconds to hum my preferred speed, then move to the crook of the piano and face the panel. "My name is Caitlin Vincent, and I'll be starting with the aria 'Durch Zärtlichkeit und Schmeicheln' from Mozart's opera *The Abduction from the Seraglio*." The smiley one nods encouragingly—bless her. The other two scrutinize my CV. I give an elegant nod to the pianist. The opening strains of the accompaniment start, and my stomach drops—the pianist is playing too fast. And, what the hell? Was that a wrong note?

I take a deep breath, digging deep to find the character I've so carefully rehearsed. The first two notes are shaky, but I force myself to gain control of my nerves. I gracefully move through my practiced arm movements and facial expressions. *I'm prepared. I'm ready. I'm exactly what you're looking for.* I reach the end of the aria and wait expectantly, the sudden rush of adrenaline making my knees tremble. With the exception of those wobbly first notes, it's the best I've sung the aria in an audition. The panelists confer quietly. *Ask for a second one,* I plead silently. *Ask for a second one.* The smiley one looks up. "Thanks for coming in." I give the pianist a beatific smile and collect my binder. Walking past the panel, I turn to thank them for their time. But they've already put my CV aside . . . they're already looking at the next one.

I walk straight from the audition room to the bathroom and change back into my travel clothes. Then it's three blocks to Port Authority station and the waiting Greyhound bus. All during the long ride back to Baltimore, I replay my audition over and over in my head. A shaky start, but then I nailed it. *I'm definitely getting cast this time.*

But an acceptance email never comes. In fact, I never hear anything at all.

* * *

I've never met a singer who enjoys auditions. Just as I've never met anyone who enjoys job interviews. Because that's what an audition is. Except worse. Because auditions aren't approved by HR. They don't use standardized interview questions. You rarely get feedback. Often, you're never even formally rejected, just ghosted indefinitely. And worst of all, there's never just one. Auditions are constant. Perpetual. For every role, every production, every training program. Audition after audition. Always with the same undercurrent of anxiety and anticipation, the same desperate but silent *Pick me! Pick me!*, and the same seemingly endless wait as you obsess over what you could have done better. Only singers working at the highest levels of the field no longer have to audition at all.

Peak audition season generally runs from September to December, with many companies holding auditions annually, both locally and in major hubs such as New York City. At the lowest professional level most auditions are "general" auditions, which means they're open to any singer who submits an application. This includes a headshot, a performance CV (that is, a list of the opera roles performed and studied), and basic biographical details, including past training and knowledge of languages. There's also almost always an application fee, usually ranging from $20 to $100.

At the general-audition level the number of applicants can be so overwhelming that companies often add a prescreening round, just to limit the field. This requires a singer to submit a recording of one or two arias for the company to review in advance. Only the singers who pass this initial round will be invited to sing an audition in person. Of course, even if you aren't invited for an audition, the company still usually keeps your application fee. Revenue's revenue, after all.

At the next level up, auditions morph from public free-for-alls into invitation-only affairs. This is standard practice at the bigger companies, which don't have time to deal with a mob of hopeful singers pounding on their door. Audition slots are instead reserved for singers who already have professional representation (i.e., an agent and/or artist manager) and will be considered for specific roles in upcoming productions. Some auditions are organized by the companies, who cast a wide net of invitations across various agencies. Others are organized by the agencies themselves, with representatives from multiple companies invited to come and hear the singers on their rosters. Not that these auditions are any less terrifying or daunting than the general ones. In fact, they might actually be *more* terrifying because they involve singing one-on-one for opera's major players, the kinds of stage directors, conductors, and casting directors who can make or break a career.

If there's one consistency to auditions, it's the *lack* of consistency. Audition venues come in all forms. Some are small and stuffy with out-of-tune pianos. Some are cavernous with hardwood floors and glorious acoustics. Sometimes there's a designated warm-up room for singers. Sometimes there's a bathroom. Sometimes there's nothing at all. A friend of mine once had to change into her audition outfit on a public sidewalk: dress, Spanx, stockings . . . all right there on the corner of Sixty-Ninth and Broadway.

Australian soprano Helena Dix told me about one audition where the venue was a small hall at the back of a shopping mall, right behind a butcher shop. Halfway through Helena's first aria, a deliveryman pushed a trolley full of raw meat between the stage and the audition panel and just stopped, gawking up at her until her final high note. He then applauded, still oblivious of the panel sitting behind him. "At least *he* was enthusiastic about my singing," Helena joked. Compare that experience to Helena's audition for the Metropolitan Opera, in which she was personally invited to fly to New York City (on her own dime, naturally) to sing for the company's casting director on the Met stage.

The makeup and temperament of audition panels can also vary widely. Sometimes a panel will include a company's artistic director—that's the executive leader responsible for a company's artistic vision and programming—sometimes it will include the stage director or conductor for a specific production. Many companies also rely on casting directors—individuals who are hired to work with company leadership, directors, and conductors to assess singers and determine final casting choices. Some panels are generous, even welcoming. Others are downright cruel. I've heard of panelists answering their cell phones in the middle of a singer's aria.

The uncertainty about what to expect during an audition is one of the hardest parts. What the room will be like, how the pianist will play, what the panel will ask—it's all unknown, all unpredictable. The only things a singer can control are what they wear (in my case, jewel-toned wrap dress, high heels, and fake eyelashes) and what they sing.

Every singer on the audition circuit has what's called a package, a group of arias that's been curated to highlight their vocal strengths while, ideally, hiding their vocal flaws. The general rule is five arias by five different composers from different time periods, each demonstrating different technical skills and representing each of the four main operatic languages (Italian, French, German, and English). Here again, *Fach* is key. If your alleged *Fach* is dramatic coloratura soprano, then all five of your arias will be drawn from the roles categorized as dramatic coloratura soprano. Because these are the roles you'll theoretically be hired to sing. (Fingers crossed the panel agrees your voice is in the *Fach* you think it is.)

Singers spend months—even years—mastering the arias in their package, from technique and diction to acting and artistic expression. But no matter how long a singer spends in preparation, they'll rarely get a chance to sing all five in an audition. Standard practice is for a singer to choose their first aria—the starter, as it's called. Then, the panel may (or may not) ask for a second aria, usually one that's contrasting in some way. And that's it.

The average opera audition lasts just ten minutes. That's ten minutes to make an impression on the audition panel, to convince them you're exactly what they're looking for. Though it actually takes even less time for a panel to form an opinion. The more realistic time frame is ten to fifteen seconds, a snap judgment based on the combination of your CV, the first few notes you sing, and the way you look. This is why the importance of appearance is hammered into aspiring opera singers during conservatory training. It's about ensuring your headshot, arias, and outfit all match the look you're trying to present and, hopefully, the one the opera company needs.

It's easy to frame audition panelists as villains. But to be fair, casting is tricky. Risky. A panel has just a few minutes to pull as much information as possible from what they see and what they hear. And the stakes are undeniably high: without the right cast, an opera production has a good chance of failure.

Evamaria Wieser has served as a panelist for thousands of opera auditions in her career and acknowledges that they can be horrible experiences for singers. A former artistic administrator for the Bavarian State Opera and the former director of artistic administration for the Salzburg Festival, Wieser currently works as both the head of the Young Singers Project of the Salzburg Festival and a European casting consultant for Lyric Opera of Chicago. "I've seen so many people suffering. Sometimes it's been like animals being sent to the slaughterhouse," Wieser told me in 2024. But it's also a necessary part of the job, she said. If a singer can't master auditions, it'll be a challenge for them to have a career.

But what is Wieser looking for when she's sitting at one of those terrifying trestle tables in an audition room? What makes the difference between getting cast and getting tossed in the rejection pile? According to Wieser, it boils down to four things. Voice, or the quality of a singer's instrument, is one. Technique is another. Interpretation of the music and presentation is third. Fourth is artistic personality, or the *it* factor. A singer needs to demonstrate all four qualities at once. "It has to be a package," Wieser said.

"But what about the look?" I pressed. "What about appearance?" This is where things get complicated, Wieser admitted. If the audition is for a role in a specific production, then appearance can certainly be a factor in casting. "The directors and/or conductors may say, 'I want this, this, this, and this.' And what can I say? It's their decision," she told me.

Sometimes a director wants a singer who looks a particular age or is a particular height or weight. I heard of one director who wanted to cast a tenor with big hands because it fit his concept for the character. The casting director found two tenors for him to consider—one with big hands and a mediocre voice, and one with smaller hands and a great voice. Guess who was cast? Big Hands.

Nothing about casting is objective. There's no benchmark of technique or vocal quality that guarantees success for an auditioning singer. Being cast is often a matter of luck—not only in singing for the right person at the right time but in matching the specific look they have in mind for a character. It might be related to height or weight. Or whether a singer looks like a stereotypical Carmen or fits into a little black dress.

But this is where the battleground around casting becomes fraught. Because in opera, the look has never just been about hair or height or weight. For the first three centuries of opera's history, the default look was also white.

* * *

I know what you're thinking. More identity politics? This was supposed to be a lighthearted romp through the world of opera, not a lecture on political correctness! Sorry not sorry—there's no escaping the broader culture wars when it comes to this battleground. Social movements such as #BlackLivesMatter and #StopAsianHate have taken existing pressure points around casting and escalated them to geyser-like levels of conflict.

The crux of the issue is this: How much of casting should be based on look when it comes to ethnicity and race? What are the rules for casting characters that are specifically identified as being *not* white in the score—characters such as Turandot in Puccini's *Turandot* or Aida in Verdi's *Aida*? And what about the rules for casting all the *other* roles in opera, the ones that aren't identified with a particular ethnicity?

Up until the early twentieth century, opera was a closed art form, reserved almost exclusively for white singers and white audiences. Singers of color existed, but they had limited career opportunities and were generally restricted to performing with vaudeville shows or segregated opera companies. This meant white singers held a casting monopoly over all roles, regardless of a character's race. Any issues of believability were simply countered by the liberal use of wigs and makeup.

Starting in the 1920s, however, color barriers began to topple. In 1925, Lillian Evanti became the first Black singer to perform at a European opera company. In 1933, Caterina Jarboro was the first Black singer to perform at a major company in America. Then there was Camilla Williams, the first Black singer to sign a contract with New York City Opera, in 1946; Mattiwilda Dobbs, the first Black singer to perform at Milan's Teatro alla Scala, in 1953; and Marian Anderson, the first Black woman to sing at the Metropolitan Opera, in 1955. Singers of Asian heritage also made significant strides. For example, soprano Yoko Watanabe was not only the first Japanese singer to perform a lead role at the UK's Royal Ballet and Opera in 1983, but also the first at the Teatro alla Scala in 1985, the Metropolitan Opera in 1987, and the Wiener Staatsoper in 1988.

And barriers are still being broken. As recently as 2022, tenor Russell Thomas became the first Black singer to perform the role of Otello in Verdi's *Otello* at the Royal Ballet and Opera at Covent Garden. Hooray for Russell, but what does that actually mean? That every other Otello in the history of the company was played by a white singer. Until 2022.

Even when opera stages were officially being integrated in the mid-twentieth century, the industry wasn't exactly all in. Opera was now technically open to singers of color, but access remained limited, largely restricted to the kinds of roles that Rudolf Bing of the Metropolitan Opera described in 1950 as "suitable parts." For Black singers, suitable parts were characters described in the score as being African or African-adjacent—characters such as the Ethiopian princess Aida in Verdi's *Aida* or the African queen Sélika in Meyerbeer's *L'Africaine*. For Asian singers, suitable parts were similarly Asian-specific: characters such as Cio-Cio-San, Goro, and Suzuki in Puccini's *Madama Butterfly*, and Turandot, Liù, and Ping, Pang, and Pong in Puccini's *Turandot*.

A handful of other "exotic" roles were also seen as fair game for singers of color. This included "Gypsies" such as Carmen in Bizet's

Carmen and Ulrica in Verdi's *Un ballo in maschera*; Moors such as Monostatos in Mozart's *The Magic Flute* and Otello in Verdi's *Otello*; and Southeast Asians such as the Indian priestess Lakmé in Delibes's *Lakmé*. In other words, the default was typecasting by race. Meanwhile, all the other roles in the repertoire—roles that didn't come with a particular ethnic identifier—were seen as being neutral. Raceless. White.

This ingrained discrimination makes us look at that list of broken color barriers with a more critical eye. Marian Anderson was the first Black singer at the Metropolitan Opera, sure, but she also played the role of Ulrica, a "Gypsy" fortune teller. Lillian Evanti's premiere in Europe in 1925 was as the Indian priestess Lakmé. Yoko Watanabe's string of debuts throughout the 1980s? All as Cio-Cio-San.

Matching up nonwhite singers with a "suitable" (stereotyped) role wasn't a hard-and-fast rule, and it's not difficult to find exceptions, especially in the case of star singers. Legendary Black soprano Leontyne Price made her debut at the Metropolitan Opera in 1961 as Leonora in Verdi's opera *Il trovatore*—a role without any ethnic identifiers. But to be fair, Price would have made her debut three years earlier if she'd accepted the Met's initial offer—to play Aida.

By the 1970s and 1980s, the divide in casting was increasingly obvious. Singers of color were overwhelming relegated to a small subset of "ethnic" roles, while white singers were earmarked for all the neutral or "raceless" ones—which also happened to be the majority. Worse, white singers were still being cast as Black and Asian characters, usually with a heavy slathering of makeup.

Then came the magic bullet that would finally solve everything—or so many thought. Color-blind casting. The premise was simple:

casting should be blind to color, made without any regard to the race or ethnicity of the performer. Instead, companies should cast the best singer for the role.

The concept first emerged in the United States theater scene in the 1980s, thanks to the efforts of the Non-Traditional Casting Project, an initiative sponsored by the Actors' Equity Association (aka Equity), the US–based union for actors and stage managers. The goal was to encourage theater companies to cast in more equitable ways, and, in particular, to cast a broader range of performers in traditionally "white" roles. The initiative was idealistic and hugely progressive at the time. And it almost immediately went wrong.

The kerfuffle started with the casting of Welsh actor Jonathan Pryce as the Engineer in the 1991 Broadway production of the musical *Miss Saigon*. Much like *Madama Butterfly* (the opera that inspired it), *Miss Saigon* isn't exactly a paragon of authentic representation. On the contrary, the show's portrayal of an American GI who falls in love with a Vietnamese sex worker during the Vietnam War is jam-packed with racial stereotypes. But in this case, the controversy wasn't about the plot. The problem was Pryce being cast as a character who was half Vietnamese.

Pryce had previously performed the role in the production's London premiere in 1989, notably wearing latex eye prosthetics to slant his eyes. Weeks before the show was scheduled to open on Broadway, however, Equity expressed concerns about his casting to the show's producer Cameron Mackintosh, arguing that an Asian or Asian American actor should have been considered over Pryce. Mackintosh immediately pushed back, claiming he was adhering to the principle of color-blind casting: Pryce hadn't been cast because of his ethnicity but because he was the best performer for the role. Facing increased pressure from the Asian American theater community, Equity nonetheless voted to ban Pryce from the production. But Mackintosh called their bluff. He canceled the show's Broadway opening, giving the middle finger to both Equity and the $24 million in advance tickets that had been sold. Mackintosh then publicly accused Equity of discriminating against Pryce on the basis of race. Forced into further consideration, Equity reversed its decision to ban Pryce. A mitigating factor was Mackintosh's assurance that an Asian American actor would replace Pryce when he left the production. And so *Miss Saigon* finally opened on Broadway in April 1991.

Was Pryce a beneficiary of color-blind casting? Absolutely. But this was also a case of following the letter rather than the spirit of the law. The goal of color-blind casting was never to create *more* opportunities for white performers, but rather the other way around. And Pryce's casting—and Mackintosh's rationale—would have ripple effects across the performing arts for the next three decades.

Today, a variation of Mackintosh's argument is regularly mounted in Opera Land whenever a company is criticized for their casting choices. "We're committed to color-blind casting, and we don't cast any role based on ethnicity or skin color," declared a spokesperson for Opera Australia after the company was denounced for casting a white soprano as the Puerto Rican ingenue Maria in a 2019 production of *West Side Story*. Or take LA Opera's similar statement following protests over their casting a white singer as an Egyptian pharaoh in Philip Glass's *Akhnaten*: "We have a long-standing policy of ignoring age, race and other physical characteristics when it comes to casting particular roles."

Or Houston Grand Opera's defense after casting white singers as Chinese characters for its 2017 production of John Adams and Alice Goodman's opera *Nixon in China*: "HGO casts performers on the basis of talent, not ethnicity."

Let's be honest. If companies were truly ignoring age, race, and physical characteristics when casting, they'd be holding auditions with singers standing behind a curtain. That's not happening. But the bigger fallacy here is that no one's actually blind to race. Not casting directors. Not stage directors. Certainly not audiences. We *all* see race. Just as we all see gender and height and weight. Even when we pretend we don't.

The premise of color blindness is especially unrealistic in opera because of its repertoire. Many of the works central to the Canon—operas such as *Madama Butterfly*, *Lakmé*, *Aida*, and *Otello*—draw on racial difference as part of their plots. It's hard to be blind to race when the story is literally about it. It's even harder when an opera is staged with race in mind.

Take *Madama Butterfly*, with its classic exotic storyline about Cio-Cio-San and her white American "husband." That plot? Definitely not color-blind. The opera's traditional staging with all those kimonos and geisha wigs? Also definitely not color-blind. Now let's say an opera company decides to cast a white soprano to play Cio-Cio-San because they support color-blind casting, and she's the best singer for the role. Except they're doing a traditional production and want her to look Japanese. Not to worry—that's what makeup and costumes are for!

Is the company still being color-blind? Not really. Is that soprano still the best performer for the role? Probably not. Because the production itself isn't color-blind—it's intentionally been designed in a racialized way, intentionally framed around a particular look. A look that isn't white. "But we don't consider race or ethnicity! We're color-blind!" the company declares with wide eyes and a hint of hysteria. Sure. Whatever you say.

The important question is, If color-blind casting is a nonstarter, then what's the alternative?

One increasingly popular approach is known as color-conscious casting. This means casting in a way that acknowledges the cultural background of the singer and the ethnicity of the character they'll portray, as well as broader social complexities around race and representation. When choosing a singer to play the Ethiopian princess Aida, for example, casting should consider the singer's voice, acting ability, and stage presence, as well as her cultural and lived experience *and* the industry's historical exclusion of certain groups.

The approach isn't without its critics. For some, it's akin to operatic affirmative action, with certain roles being reserved for singers of color because of their look rather than their talent. Consider conservative writer Heather Mac Donald, who sarcastically asked in a 2021 column whether casting directors will "need a spectrometer to decide if a performer is sufficiently 'colored' to fill a role." She continued, "The next step in imaginative emasculation is obvious. Only elderly actors can play King Lear, only hunchbacks can sing Rigoletto or play Richard III, only fat people can play or sing Falstaff, since using stage make-up and body suits to transform non-old, non-handicapped, and non-fat actors into those roles represents ageism, fat-shaming, and ableism."

It's an extreme take but one that brings up legitimate questions about the nature of performance and what it means to play a character onstage. After all, acting is *acting*. The whole notion of the thing involves assuming different identities, different personalities, and different appearances.

It's also a slippery slope because identity and appearance don't necessarily go hand in hand. Deciding that a singer has the right look to be cast as a certain character means drawing on a swath of generic visual identifiers, none of which may reflect their actual experience or self-perception.

And where does one draw the line? Carmen is described as a "Gypsy." Does that mean the role should only be played by mezzo-sopranos with Romani heritage? Does Cio-Cio-San have to be played by a Japanese soprano? Or is it okay to cast a Korean soprano? Or a Chinese one? Or, as arts journalist Anne Midgette asked in 2017, does that imply that "all Asians look alike?" What about the other operatic roles that have specific identifiers or national characteristics? In Mozart's opera *Così fan tutte*, the characters Guglielmo and Ferrando are Italian. Does that mean only Italian singers need apply?

There's no obvious answer or solution. But this battleground also isn't going away. Casting in opera continues to be far from equitable—not least because no one agrees what equitable casting is. Meanwhile, roughly seventy-five years after Rudolf Bing first referred to "suitable parts," trends of racial typecasting still persist, shaping and limiting the careers of many Black and Asian singers.

* * *

In December 2023, I spoke with soprano Yunah Lee, whose career has been defined by her performances as Cio-Cio-San in *Madama*

Butterfly. Born in South Korea, Lee attended Juilliard for her master's degree and then made her professional debut in 1995 at New York City Opera. Lee told me she was cast in a range of roles in the first seven years of her career, including star turns as characters such as Mimì in *La bohème*. But everything changed in 2002, when Lee was cast as Cio-Cio-San for the first time. After that production, said Lee, "There were no companies asking me to sing anything else but *Butterfly*. Over two decades."

A quick glance at Lee's performance CV is a jarring case study in pigeonholing. It's Cio-Cio-San after Cio-Cio-San—approximately 170 performances in more than forty productions of *Madama Butterfly* between 2002 and 2019. Not surprisingly, Lee has mixed feelings about the role. "I'm grateful to *Butterfly* because I made a career out of it," she told me. "But artistically, I was not really satisfied. So that has been my struggle. I would still sing *Butterfly*. I just don't want to sing *only Butterfly*."

Mezzo-soprano Nina Yoshida Nelsen described similar limitations in her career because of her Japanese American heritage. She told me she was cast in just three non-Asian roles in the ten years after she made her professional debut in 2009. Like Yunah Lee, *Madama Butterfly* has also been a constant operatic albatross around Yoshida Nelsen's neck. Between 2009 and 2019, she sang 150 performances as Cio-Cio-San's maid, Suzuki. I counted at least three productions where Yoshida Nelsen even shared the stage with Lee as Cio-Cio-San.

"I've often wondered what would have happened if I took *Yoshida* out of my name and had just been known as Nina Nelsen," she speculated in an article for the Asian Opera Alliance. "Would my career have had a different trajectory? Would people have seen me as more ethnically ambiguous? After all, I'm only half-Asian. Would I be where I am today?"

Many Black singers experience similar kinds of pigeonholing. Black women are still frequently cast as "exotic" characters and femme fatales, rather than heroines or ingenues. Meanwhile, Black male singers are often earmarked as fathers, brothers, and villains rather than romantic leads, a holdover from historical concerns about staging interracial romance with white lead sopranos.

Then there's the matter of *Porgy and Bess*. With music by composer George Gershwin and a libretto by DuBose Heyward and Ira Gershwin, *Porgy and Bess* is set in Catfish Row in 1920s South Carolina and follows disabled beggar Porgy as he tries to rescue his love interest, Bess, from her violent lover. The music is spectacular, but the story deeply problematic, often devolving into stereotypical and demeaning portrayals of Black culture. Even so, following its premiere in 1935, *Porgy and Bess* would become one of the most popular American operas of the twentieth century—and a godsend for Black singers trying to gain a foothold in the industry thanks to a legal stipulation that any staged production use an all-Black cast.

As with *Madama Butterfly*, a singer can make an entire career out of *Porgy and Bess*, simply jumping from production to production. But once a singer is associated with the opera, they often struggle to be cast for anything else. In a webinar hosted by Long Beach Opera in 2020, baritone Kenneth Overton recalled being told to avoid *Porgy and Bess* when he was first starting out. But after ten years in the industry, he decided to take the chance: "I said, 'Well, I'm established enough to take it. I want to take it. It's a badge of honor.'" Overton was quickly inundated with offers to sing Porgy, not only in the United States, but in Mexico, Canada,

Denmark, Germany, Ireland, Poland, and South America. After singing more than a hundred performances in the role, Overton finally called his agent and told him to reject any further offers, saying, "If I'm a viable artist, I'll survive without it."

There's a shared recognition that certain operas constitute a professional trap. It's one reason why many Black singers refuse to sing *Porgy and Bess* and many Asian singers similarly decline to audition for *Madama Butterfly*. But for some, it's seen as a choice between having a demarcated career and having no career at all. Because there's also an understanding that the majority of roles in opera are still inherently seen as "white." That's the default image that pops into the head of the casting director or the stage director in the audition room. That's the look they're shooting for, the look they think will be believable—even if they don't consciously realize it.

In 1977, Black soprano Leona Mitchell wasn't cast in the role of Donna Anna in Mozart's *Don Giovanni* at the UK's Glyndebourne Festival because the director allegedly didn't think a Black singer would be plausible as a Spanish aristocrat. In 2023, Singaporean singer Wei En Chan described being rejected for the role of King David in Handel's opera *Saul* because King David "wasn't Asian." Yunah Lee recalls multiple instances of being told she didn't have the right look to play certain characters. An offer to perform the role of Tatiana in Tchaikovsky's opera *Eugene Onegin* fell through, she told me, because the director couldn't "see" her as the Russian ingenue. According to Lee, her European agent was even more explicit, telling Lee he couldn't present her for anything other than Asian characters like Liù or Butterfly because he "couldn't see her doing anything else." Tenor Frederick Ballentine, who's

Black, described something similar in a 2019 interview with the Associated Press. "I have experienced a few times where people said, 'I just don't know if we could see you in that.' Or 'Are you sure you could play that, does that quite work?' They'll dance around it but not say the actual thing."

Progress is slow, and the frustration of many singers of color is palpable. "If you're being hired to sing Butterfly or if you're being hired to sing Suzuki, you're good enough to sing Mimì in *La bohème* or Maddalena in *Rigoletto*," Nina Yoshida Nelsen told me. "There's no reason why a company shouldn't be seeing you for those roles as well." Until singers of color are being considered equally—until the industry is truly at the point of equity—Yoshida Nelsen believes casting should be based on the premise of "Yes, and." *Yes* to being cast in racially specific roles such as Cio-Cio-San and Aida. *And* to also being cast in traditionally "white" roles.

Yoshida Nelsen started applying this approach in her own career in 2021, after years of being pigeonholed as Asian characters. "If I'm specifically going to do an Asian role at a certain opera company—which I'm happy to do—then my agent will now ask the company what other opportunities they have for me in future seasons that are non-Asian. They need to understand that they're pigeonholing me unless they also bring me back for something else."

* * *

There will always be the look that fits a character as they're described in the musical score. But there's also the look that fits a director's concept for an opera. As we know, this is something with more than a little wiggle room. No one's forcing directors to stage operas in a particular way, let alone forcing them to look at characters such as Carmen and Cio-Cio-San in the same way long-dead composers and librettists once did. Casting isn't fixed or set. It's dynamic, changeable. A choice that's being newly made in the course of every production and every audition.

And what's the worst that could happen if the look that finally won the audition this time was a bit different? A bit unexpected, even unbelievable? What's the worst that could happen if the Carmen was curvy? Or the Russian ingenue was Asian? Or the plus-size soprano actually wore a little black dress?

Maybe if we finally see it, it won't be so hard to believe it.

CHAPTER 5

The Show

— or —

What Happens in Rehearsal Stays in Rehearsal

All the elements are in place. All the ingredients finally ready to be whisked together: the score, the staging, the creative team, the cast. Every element comes with its own set of tensions, and each is a critical cog in the machine of the final performance: the show that's destined to be presented in front of a live audience.

But we can't dive into the glamour and adrenaline-driven high of an opera performance without first examining the path that leads to opening night. The performance is only the product, after all. There's no product without the process.

For every painting that makes it onto the wall of the Metropolitan Museum of Art, there's a turpentine-spattered studio strewn with dirty paintbrushes and half-eaten sandwiches. For every book about opera, there's a messy desk covered with teetering stacks of reference books and frantically scrawled Post-it notes. And for every performance—for every standing ovation and bouquet tossed at the star soprano—there are rehearsals. These are the muddy trenches of the Opera Wars but also a battleground in themselves—the gauntlet that must be run and overcome before the curtain goes up.

* * *

Rehearsals are the nexus of every decision, choice, and compromise that's made in constructing a performance. They straddle the liminal space between the version of an opera that'll eventually exist onstage and the version that'll only ever exist in the minds of the cast and creative team. Forget Schrödinger's cat—this is Schrödinger's opera, a transitional state during which a show is simultaneously dead and alive, and the final verdict is only revealed on opening night.

But rehearsals are also largely mysterious domains—what Susan Letzler Cole called "a hidden world" in her 1992 book, *Directors in Rehearsal.* Only a select few ever learn the secret handshake that grants access to this oh-so-private realm. There's the stage director, of course, alongside the conductor, the designers, the cast of singers, and the instrumentalists. But our exclusive club also has a few new members, including the stage manager (and team), who organizes the practical logistics of the performance on and off the stage; the props manager (and team), who manages the physical objects that'll be used in each scene (think Don José's dagger of choice in *Carmen*); the *répétiteur*, that is, the rehearsal pianist and vocal coach who will accompany the majority of the rehearsals instead of the orchestra; and the company manager, who liaises with the company bigwigs and generally ensures rehearsals aren't going sideways.

Every rehearsal process is unique, shaped as much by the distinct personalities of the creatives involved as by the practical logistics of the opera being staged. The rehearsals for an opera with two singers and a single backdrop are a very different animal from those required for a five-act grand opera with a cast of seventy-five and a hundred-foot-tall pyramid in the background.

Timelines can also vary, with the length determined by the presenting opera company in concert with the current state of their bottom line. Company leadership must weigh the collective costs of renting rehearsal space and paying the fees of key personnel to calculate how many rehearsals are actually needed. Here the notion of "need" is somewhat subjective, though as a general rule company leadership always needs fewer rehearsals, and the creative team always needs more.

On average, a new production of an opera might be allocated four or five weeks of total rehearsal time. A new production of a *new* opera—that is, one that's being hastily written by a composer and a librettist—may get a few extra weeks on top of that. In comparison, a revival production—that is, a production that was designed, built, and staged in a previous season and has been hauled out of storage to be performed with different singers—may be allocated just two or three weeks. Take the revival production of Verdi's opera *Rigoletto* staged by Lyric Opera of Chicago in 2024: just nine days of rehearsal over three weeks.

Though even nine days can sometimes be a luxury. I spoke to one stage director who was hired to revive a production of Mark Adamo's opera *Little Women* with just four days of rehearsal.

Luckily, most of the singers had sung the opera before and were well familiar with their roles and the production design. But the staging, the director told me, mostly involved him playing traffic cop: "'You stand here. You pick up the book there. You die there.' It's all we had time for. The production was a success, so some would say we got the job done, but with such a talented cast, I can't help but imagine what would have been possible with more time."

No matter how much time is allocated to rehearsals, however, the same components are always involved. Every process starts with the music. It's customary for the very first rehearsal to include a full sing-through of the entire opera with the conductor, singers, and rehearsal pianist. Some additional music-only rehearsals will then be scheduled, including one-on-one sessions for the principal singers and conductor, as well as rehearsals of larger group numbers and sessions for the chorus.

Every singer is expected to arrive on day one with their music already learned and memorized, but music rehearsals provide an opportunity to polish and refine, and, most important, to incorporate the artistic preferences of the conductor. How fast does the conductor want to take a certain aria? What vibe are they thinking for a particular duet? Music rehearsals are also a chance for singers to hear the other members of the cast—some of whom they'll be meeting for the first time—and potentially to adjust their musical interpretation to align with that of their colleagues.

The culmination of the music rehearsal stage is the *Sitzprobe*, which translates from the German as "seated rehearsal." This is the first time the singers rehearse with the full orchestra, and the two cohorts collectively work through the music of the entire opera under the close supervision of the conductor. As per the name, singers generally remain seated—at least until it's their turn to sing—and usually have their well-thumbed musical scores on a music stand nearby, just in case they need to add additional notes or markings. A particular quirk of the *Sitzprobe* is the expectation that singers will dress to impress, not only as a sign of respect for the process but so they can schmooze with any donors in attendance.

After the music comes the staging, which constitutes the bulk of every opera's rehearsal process. Staging rehearsals are the purview of the director and usually take place in a rehearsal space that conforms to the rough size and shape of the actual stage. The director starts off the first staging rehearsal with an overview of their chosen concept, often including sketches of the sets and costumes. Then they'll dive straight into the practical logistics of "blocking" the show, including setting basic entrances and exits—that is, when and where singers come onstage during each scene—as well as the broad strokes of what each singer will do while they're there.

A key focus of blocking is ensuring singers don't "bump into the furniture," as playwright Noël Coward allegedly once quipped—a task that can be particularly challenging when dealing with a chorus of sixty singers who all need to be onstage at the same time. But a further priority of staging rehearsals is to help singers establish the arcs of their characters, finding the dramatic motivation for why they're singing what, when, and how. Accordingly, once the entire opera has been roughly blocked—meaning the singers can stagger through the outline of each scene from start to finish—the next step is to go back to the beginning and incorporate nuances. This means adding more detailed physical movement (also known as stage business) as well as in-depth character work. How should Rodolfo react when he meets Mimì for the first time in *La bohème*, for example?

Whom should he be looking at? How should he be standing? What should he be doing with his hands? And above all, why?

Once these details are incorporated and finalized in each scene, the name of the staging game becomes repetition: rehearsing scenes over and over until the physical movements and characterizations become second nature. This is the only way to ensure the singers can juggle the physical, mental, and emotional components of an opera during the actual performance, including staying in character, making the right entrances and exits, finding the right spotlight, staying in view of the conductor, and remembering all that intricate stage business. Oh, and also managing the complex physical coordination involved in, you know, the actual singing.

After music and staging, rehearsals shift to technical matters, with the cast and crew officially saying goodbye to the rehearsal room and hello to the stage. In what is known as Load In (or Bump In, if you're speaking Australian), all the sets, costumes, wigs, props, and equipment for the production are physically hauled into the theater. Stage lights are hung and adjusted, singers are assigned dressing rooms backstage, and the stage floor is marked with colored tape to indicate where each piece of scenery and furniture will be placed. Now comes the challenge of integrating all that carefully rehearsed blocking with moving set pieces, costume changes, and shifting lights, not to mention navigating the gaping hole of the orchestra pit in front of the stage, which now threatens a broken limb for any careless singer.

There are so many technical logistics to manage that most companies schedule multiple days, if not an entire week, of technical rehearsals (aptly called Tech Week). Common milestones include a so-called Cue-to-Cue, during which the director and the designers run through each lighting transition and set change from the specific "cue," or musical spot in the score, that prompts the action. Then there's the Piano Tech, or the first time the singers rehearse onstage with piano accompaniment and can fix their blocking to accommodate the now-present set pieces and spotlights. A Piano Tech with Costumes is more of the same but with costumes (obviously) and frequently involves running the entire show from start to finish. The *Wandelprobe*, literally translated from the German as "wandering rehearsal," adds in the orchestra, with the singers wandering through the basics of their blocking while the conductor checks the balance of volume and sound with the instrumentalists.

Over hours and hours of technical rehearsals, of continued adjustments to lights and staging—and occasional panic attacks from the director and the designers—all the kinks, quirks, and issues with the production will be resolved. And just in time, because the next rehearsal milestone is the Orchestra Dress Rehearsal, a full run of the opera that aims to replicate the conditions of an actual performance. This means sets, lights, costumes, hair, makeup, and orchestra—everything except for an audience. After this rehearsal, there may be a few more tweaks, a few more changes, and certainly a few more comments and criticisms from the director. But the Final Dress Rehearsal is swiftly approaching. This will be the last run-through of the opera prior to the first performance and typically functions as a kind of preview event for invited audiences such as donors and school groups. After this, the show is considered frozen, with no further changes to be made either before or after opening night.

When laid out as a series of milestones—or more often in practice as a color-coded spreadsheet—the opera rehearsal process seems systematic, even clinical. Time crunch aside, there's an extensive but ultimately manageable to-do list that simply needs to be completed for a show to progress from the rehearsal room to the stage. However, this orderly outline is also missing a critical element, one that inevitably throws every rehearsal process into complete and utter chaos: the people.

* * *

Opera has been called the original team sport. Dozens if not hundreds of different artistic and technical personnel must work together as a unit to make each performance a reality. To extend the sports metaphor—at least as far as this decidedly nonsports-minded author can take it—every team sport also has its coaches. In this case, it's the director and the conductor.

As the designated leaders of the production, the director and the conductor collectively set the tone of the rehearsal room and shape the cumulative way a performance is built from the ground up. But this is where the sport can be less a friendly game of football and more like the Hunger Games—even before the singers have come onto the field.

On paper, the delineation of duties between our two head coaches is fairly clear-cut. The conductor is in charge of the music and therefore responsible for music rehearsals. The director is in charge of the staging and therefore responsible for staging rehearsals. Consider the lines drawn and borders established. But opera also isn't an art form that's so easily compartmentalized. It's defined by the *simultaneous* integration of music and staging—by what the audience sees and hears merging at the same time. This means those seemingly clear lines between the realms of the director and the conductor frequently blur, overlap, and clash.

First, there are the inevitable practicalities to iron out, questions such as where and how should the singers be placed onstage to ensure they can see the conductor in the orchestra pit and still be heard by the audience. Will the soprano be able to sing her aria if she's staged to be lying on her back? Will that tricky ensemble number fall apart musically if the singers aren't locked in place, eyes glued to the conductor?

Squabbles over practical logistics can often lead to more heated discussions, ranging from basic disagreements over the meaning of a certain aria or line of text to more philosophical arguments about how an opera should be interpreted and staged. Things can get particularly tense when a nontraditional *Regietheater* concept is involved.

I remember directing a production of Mozart's *The Marriage of Figaro* in college and having repeated (and occasionally shouted) arguments with the conductor because he disagreed with my concept. Much to his dismay, I'd decided to break from the opera's traditional setting of eighteenth-century Seville and instead reimagine it as a take on John F. Kennedy's 1960 presidential campaign. Despite months of meetings and rehearsals, the conductor and I never resolved our differences. In the end, I simply proceeded with my plans for bouffant wigs and skinny ties, while he glowered at me from his podium in the orchestra. If an amateur college production involving no money, no stakeholders, and even fewer stakes could produce so many sparks, imagine the fireworks at a professional company where an internationally renowned conductor and equally famous director are grappling for artistic control.

Amid these kinds of conflicts, a fundamental question always lingers just below the surface, one that recalls the classic battleground between composers and librettists. Whose opinion (and domain) matters *more*? Does one coach have slightly more authority? Is one crown slightly more bejeweled? Opinions differ, and I, for one, plead the Fifth.

But regardless of whether you're Team Director or Team Conductor, the general consensus is that most coach-to-coach disagreements are exacerbated by poor communication, which is, in turn, aggravated by tight rehearsal timelines. While directors are present for all staging rehearsals, conductors often fly in and fly out while juggling other freelance gigs. Depending on scheduling, the director and the conductor may not even physically be present together for the majority of the rehearsals, leaving limited opportunities for creative conversations.

Too many missed conversations can lead to nightmare rehearsal scenarios, such as the one described by British soprano Susan Bullock in a 2024 interview: "Sometimes I've done Brünnhilde [from Wagner's *Ring Cycle*] with conductors who haven't turned up until the show. I've spent weeks working in a room with the director, and the conductor hasn't been there. And when I get onstage, [the conductor is] suddenly freaking out, saying, 'You can't do that staging, it doesn't work.' Because they haven't been part of it and they don't know why I'm doing what I'm doing, why I'm in that position on the stage. And then the battle commences, trying to appease everybody and not screw up what I've done for eight weeks."

Conductor Lidiya Yankovskaya told me she always tries to stave off potential disagreements as early as possible, usually by scheduling a meeting with the director before rehearsals begin. This, she said, gives them a chance to discuss their individual concepts for the opera and work through any tricky practicalities or conflicts—all, importantly, while out of earshot of the singers. "These are conversations that have to happen," Yankovskaya told me. "It's a collaborative process. Often actually having two people who see things very differently can be more valuable than having the same perspective in the room."

Yankovskaya was the music director of the Chicago Opera Theater from 2018 to 2024 and has extensive experience working across both opera and symphonic music. From her perspective, some conductors and directors aren't necessarily suited to opera—or prepared for the level of collaboration that's required. It's often when conductors and directors aren't actually "interested in the art form," she said, that things turn disastrous.

"Sometimes you have conductors who don't understand what theater is and don't understand how working with singers is different from working with instrumentalists. And sometimes you have directors who aren't interested in musical storytelling. Whether a director chooses to go with the composer or push against the music, they must be aware of the emotional subtext and dramatic timing that's created through the music. One can't direct an opera from the libretto alone. That's where the conflicts arise."

The best-case scenario for directors and conductors is one of complete collaboration, in which each respects the expertise and domain of their counterpart while pursuing a shared artistic goal. However, even when our two head coaches establish the perfect working relationship, there are still limitations. Hurdles even. Because the best coaches are only ever as good as the players on their team.

* * *

We've all played God in our time—or, to be more accurate, we've all played Director and Conductor. Every child has enacted a melodramatic storyline with Barbie dolls or staged a mock battle between G. I. Joe action figures and villainous Decepticons, or even just organized a good old pretend game of Cops and Robbers or Restaurant. Like the tempestuous gods of old, every child has controlled the fate and destiny of those within their dominion of power, determining with tyrannical precision exactly how each character should behave. But the practical logistics of rehearsing and staging an opera aren't as simple as navigating a Barbie Dreamhouse or even managing a hectic day at the local pretend café. Because in opera, all those dolls—all those Transformers and demanding imaginary customers—also have agency. Worse, they have *opinions.*

Every director and conductor has a different approach for working with singers and trying to squeeze out the precise performance they want. Manipulation, flattery, yelling, coaxing—every approach is unique to the combination of personalities and egos in the room, as well as the preferred style of the leaders in charge. "Every production has a different dynamic," director Claus Guth told me. "Some productions I create with singers that I know, so we're immediately in a family atmosphere. Others are with singers I never saw before in my life. They're all very different worlds."

The first rehearsal always sets the dynamics of the "world" that'll be evoked over the course of rehearsals. It's the equivalent of a group blind date in which everyone is also having their first day at a new school and trying to figure out where to sit in the cafeteria. It's all nervous energy and snap judgments, with everyone taking the temperature of everyone else while simultaneously struggling for a foothold in the newly formed social hierarchy.

Accordingly, for Guth, that very first rehearsal is far more nerve-racking than even the first performance. "It's the moment where you reveal your concept, your ideas," he told me. "You have maybe thirty minutes to explain something that you've been working on for two or three years. It's always a tricky moment because, if it goes wrong, it'll take a long time to get singers back on board." The singers, after all, are the ones who realize the director's vision through their acting and singing. And if they're not on board, it shows.

Guth's concepts are often nontraditional—remember his *La bohème* in space?—and early in his career, he frequently encountered resistance from the singers tasked with making his vision a reality. Sometimes they had opposing views about their characters or the logistics of the blocking, but most often, they took issue with his concept. In such cases Guth's task in the rehearsal room was to try to work past the disagreement and persuade the singer to commit to his vision despite their trepidation. This was especially challenging, Guth said, if the singer already had preset expectations about a character or storyline.

"You try to convince by words, but in most cases, words don't fix it," he told me. "I have to convince the singer to just try it once, and then [we] can discuss how it feels. You need to be stubborn and calm and patient and wait until it clicks." Most of the time, Guth said, it does eventually click. But if he's tried every possible approach and the singer still won't budge, there's only one option left: "One of us has to say goodbye," he said.

The interpersonal stakes in the rehearsal room are particularly high for directors because of the sheer scale of the task to be accomplished. The singers need to learn and internalize all the relevant blocking, stage business, and characterization for their roles, which, in turn, relies on the director effectively communicating their vision while also organizing and managing limited rehearsal time. The conductor has an equally significant job to do in shaping the musical interpretation of the opera and drawing out the best vocal performances. But the music already exists on the page—and the singers already know it (at least in theory). The staging doesn't. So, even if everyone accepts the director's concept in record time, a daunting amount of work is still to be done.

But how does one go about staging a three-hour opera in just three or four weeks of rehearsal? What's involved in the actual *directing*?

Like the rehearsal rooms themselves, every director is different. Some are meticulous planners, mapping out every aspect of the blocking prior to the first day of rehearsal. Every gesture, every movement, every stride across the stage—everything's predetermined, notated in the score, and precisely relayed to the singers. Other directors take a more organic approach, arriving at rehearsals with a general plan for staging each scene and then working out the finer details with the singers in the room.

Claus Guth's preferred approach is a combination of planning and improvisation. "I'm extremely prepared," he told me. "I usually have a score where I have a note for what I want to do in almost every bar of music. I always do this homework. But then, in the rehearsal, as soon as I see anything developing that's more interesting than what I planned, I set aside what I've prepared. I might meet back with my concept fifty pages later." Guth explained that he sees his job as giving the singers an initial push in a certain direction. Then, ideally, "the singer starts running with much nicer ideas than I would have had," he said.

For stage director Lawrence Edelson, who's also the general director of the Chicago Opera Theater, the goal is to shepherd the energy and talent that's in the room, rather than impose explicit instructions. "It's important that we make the time to ask the questions that ensure we're coming together to tell the same story. Once we get to staging, there may be some physical things that have to happen for the logistics of the scene to work. Those moments are anchors in my mind," he explained. "But I find it most effective to provide a framework for the performers to create the staging with me. We'll try things many different ways. We'll bounce ideas off each other. My goal is setting up a rehearsal room where everyone feels comfortable to play and experiment. It's not that I don't have strong ideas, but the ideas I have become stronger through collaboration with the artists who'll bring the story to life onstage."

Director Peter Kazaras also prefers a collaborative approach and never blocks out the stage details in advance—though he knows a number of directors who do. As a former singer, as well as the former artistic director of the Seattle Opera Young Artists Program, Kazaras has a keen sense of what singers can potentially bring to a rehearsal room and feels that a director's primary job is to create space for them to discover new things in the moment. "I firmly believe that a lot of the great ideas come from singers. Sometimes it's your job to help them express what they want to put across, and sometimes it's your job to help them solidify an idea that's not really formed yet," he said.

However, Kazaras acknowledged that directors must also sometimes err on the side of wrangling, particularly when dealing with strong personalities. He mentioned one production in which his two romantic leads despised each other and weren't successfully hiding it onstage. "It was already after the piano dress rehearsal, and I'm backstage trying to work on the final scene with the two of them. I said, 'How can you do this so it doesn't look like you hate each other?'" Kazaras recalled the tenor accused the soprano of being frigid, the soprano called the tenor an asshole, and both singers stormed out. With opening night imminent, Kazaras finally intervened with each singer individually: "I said, 'You're professionals. Figure this the fuck out.' And they did. They gave a good performance. But, man, it was difficult."

The unique world that exists within the rehearsal room is built and maintained by the people who are in it. So, not surprisingly, rehearsal rooms can also have a dark side. In some cases, a very, *very* dark side. After all, take any scenario involving artistic temperaments, uneven power dynamics, and a looming deadline, and the conditions are ripe for bad behavior.

"Sometimes you're lucky, and you get into a rehearsal room, and it's led by wonderful leaders, and the cast is just clicking, and you're making art. That's amazing. And that's about five percent of the time," one singer told me. "The rest of the time there's usually at least somebody who's making it difficult for a lot of people."

Singers can often be the reason a rehearsal room takes a toxic turn. Think of the stereotype of the narcissistic diva who struts around making increasingly outrageous demands. American soprano Kathleen Battle was notorious for her operatic temper tantrums in the 1980s and 1990s, so much so that stagehands at the San Francisco Opera were said to have made T-shirts with the slogan I SURVIVED THE BATTLE. The soprano's reputed transgressions included arguing with conductors, storming out of rehearsals, throwing singers out of dressing rooms, and even once allegedly calling the management of the Boston Symphony Orchestra to complain that her hotel restaurant had added peas to her pasta. According to reports, Battle's very public firing from the Metropolitan Opera in 1994 due to "unprofessional actions" was met with cheers and applause from other singers at the company.

There's no excuse for bad behavior—and really, what kind of monster doesn't like peas?—but we can extend some empathy to those singers who have outbursts behind the scenes. Remember that singers must internalize the competing elements of staging, character interpretation, music, and vocal technique and then present a compelling performance in front of a live audience. Stress levels are high, and insecurities are inevitably rife. "It's the ones who feel insignificant in themselves that feel they have to pull that kind of power," one singer told me.

But more than from the singers, bad behavior most frequently originates from the leaders of the rehearsal room: the director and the conductor. This poisoning of the atmosphere can range from bullying, threats, and verbal abuse to far more litigable offenses. One soprano I interviewed described an encounter with a director who called her "fucking stupid" during the dress rehearsal. "He called someone else a cunt. He told another singer he wanted to see her clitoris when she was onstage. He was just a ticking time bomb."

The singer dodged the director's violent mood swings for the majority of the rehearsals, but everything came to a head at the final dress rehearsal. "He started to get more and more aggressive [toward] me," she said. "But none of my colleagues stood up for me.

Everyone was worried about their own job. So I just walked out." The choice, she acknowledged, reflected her privilege as a fairly high-level artist in the field. She still sang the performances but was able to remove herself from the toxic dynamics of the rehearsal room without any professional consequences. "At that stage in my career, I knew myself as an artist. I knew what my values were. I feel fortunate I had the confidence to walk out when I know not everyone would."

Another soprano described a run-in with a conductor who was so verbally abusive that the singer almost backed out of the contract. She decided to suffer through, mostly for the sake of her career. "No one wants to mess with conductors. Even if they humiliate you—artistically, personally, dramatically—you can't really say anything to argue back. Because you don't want to lose that job or future jobs," she said. "They don't want to offend the singers that have important reputations, so they don't touch the divas. But they always pick on the weakest ones. The youngest ones."

The particular vulnerability of younger singers to volatile directors and conductors was a recurring theme in my interviews. "Singers have this feeling of being replaceable," one said. "Until you're at a certain point in your career where you feel like you have some level of security, people won't stand up for themselves." Another told me they try their best to protect the other singers whenever they see the dynamics of a rehearsal spiraling downward: "If I'm in a room, and I'm anywhere near playing the title character or I'm one of the leads, I feel a responsibility to advocate for the other people in the room who don't deserve to receive abuse," they said.

Another more disturbing theme in my interviews was the propensity for opera companies to ignore or even defend the bad behavior of directors and conductors. One singer I spoke to was forced to fend off the sexual advances of a conductor during a production. Irate at her rejection, the conductor bullied her for the remainder of the rehearsals and then tried to disrupt her singing during the actual performances. "I went to the director of the company and told him about it. He said there are seven other women who've also complained," the singer said. "But they're not doing anything. He still gets to conduct. He still gets to destroy me, even onstage in front of an audience. They won't say anything because he's an artistic genius and, you know, great artists are always capricious. They say I should just be more flexible."

It's a well-known rationale in Opera Land, among other artistic realms, that genius is sufficient justification for abuse—and that the art that's produced matters more than any harm caused in the process. But with the rise of the #MeToo movement in the United States, there's been growing scrutiny over what exactly happens behind the closed doors of rehearsal rooms. Since 2018, a spate of public allegations have been made against major industry players, who've alternatively been accused of bullying, physical violence, sexual misconduct, and worse. The long list of alleged perpetrators includes James Levine (1943–2021), the longtime conductor of the Metropolitan Opera; Plácido Domingo, the Spanish tenor-turned-conductor and former general director of both Washington National Opera and LA Opera; and Stephen Lord, the former principal conductor of Michigan Opera Theatre (now Detroit Opera), among others.

For many current and former singers, the names plastered across newspapers and social media haven't come as a surprise. Instead, the more common reaction is a knowing grimace. I interviewed one singer who recalled a decades-old interaction between a soprano colleague and a conductor who'd later be swarmed with allegations of sexual misconduct. "We'd just finished rehearsing a scene and were relaxing, sitting around, and she froze. She turned and told me not to leave her side, saying, 'He's here.' I asked, 'Who?' She indicated the door, and within just a few seconds, this Very Famous Person was standing in front of her, looming over her, and she was sweating. I never saw this woman sweat at all when she was singing, but she was sweating. I just sat there, not moving, and quite obviously not about to move. Eventually he left."

There's been so much cumulative bad behavior—and negative publicity—that many opera companies are toeing a more careful line with rehearsal rooms. But the industry response has also been inconsistent. Companies in the United States have scrambled to implement new HR policies and behavioral guidelines, many of which seem designed to protect the company as much, if not more, than the cast and crew. But companies in countries such as Germany and Italy haven't come on board in the same way. "#MeToo doesn't exist in Europe," one singer flatly told me. Another agreed, "Some of the most challenging and traumatizingly abusive rehearsal rooms I've encountered have been in the last few years in Europe. I think it's because there are no unions. There's no HR department. It's your word against the director or conductor or colleague."

It's a symptom of opera's freelance work structures that rehearsal rooms are so unpredictable—alternatively safe or unsafe spaces depending entirely on the individuals involved. But even the grimmest and most toxic of rehearsal rooms is only ever temporary. Eventually, for better or worse, the gauntlet is run: every scene is staged, every musical number is polished, and every rehearsal milestone is met. The next step is to leave the trenches behind and finally go over the top.

As of opening night, the director's job is officially done, and the conductor is firmly situated in the darkened recess of the orchestra pit. The technical workings of the production are left to the stage manager and their team, who'll manage the practical logistics of every set change and lighting cue as it happens. But artistically? Dramatically? The show now belongs to the singers.

* * *

Every show—every live performance—begins from a state of heightened anticipation. In the hours before the curtain goes up, the singers are summoned to the backstage labyrinth of the theater for hair, makeup, and costumes. They'll warm up their voices in their dressing rooms, meditate, do some yoga—perhaps be quietly sick in the nearest trash can. They might have a quick "fight call" with the stage manager to double-check the choreography of a staged scuffle or alternatively, run through the precise canoodling of an onstage love scene. And then, they wait.

Roughly thirty to forty minutes before the show is scheduled to begin, the doors to the theater open to the public. Tickets are scanned, coats are checked, and each member of the audience files into the auditorium, eyes scanning past alphabetically marked rows in search of assigned seats. There's the awkward but inevitable close-quarters shuffle past the audience members already sitting down, and finally, the settling in: flipping through programs, appraising everyone else's opera wear, and basking in the gentle murmur of three hundred preperformance conversations. And then, they wait.

The tuning of the orchestra is the musical equivalent of a kick-off and a not-so-subtle nudge for the audience to wrap up any lingering chitchat. The musical note A is played by the oboe, a gleaming thread of sound that cuts through the din of the theater.* Each section of the orchestra then adds to the growing but controlled cacophony in turn: first, the brass, then the woodwinds, the low strings, and the high strings. After a final explosion of overlapping musical notes and phrases, the orchestra stops. And then, *they* wait.

At last, a spotlight flickers on the empty podium in the orchestra pit, cuing the entrance of the conductor, who acknowledges the applause of the audience with a benevolent bow. The conductor turns to face the score resting on their music stand. A few final heartbeats of silence. Stillness. The conductor slowly raises a baton and, with a single fluid movement, marks the downbeat of the first note of the opera. The performance has finally begun. Now anything can happen.

Part of the magic of live performance is that it's fundamentally out of control. No matter how precise or obsessive the rehearsals, no matter how exacting the blocking or tempos set by the conductor, every performance possesses an inherent wildness. There are just too many elements involved—too many people, too many set pieces, too many things to go wrong—for any semblance of predictability or order.

I spoke to a singer who once broke her leg in the middle of a performance. Another who broke a toe. Another who sprained a rib. Another who had a miscarriage. I heard about audible farts,

---

* Why the note A? Because all the stringed instruments in the orchestra have an A string. And why the oboe? Because oboes are so notoriously difficult to tune on their own that it's abundantly easier for the rest of the orchestra to tune to match them instead.

flubbed lines, missed entrances, prop guns going off, singers falling into the prompter's box, and even a set piece taking off part of a soprano's nose (just the tip, apparently).

One singer recalled standing on the third story of a massive onstage "house" in the middle of a performance when the entire set started unexpectedly moving on its remote-controlled track. "We're singing and the house suddenly lurches and is headed for the orchestra pit. The whole fucking thing began to move. House, stairs, rooms—everything going toward the pit without stopping. And we're just hanging on to the sides like, 'What the fuck?!'" After finishing the scene and staggering offstage, the singer learned the cause of the near disaster: one of the stagehands had accidentally tripped while holding the remote control.

External variables can easily add a touch of chaos to a live performance, particularly malfunctioning set pieces. Then there's the uncertainty associated with the staging. Will everyone remember the precise stage business that's been endlessly rehearsed and rehashed? Will the fake punch land? Will the faux kiss work? And, when some aspect of the blocking is unavoidably forgotten or confused, will everyone adapt and adjust in the moment . . . ideally, without the audience noticing?

During a performance of a Gilbert and Sullivan operetta, I once took a step too far back onstage and tripped over a prop picket fence behind me. I then got stuck, my legs, petticoats, and gown all firmly wedged between opposing pickets. I desperately reached out an arm to the other singer onstage for assistance, but she could only look at me with horror: ironically—and inconveniently—her costume in the scene was a straitjacket. Against a soundtrack of growing laughter from the audience, I finally extricated myself and continued the scene.

But more challenging even than blocking disasters or precariously low picket fences is the mental battle of a live performance. Knowing the staging and the music at an intellectual level is one thing, but an internal war wages within every singer who steps out on the stage, a clash between self-confidence and crippling self-doubt. *Will I be able to combine my staging, music, technique, and character in front of a live audience? Will I be able to deliver when it matters?*

Bring on the nerves.

Psychologists have long recognized that some nervousness is a necessary ingredient for a good performance. Back in 1908, psychologists Robert M. Yerkes and John Dillingham Dodson proved an empirical relationship between mental or physiological "arousal" and an increase in performance quality. But only up to a point. Too much arousal, they found, and quality inevitably plummets. Admittedly, Yerkes and Dodson were experimenting on mice, but their findings were still subsequently deemed psychological law (literally, the Yerkes-Dodson law). Translated to opera, this means every performance is a delicate balancing act, in which singers try to summon the necessary nerves to put on a good show while simultaneously dodging the all-encompassing stage fright that could destroy it.

Stage fright can take different forms depending on an individual's brain chemistry. The most common physical symptoms include stomach butterflies, increased heart rate, shortness of breath, trembling legs, sweating, and a compelling urge to use the toilet (because both fight *and* flight are equally tricky with a full bladder). Then there are all the delightful psychological symptoms, such as fear of failure, fear of embarrassment, fear of mediocrity, fear of memory loss, and—my personal and well-practiced favorite—an unavoidable sense of dread.

Any combination of these physical and mental symptoms can potentially inhibit a singer's performance onstage, making them lose focus or fumble in the moment. But stage fright and nerves can also negatively affect the Voice. Operatic voices are capricious, volatile, and easily susceptible to disruption from both internal and external forces. Acid reflux, period cramps, sore muscles, missed sleep, too much talking, too much caffeine—any of it can easily move the needle from a good singing day to a bad one—and that's before even adding debilitating symptoms of stage fright such as a racing heart or hyperventilation. "It's a scary thing. There's a fear that our very delicate voices will betray us," one singer told me. And while that's the worst-case scenario, it's been commonly known to happen. Singers *are* regularly betrayed—*are* regularly failed by their voices in the middle of a live performance.

Given the stakes, it's perhaps no wonder that many opera singers resort to superstition to manage their preshow jitters. Consider the ubiquitous backstage blessing "Toi, toi, toi," an onomatopoeic expression that evokes spitting three times to ward off evil spirits, specifically any that might wreak havoc on the upcoming performance. But that's not all. Special bobby pins, lucky bras, obsessive preperformance rituals—everything's fair game in the delicate dance between trust and terror.

I heard of one singer who always has to spit out their toothpaste in a certain way. Another who has to put their car keys on the kitchen table just so. One singer told me about a brief but intense fixation with bubble tea. "One time I sang really well after having bubble tea. Something about how the tapioca pearls coated my throat," she explained. "So I started to think that I couldn't do it without bubble tea. That I *had* to have it before every show." The singer told me she gained ten pounds in two months. After that, she swapped out bubble tea for meditation.

My personal singing superstitions included sleeping with a copy of the score under my pillow—to facilitate osmosis, I reasoned—and then putting on my stage makeup while watching an episode of the 1987 BBC sitcom *Blackadder the Third*. I also religiously ate the same meal before every performance: a large bowl of penne pasta with olive oil and Parmesan cheese. Did these rituals make a difference to my singing? Probably not. But they certainly helped manage my unavoidable sense of dread.

Australian soprano Helena Dix has a somewhat more reasonable preshow ritual, though she admitted to me she's still highly regimented about it. She always gets a good night's sleep, hydrates early in the morning, and then completes a thirty-five-minute cardio kickboxing routine ("Coach Kozak on YouTube"). When she arrives at the theater, she works through a mental checklist of staging notes and then tries to find a place of mental calm. "I always say to myself that life still carries on outside the theater," she said. "If I sing a wrong note, it's insignificant in the grand scheme of things. Life will still carry on."

Tenor René Barbera takes a similarly philosophical approach to manage fear when performing. "The stakes are created in our heads," Barbera said. "When I go out there, there's no risk. No one's going to die. I'm not a brain surgeon about to operate on someone. We're just playing onstage. I think a lot of people take on a responsibility that's not theirs to take on."

It's the true tell of a successful opera singer, one insider told me. Not whether they have the necessary acting ability or vocal goods, but whether they can win the mental battle. "The ones that actually make it aren't the most talented. It's the ones who can cope with that level of pressure and stress," they said. "It's not about being gifted. It's about being able to channel their energy and deliver in that one moment."

Even then, it's still never an easy thing. When you're standing alone onstage in a blinding spotlight with hundreds of eyes watching you from the seats of the auditorium, sometimes all you can do is take a deep breath and pray your voice is where you left it. Most of the time, if a singer has rehearsed, prepared, and overcome any temporary panic, the voice *is* there, and everything else falls into place.

But sometimes, performing also becomes more than a matter of managing in-the-moment staging adjustments or hiding an inadvertent swallow of fear at an approaching high note. Sometimes everything aligns at a higher level—not just physically and dramatically but emotionally and mentally. Sometimes a singer reaches a state of complete focus, of total immersion in the performance. There's no preoccupation with the conductor's tempo or the intricacies of the blocking or even an awareness of time passing. There's only a sense of being in the moment onstage and, with it, a visceral feeling of achieving peak performance. Psychologists call it the flow state. And for singers, it's nothing less than magic.

Finding the flow state is rare. It might only happen a handful of times over hundreds of performances. But when it *does* happen, it's so thrilling, so joyous, that it makes up for any unpleasantness that happened in the rehearsal room or even that brief bout of nervous vomiting that just happened backstage. "It's the ultimate feeling. I do all of this work for that one second, and it's all worth it. It's such a rush," one singer told me. Another said, "I live for those moments."

And when those moments happen—when a singer achieves that elevated feeling—the audience often feels it, too. In a 2003 study, psychologist Arnold B. Bakker found that flow states can be contagious, that the feeling of flow can cross over and be shared by different people at the same time. Extend Bakker's hypothesis to the opera house, and audience members can easily be caught up in the same sense of distorted time, engulfed in the same complete and utter focus: all eyes fixed on the singer, heart rates and breaths in sync . . . nothing else in the world but the voice, the story, and the stage.

If you as an audience member are immersed in one of those electric moments, you often have a physical reaction. Perhaps a tingling throughout your body or sudden chills at the back of your neck. Maybe you start crying without realizing it or notice you've been holding your breath. You're, in a word, moved. And when the thrill of that moment is over, there's an undeniable catharsis, an emotional release. Almost as quickly, there's a desire for more—more of that energy, that shared experience, that total immersion.

These are the moments opera fans gush about, tossing around words such as "transformative" and "transcendent" in an attempt to describe an experience that's inherently indescribable. These are the moments that make people come back to the opera house again and again, hoping for another hit of that elusive, magical feeling. These are also the moments that opera companies are desperately trying to sell.

But how does one bottle something as ephemeral as chills or being lost in the sound of a singer's voice? How do companies explain what they're offering—what they're selling—when only those who've already experienced it even know what they're buying? Is it even possible to translate the thrill of a performance into a sustainable business?

Time for our next battleground.

CHAPTER 6

The Company

— or —

Show Me the Money

Nestled in a quiet corner of Opera Land is a cemetery for the fallen. It's not a cemetery for singers or directors or conductors, or even for all the characters who are murdered onstage. No—this is the graveyard for opera companies.

There are thousands of graves, dating back to the art form's earliest beginnings. Death by mismanagement. Death by embezzlement. There's an entire row dedicated to the companies that crumbled after the Great Recession of 2008. Another for the ones that composer G. F. Handel personally drove into ruin in the 1700s. Even my own little company has a grave. Not enough money or status for a proper headstone—just a small wooden marker with an epitaph scrawled in permanent marker: R.I.P. THE FIGARO PROJECT, 2009–2014.

Some company deaths are long and lingering, such as New York City Opera (1943–2013), which had funeral bells tolling as early as the

1960s before finally expiring in 2013.* Other deaths are more unexpected, akin to a piano falling out of a window onto an unsuspecting passerby. Take New York's Gotham Chamber Opera (2000–2015), which closed almost overnight after the newly appointed executive director discovered six figures of hidden debt—something the previous executive director had apparently neglected to mention or was unaware of. And more than a few deaths are downright suspicious. Consider London's Haymarket Opera House (1705–89), which was conveniently destroyed in a fire around the same time its managers were embroiled in legal woes and £68,000 in debt.

Whenever a company dies, pointing fingers of accusation are never far behind. Critics and audiences stand over the grave, wringing their hands and writing passionate op-eds about what could or should have been done. As time passes, a few dedicated mourners will return for the occasional visit, picking moss off a headstone and reminiscing about a beloved production once staged by the company. But for the most part, this cemetery remains empty of visitors. It's an unwelcome reminder of the impermanence of companies, of just how quickly they can disintegrate and self-destruct. Because opera companies aren't actually institutions, though many pretend to be. And while the official cause of death often varies (at least in the coroner's report), there's usually the same underlying cause, the same singular battle that was fought and ultimately lost. A desperate, bloody fight . . . for money.

* * *

* In *Night of the Living Dead* style, the company was revived by new management in 2016.

Opera companies come in assorted shapes and sizes but can loosely be categorized by budget and size. At the top we have the industry behemoths, the kinds of companies that, as one director told me, squat over the rest of the field like gigantic tarantulas. Think heavy hitters such as New York's Metropolitan Opera, the UK's Royal Ballet and Opera, and Milan's Teatro alla Scala (known as La Scala), which present up to two dozen different productions a year and have operating budgets (and expenditures) in the hundreds of millions. In the shadow of such leviathans are many more midrange companies—those with respectable budgets of seven or eight figures and equally respectable performance seasons of roughly five to seven productions a year. Then, for every midrange company, there are a handful of tiny companies, some of which wink in and out of existence with equal rapidity. These might present between one and three productions a year and have modest—if not microscopic—annual budgets: perhaps a few million dollars, a few hundred thousand, or even far less.

Consider the statistics: in 2024, industry body OPERA America counted 204 professional "member" opera companies operating across 138 cities in the United States and Canada. But only eleven of these had an annual budget greater than $15 million. And only one, the Metropolitan Opera, can be considered a true colossus.

Different companies use widely different organizational systems, with the main options being repertory, *stagione*, or the festival model. A repertory company (the model most commonly seen in Europe but also used by the Metropolitan Opera) will stage several different productions over a given week, similar to the daily shifting menu in a school cafeteria: Monday is *La bohème*, Tuesday is *Carmen*, Wednesday is *The Marriage of Figaro*, and so forth.

In comparison, a *stagione* company (the term translates from the Italian as "season") stages productions in a sequential manner: all the rehearsals and performances for *La bohème* in a single batch, followed by all the rehearsals and performances for *Carmen*, followed by all the ones for *Figaro*. This is the default system for most companies in the United States. Finally, we have the festival model, in which a company presents all of their productions in a condensed period. The Santa Fe Opera and UK's Glyndebourne Festival, for example, exclusively run over the summer months.

But no matter its size or structure, every opera company grapples with the same financial headache. Because while the combination of text, music, and staging may lead to an exalted theatrical experience, it's also mind-bogglingly—soul-crushingly—expensive.

It's no coincidence that my own little opera company was born as a direct result of another's financial ruin. In March 2009, the Baltimore Opera Company filed for bankruptcy after fifty-eight seasons—one of a string of companies slain by the Great Recession. For many, it was a devastating loss. This was the company once run by American soprano Rosa Ponselle, that once hosted operatic royalty Beverly Sills and Birgit Nilsson! Cue the hand-wringing and teeth gnashing. But for me, a few months from graduating with my master's degree from Baltimore's Peabody Conservatory, the devastation wasn't so much about the loss of a seeming institution. Rather, it was about the loss of my anticipated career path—the pipeline I'd planned to take from point A to point B as a professional singer—because Baltimore Opera had an opera chorus.

An opera chorus is a group of professional singers who are hired to sing all the "group" parts in an opera: the generic crowd of Capulets and Montagues in Charles Gounod's *Roméo et Juliette*, for example. It's hardly a starring role but a good solid gig, and one that notably comes with union protections. A shrewd singer can even cobble together a fairly decent income from a chorus contract combined with church singing jobs and concerts with local orchestras.

So, I never had any doubts about the plan. I'd graduate from Peabody, stay in my cheap Baltimore apartment, get a chorus contract at Baltimore Opera, and use that ever-so-slight financial security as the foundation to build my singing career on the East Coast. But with Baltimore Opera's closure, my path to fame and solvency suddenly vanished. How would I gain performance experience? How would I make the jump to the big pond when my own small pond had just dried up?

It takes a certain amount of hubris for a twenty-four-year-old with no business experience to conclude, "I'll just start my own opera company." But that's more or less what I did. And let's not suffer any illusions. My motives for starting a company were largely selfish. I had no interest in advancing the art form or even building a company with a long-term future. I merely wanted a platform that would allow me—and my friends—to augment our performance CVs until the opera industry recovered. Then, we'd all jump back onto our original career paths.

So, I picked a role from my *Fach*: Susanna in Mozart's *The Marriage of Figaro*. I called up a few singer friends—all equally panicked about Baltimore Opera—and asked if they'd be interested in learning a role. The idea, I told them, was to stage a concert version of Mozart's opera the following spring. Within a few days, I'd confirmed ten singers for the cast, all grateful for the opportunity to perform in a low-stakes setting.

I knew we'd need some money to get the show together, but I figured a few thousand dollars would be more than enough. (Cue hysterical laughter from opera administrators everywhere.) I applied for an alumni grant from Peabody and supplemented it with a few hundred dollars raised from a recital at a local church. Here again, the hubris is somewhat astounding. Not only that I decided to start an opera company, but that I assumed it could be done for $2,000.

To be fair, the overhead for our first show *was* exceedingly low. None of the singers were paid, nor any of the administrative staff—an achievement that required little negotiation since I *was* the staff, along with a friend who dabbled in ad hoc graphic design and my boyfriend,* who edited the videos for a social media campaign. The venue was also free—a church where my boyfriend was the baritone soloist—costumes came from everyone's own closets, and the set was similarly DIY, consisting of a line of music stands commandeered from Peabody and a few handmade props. For marketing, I spent $60 to print a stack of four-by-six postcards advertising the show and filmed a series of teaser trailers for Facebook. The biggest expense for the entire production was the conductor and the pianist. Both were active professionals in Baltimore who, while indulging my ambitions, were absolutely not going to provide their services for free.

But even with the money sorted, there was still a problem. We had no spare cash or technical capacity to project supertitles in the church venue, and there was no way a group of aspiring opera singers were going to learn *The Marriage of Figaro* in English instead

* Reader, I married him.

of the canonical Italian. But how could we get an audience to sit through an opera they couldn't understand?

My solution to what initially seemed an intractable problem was simple, if not heretical. I messed with the score. I cut all the opera's original recitatives and replaced them with new English dialogue. And since I was already messing with the music, I figured I might as well mess with the story. I added a new plot involving the opera's librettist, Lorenzo Da Ponte, who develops writer's block and faces a mutiny from his characters.

Did I realize I was committing operatic sacrilege? Maybe a bit. The biggest clue is on the postcard we used to advertise the show. It's not an image of a generic love theme or the main characters snuggling in eighteenth-century garb. No—it's a picture of a nuclear bomb explosion. And I called the production not *The Marriage of Figaro*, but *The Figaro Project*. I'd say I knew exactly what I was doing.

But it didn't matter. Because I was focused entirely on my artistic vision, on presenting the opera in a way that would benefit the singers who were performing (especially me). I didn't care what the audience said or what the board of directors said. Here it helped that we didn't actually have a board yet. I didn't even care about ticket sales since we weren't charging for admission. Looking back now, I wonder if it was more than mere hubris. Maybe it was also fearlessness. Or ignorance. Maybe all three. It simply never occurred to me that opera couldn't be done this way.

By our second season, I was no longer as charmingly oblivious of the realities of running an opera company—one that I'd officially named The Figaro Project in a nod to our first production. Expenses were still low, relatively speaking, and programming was still driven by the potential benefits to me and my friends, all now members of the company's ongoing troupe. We'd also been granted nonprofit status, built an official website, and even come up with a snappy mission statement. But I was starting to feel pressure, an urgency to find more money. And then more. Because opera companies can't actually survive on gut instinct and a slightly self-serving artistic vision. For most companies, producing opera is inherently, fundamentally, and inextricably commercial.

* * *

The most important thing to understand about the business of opera is that it's nothing close to an actual business. At least not a successful one. Most viable businesses generate profits from the product they sell. But not only do opera companies rarely make any profit, they rarely break even. As one opera insider told music journalist Zachary Woolfe in 2011, "The best opera house heads are the ones who 'lose money responsibly.'"

But why is opera such bad business? How expensive can it actually be?

Take out your calculators, class.

We'll start with the cost of the people. At the highest levels, an opera singer in a principal role might get paid $10,000 or more per performance. The singers for the smaller roles are also paid—perhaps starting at $800 to $1,000 per performance—as are the singers in the chorus. The standard union rate for a chorus contract with Detroit Opera is $23 for every hour of rehearsal, then an additional $173 for every performance—not a small expense when you have a chorus of fifty singers booked for three weeks of rehearsals and four performances. Meanwhile, a single instrumentalist in a top-tier opera orchestra might rake in $150,000 a year—at least, that's what the Metropolitan Opera offered in their 2024 job listing for a new cellist. The combined cost of singers and instrumentalists can easily skyrocket depending on which opera is being staged. An opera such as Puccini's *La bohème* requires seven principal singers, a chorus of thirty (plus a children's chorus), and roughly fifty instrumentalists. *Götterdämmerung* by Richard Wagner, on the other hand, requires thirteen principal singers, a chorus of one hundred, and an orchestra of ninety. Cha-ching.

Next comes the cost of the creative team—the director, the conductor, and the designers. For a brand-new production at a major company, a top director might earn as high as $80,000, while a leading conductor can net up to $40,000. According to the United Scenic Artists labor union, fees for individual designers can be similarly considerable, ranging from $8,000 to $30,000 depending on the number of sets involved. Now add the fees for technical personnel, including in-house technicians, carpenters, painters, electricians, stage managers, prop managers, and stagehands. Multiply by the total number of productions in a company's season, and you're looking at an annual bill that—to quote Bing Crosby in *White Christmas* (1954)—falls somewhere between "ouch and boing."

And that's just the cost of the people involved in the actual shows—don't forget the company administrators running things behind the scenes. At the very top of the administrative ledger is the executive leadership team, or the Big Bosses. At many companies, this translates into two distinct roles: the CEO, also sometimes called the executive director or general director; and the artistic director, also sometimes called the music director. While the CEO manages business and commercial operations, the artistic director is responsible for artistic vision, including programming and casting. In some organizational structures, the two positions are merged into a single role. At others, such as the Royal Danish Opera, business matters are managed by a stand-alone department. But either way, with great power comes great responsibility—and a paycheck to match.

Next, we have our middle tier of company management. This includes the marketers, who send out media releases and post on Instagram; the staff on the donor relations team, whose job is asking (if not begging) for money; the operations team, which manages venues and facilities; and the artistic administration team, which manages day-to-day planning and production. There's also often an outreach and education team, a diversity and equity team, an in-house music staff, and more. Depending on its size, an opera company might employ hundreds of people, none of whom will ever set foot on an actual stage. All in all, across artistic, technical, and administrative staff, a company might spend as much as 75 percent of their annual budget on personnel alone.

Is your calculator smoking yet? Mine certainly is.

Next we need to consider the cost of the physical productions, including the sets, costumes, furniture, props, and lighting equipment. Many operas have multiple acts and settings, each of which requires a different combination of painted or projected backdrops, physical structures, and props to set the scene. And none of it comes cheap. Timber, fabric, foam, paint, plastic, not to mention time and labor—according to set designer Charles Edwards, constructing the physical set for an opera costs as much as building a new house.

Costumes can be equally complicated (and pricey), with multiple outfits potentially required for every singer onstage, including the principals as well as the chorus. What's the cost of materials to build a single period costume that not only looks good from a distance but is durable enough to last for dozens of performances? Hundreds, if not thousands, of dollars.

The total cost of a production most depends on *how* an opera is being presented. A key consideration is whether a company is building a new production, building a new production with other companies (called a coproduction), staging a production they built in a previous year (called a revival), or renting a production owned by someone else.

Building a new production from scratch is the most expensive venture because a company is solely responsible for all the initial costs, from constructing the sets and costumes to covering the fees of the director and the designers. According to a report by LA Opera, a new production can easily cost $1.5 million. And that's before adding singers or instrumentalists. This means new productions are usually a luxury reserved for companies that operate at the behemoth or near-behemoth budgetary level. Even then, new productions are generally so expensive that it's hard to justify the investment unless a company can eventually recoup its costs. This is where revivals come in.

After a new production is built and performed, the sets, costumes, and props will be placed in storage with the aim of being "revived" in a future season, meaning they'll be dusted off and used for a new set of performances with a different group of singers. A stage director will be hired to revive the blocking on the new cast (either the original director or a new one credited as the "revival director"). The original designers will also be rehired—or, if they're unavailable—a set of revival counterparts. But the bulk of the production already exists—and most important, it's already been paid for. And every time that production is revived, the sting of the initial investment gradually lessens until, eventually, the production has paid for itself.

Take the production of *La bohème* that was directed and designed by Franco Zeffirelli for the Metropolitan Opera back in 1981. It's extravagant and luxurious, with period costumes and detailed stage settings—there's even falling snow in the third act. That exact production has been revived by the company almost every single year since it was built, including, most recently, in 2025. While the initial cost of the production ran into the millions when adjusted for present-day inflation, revivals brought in a staggering $140 million in ticket revenue between 1981 and 2006 alone. Not bad.

However, not every new production is fated for success, and companies must be careful when making such an expensive gamble. Pick the right combination of opera, director, and designers, and you might end up with a production like Zeffirelli's *La bohème*, popular enough to be endlessly revived for forty-odd years. Pick the wrong combination, and the result can be financially calamitous.

In this regard, the Metropolitan Opera's 2010–12 production of Wagner's *Ring Cycle* is something of a cautionary tale. Wagner's work is a mammoth undertaking: four separate but thematically linked operas featuring gods, giants, dragons, dwarfs, and incest. Helmed by director Robert Lepage, the Met's new production was noteworthy for its cutting-edge digital technology—interactive video projections, real-time audio and motion sensors!—as well as its sheer scale. The physical set, dubbed the Machine, consisted of a series of thirty-foot aluminum planks that interlocked into different configurations and collectively weighed a whopping forty-five tons. And the price tag was just as massive. The stage unit alone cost $16 million to construct and test (plus another $1.4 million to reinforce the Met's stage), while some estimated the cost of the entire production at $45 million. Luckily, the company recouped their investment and revived that production every season, right? Not so fast.

Critical response was, for the most part, resoundingly negative. Particular ire was directed at the Machine, which loomed over the singers, made distracting clunking noises, and suffered frequent technical malfunctions. In a 2012 review, Alex Ross of *The New Yorker* described the enterprise as "the most witless and wasteful production in modern operatic history." Not exactly the blurb the publicity team was hoping for. As of 2025, the complete four-opera cycle had been revived just once. The rest of the time, that forty-five-ton set has been sitting in storage—perhaps camouflaged behind a few prop trees—with the unspoken agreement being not to mention it unless absolutely necessary.

Given the financial risk of new productions, coproduction has become increasingly popular in recent years, especially for mid-range companies. Here the initial investment for a new production is shared by multiple companies, with costs decreasing as more companies enlist. The challenge is getting all the coproducing companies to agree with one other, not only on budget, creative team, and concept, but on the nitty-gritty of how the expenses will be divided. Many companies that plan for a coproduction end up with unexpected bills when negotiations inevitably break down.

This brings us to the final option for productions—the rental. It's a common approach for smaller companies that aspire to present opera on a grand scale but don't have the requisite cash to build their own productions. So, instead, they rent the physical components from another company—or sometimes more than one. Take the set for *La bohème* that's available to rent from Florida's Sarasota Opera. Four performances cost just $15,000, plus a security deposit, insurance, shipping, and a small royalty to the original set designer. No costumes are included in the deal—Sarasota recommends renting those from Utah Opera—but the total expense is still eminently more manageable than, say, $45 million for a new *Ring Cycle*.

Now, take a moment to dab your perspiring upper lip . . . because we're not quite done with our calculation.

In addition to the people and the production, you can't perform an opera without a venue. That means buying or renting a physical theater that can accommodate multiple sets, chorus singers, an orchestra, and an audience. All those music and staging rehearsals from the last chapter also need a designated space—one that's large enough to accommodate the same hundred or so singers and instrumentalists. And if a company has decided to build a new production from scratch? Tack on the cost of workshop space to construct those shiny new sets and costumes, along with storage facilities to keep them safe until they're revived. Then there's all the nonartistic nuts and bolts of facility maintenance, such as making sure the theater infrastructure is up to code and stages appropriately reinforced as needed.

Time to tally up the total. Personnel expenses, production expenses, venue expenses, plus overhead and maintenance. Plus the cost of marketing campaigns, printed programs, and an opening-night gala with canapés for the donors. Plus corporate insurance, cybersecurity, computers, a website, and a customer-relationship-management platform. Best to also add in the cost of an accountant, to make sense of all those spreadsheets and crumpled receipts.

My calculator isn't smoking anymore. It's melted away entirely.

But not to worry, you're thinking. Yes, opera is shockingly expensive, but it's still a product that audiences are buying. Aren't tickets covering most of these costs?

Before visions of balanced budgets start dancing in your head, let's take a peek at ticket sales. What if we assume eight performances of Puccini's *La bohème* in an eight-hundred-seat theater, with ticket prices running between $50 and $200?

Are we breaking even? Getting close to it?

Not a chance.

The costs of opera are so horrifically high that ticket sales are only ever a fraction of what's actually needed. For major companies, tickets might cover 25–40 percent of expenses, if that. For smaller companies, the benchmark is even lower. At Opera Philadelphia, ticket sales amounted to just 13 percent of the company's revenue in the 2023–24 season. In other words, even if a company sells out every single performance of *La bohème* at the top tier of ticket prices—even if they sell out their entire *season* of performances—it'll barely move the dial. And things are only getting worse. All the costs associated with opera production are increasing, almost exponentially: sets, materials, labor, venues. "Each year we must find two and a half to three million dollars of new revenue just to do exactly the same thing as we did the year before," said Matthew

Shilvock, general director of San Francisco Opera, in a 2024 interview with *San Francisco Classical Voice*.

"There are so many things that add to your structural running costs, and that never goes away. The needs keep growing. The numbers just keep going up," said Andrew Jorgensen. The general director of Opera Theatre of Saint Louis, a festival opera company based in Missouri, Jorgensen is no stranger to financial pressure. When we met over Zoom in 2024, he'd just spent his lunch hour signing a stack of birthday cards for donors (more on them later). "Every organization is starting from the strength of its own balance sheet," he told me. And Opera Theatre of Saint Louis is in a better position than most—the company draws a third of its annual budget directly from an endowment.

But even when a company has this kind of financial cushion, it's little more than a Band-Aid over an increasingly gaping wound. Even a healthy endowment can only take a company so far, akin to a finger in the dike of compounding financial uncertainty. Because even as costs are going up, the "product" that's being produced in Opera Land—and the amount of labor required to produce it—is largely staying the same. In the world of economics, they call it Baumol's cost disease, and opera is stricken with it.

There are three treatments for this particular disease, at least according to economists. The first is to increase productivity. For an opera company, that means presenting more performances. The second is to raise prices: charge more for tickets. But in practice, neither of these options is particularly viable. Increasing productivity is one thing in theory, but companies can only book the number of performances that'll actually sell. Many are already struggling to fill seats for the performances they're currently presenting. At the same time, companies can't simply raise ticket prices to offset their losses. Opera already suffers from being viewed as elitist and expensive, and its existing audiences are arguably at the limit of what they're willing to pay. That leaves one last potential treatment: cut costs. But what exactly can be cut? And how?

We know from our earlier calculations that personnel take the biggest chunk out of a company budget. But that's largely a fixed cost, one that remains the same regardless of how well (or not well) a company sells a show. After all, the number of singers and instrumentalists required to perform *La bohème* hasn't changed since Puccini's opera first premiered—the only difference is that fees have gone up. Administrative roles aren't easy to cut either. A company might save some cash by firing its social media manager, sure, but then who's going to promote its operas on Facebook and Instagram?

That leaves trimming costs from the physical productions themselves. Maybe swapping those lavish sets for a minimalist design or trading that hand-stitched ball gown for an Old Navy summer dress. It's possible but risky. Cutting costs onstage usually means cutting quality, not to mention losing the glamorous visuals that many audiences expect to see. Get rid of the sequins and the spectacle, and a company risks losing its audience.

And so, the gap between costs and revenue grows with every passing season—with no obvious solution in sight. Can we blame an opera administrator for waking up in a cold sweat?

* * *

When I spoke with stage director Mary Birnbaum in 2024, she'd recently started a new position as the general and artistic director of Opera Saratoga, a company in upstate New York that runs an annual summer festival. It was a significant transition for her after a decades-long career as a freelance director and also her first executive-leadership role in an opera company.

Birnbaum arrived at our Zoom call a few minutes late, breathlessly apologetic—she'd been meeting with a prospective donor, and the discussion went long. "But did you get the money?" I asked.

"Not yet. But it's promising."

Even just a few months into Birnbaum's tenure, money was already the most pressing issue on her mind. "Everything is about money. All the pressure is financial," she told me. "Right now, I'm just pounding the pavement to make up the budget for the summer. Artistic excellence is one thing, but at the same time, I will sleep so soundly at night when I know we can pay people."

Birnbaum's experience isn't unusual, let alone novel. Opera companies worldwide have always faced the same perpetual panic about their annual budgets. Even when opera first emerged as a commercial enterprise in the 1630s, it was already mostly incapable of generating enough revenue to cover its expenses. Instead, there was always a king or prince or nobleman who could pull out a jingling purse and hand it to the debt collectors pounding at the stage door. There's always been a gap to be covered. Debts to be paid. Nowadays, the only real difference is who's stepping in with the purse.

In Europe, it's the government. Countries such as Germany, Austria, Sweden, and Denmark are known for their operatic generosity and provide companies with subsidies that cover 56–80 percent of their annual budgets, if not more. In 2019, Germany's Komische Oper Berlin received nearly 90 percent of its budget directly from the city of Berlin. Such countries as England and Australia have a similar culture of government funding, albeit at a lower level. The national flagship company Opera Australia receives roughly 20 percent of its budget from the government. Nothing to sneeze at, even if it's small potatoes compared to what Komische Oper Berlin gets.

But just because funding comes from the government doesn't mean it's stable. Since the 1990s, subsidies for the arts have steadily decreased across Europe. Spanish opera company Teatro Real saw its government subsidy drop from more than half its budget in 2009 to less than a third six years later. Even so, it's no wonder American companies gaze longingly across the Atlantic Ocean. In the United States there's no precedent for *any* kind of ongoing government support. At most, a respected high-level company such as Seattle Opera is lucky if 5 percent of its budget is covered by government grants. That's it.

Where does the rest of the money come from? Donors.

Now, if you're like me, a particular image comes to mind when you hear the word *donor*. Coiffed white hair, a skirt suit from Bergdorf Goodman, pearls, perhaps a tasteful facelift or two. A stereotype, if not an inaccurate one. The truth is that opera donors come in as many different shapes and sizes as do companies. But the big ones—the mega-donors, as they're known—have one thing in common. Gobs and gobs of money.

Mega-donors are the lifeblood of opera companies in the United States, and they're particularly crucial for the biggest ones. Because when you're trying to raise half of your $80 million budget for the year, you can't waste time running a bake sale or trying to squeeze cash from the folks in the cheap seats. No—you need to hook a whale. A whale such as Ann Ziff, who donated $30 million to the Metropolitan Opera in 2010. Or Alberto Vilar (1940–2021), who pledged $225 million to various opera, classical music, and ballet projects in the 1990s. (In an appropriately operatic twist, Vilar was eventually sentenced to nine years in prison on charges of money laundering and fraud.)

Oftentimes, donors provide funding to cover a company's operational expenses. Others prefer to use their money for specific productions. Take a look at the printed programs at most major opera companies and you'll inevitably find a line in small but regal font: "This production was made possible by generous gifts from so-and-so." In exchange for their contribution, donors get more than a few perks. There are the tax deductions, as well as the intangible prestige that comes from being the patron of an opera company. Then there's the access, the opportunity to schmooze with star singers and conductors who've been hauled out of rehearsals to give a personal thank-you. But some donors also want a seat at the table in exchange for their support, a chance to weigh in on a company's artistic direction. This usually translates into a position on the board.

As nonprofit organizations, opera companies are required to have a board of directors, or equivalent, which exercises high-level oversight over the Big Bosses on the executive leadership team. The form and function (or, ahem, dysfunction) of a board depends on the company and the personality quirks of its appointed directors. Many boards are "working" boards, which means the directors actually *do* something, usually supporting the strategic objectives of the company in some way, while also serving as a collective governor for the executive and artistic directors. Even then, however, the most important role of the board remains that of piggy bank. According to a 2015 report by *The New Yorker*, the expected contribution for a high-level board member at the Metropolitan Opera was $500,000 a year. Minimum.

Not that this system of private subsidies doesn't have its issues. For one thing, big donations rarely come without strings. Board members and one-off donors can easily make demands about repertoire, casting, and staging in exchange for their $2 million check. If the company doesn't acquiesce, the donor can simply walk away. But there's also a bigger problem with this model of patronage, and it boils down to this. Even the very, very rich have an annoying habit of eventually dying.

With every donor lost—either from temper tantrums or old age—an opera company needs a replacement. And mega-donors aren't exactly available at the farmers market. A company might need to court hundreds of potential donors just to find one whose pockets are sufficiently deep to reach mega-donor status. "One of the scariest things is how large a percentage of our budget is dependent on less than a dozen mega-donors," said David Gockley, then general director of San Francisco Opera, in a 2009 interview. "It is frightening to be in so precarious a financial situation every single year." Precarious, mind you, even with the security of San Francisco Opera's endowment, which was valued at nearly $150 million in 2014.

As one company administrator told me, it's also increasingly difficult to even make the case to potential mega-donors: "The way people think about philanthropy today is very different than in the past. More people are now wanting to support social services, health, medicine, equity . . . There are fewer donors who want to support art for art's sake or give to the institutions that make a city great."

It's a daunting prospect for individual companies, let alone an entire industry. And it means the financial hustle never ends.

Darren Woods was the general director of Fort Worth Opera from 2001 to 2017 and is currently the artistic director of the Seagle Festival, a summer festival company in upstate New York. He told me the job of running Fort Worth Opera was 95 percent fundraising. "The artistic part? The fun part? That took up five percent of my time." As a former commercial banker who later turned tenor, Woods never had any illusions about what was required: "If I weren't wearing a suit every day and making a call on a foundation or a corporation or an individual or taking someone to lunch, I knew I wasn't going to be successful. You have to see to it every day. It's constant."

This is where The Figaro Project started to wobble. We'd built up a tiny pool of donors, but they only gave a few hundred or, at most, a few thousand dollars at a time. Our largest donations weren't even in cash but were in-kind support, usually through free or subsidized venues. The main shows we presented in our second and third seasons, for example, were in a local university theater, with free access granted in exchange for a fifty-fifty split of ticket sales.

There's no question I was sabotaging the company to some extent by trading away half our ticket revenue. But we'd gotten bigger with every season, my programming more ambitious, and the notion of mega-donors wasn't even on my administrative radar. So I traded away our income and tried to make up as much as possible from other sources. One go-to was performing at a cabaret series in Baltimore's Little Italy that gave performers the take from the door ($10 cover per person), plus a meal at the end of the show. If we got thirty or forty people to attend one of The Figaro Project's cabarets, it was a nice little wad of cash to add to the company accounts. Plus, what starving artist doesn't appreciate a free plate of veal piccata?

But it wasn't enough. It was unsustainable, and I knew it. But I also never imagined The Figaro Project would last beyond one or two seasons. I never imagined it would receive preview coverage in *The Baltimore Sun* or be acclaimed as one of Baltimore's best small opera companies by the local CBS affiliate. Or that singers across the mid-Atlantic would be emailing me to ask when we'd be holding auditions. ("Never," I said firmly.)

In our fourth season, our main production was the world premiere of *Camelot Requiem*, a new opera about the aftermath of the assassination of John F. Kennedy. The music was by composer Joshua Bornfield, and I'd written the libretto—my first one. I was also starring as Jackie Kennedy, while simultaneously managing the scheduling, finances, rehearsals, costumes, and marketing. It was an enormous undertaking. And far more expensive than anything we'd done before. There were ten principal singers, plus a conductor, a stage director, and a small orchestra. We used wigs and vintage costumes, including historical replicas for Jackie and Lady Bird Johnson built by a local costumer. There were months of music and staging rehearsals, alongside a massive marketing push. Our luckiest marketing coup came when I was summoned for jury duty and hit it off with a local news reporter who was picked for the same case. (Our verdict? Guilty.) A few weeks later, The Figaro Project got a feature spot on local news.

By all accounts, it was a hugely successful production. Critic Tim Smith of *The Baltimore Sun* called it an "admirable premiere . . . intriguing and largely persuasive." "The Figaro Project stuns with *Camelot Requiem*," noted another reviewer. The venue was almost entirely sold out for both performances—a few audience members even had to move up to the balcony just to get a seat.

But by the end of the run, the company coffers were almost completely empty.

* * *

It's always been a comfort to me that I'm not the first opera administrator who struggled to balance art and money. In fact, this precise juggle presents the biggest hurdle for *every* company. One side needs to focus on the art—on what's being presented onstage. But there also has to be the other side, someone who says, "Sounds great, but how much is that going to cost?" Marrying those two seemingly contradictory points of view comes down, once again, to math.

At every company, there's a formula, a specific calculation used to decide which operas will be presented; which singers, directors, designers, and conductors will be hired; and the total price tag for all of it. And it's not just a matter of two plus two equals a season. There are a multitude of variables to consider, including the ratio of surefire operatic hits to riskier ventures; the balance of productions to be rented, revived, coproduced, or built from scratch; and the size of every orchestra and cast for every show. To make things more complicated, most companies are also planning multiple seasons at once, usually three to five years in advance. And in the midst of these discussions, there's the looming knowledge that, even if a season is a bona fide success, the company will still be roughly 50 to 60 percent short of the budget needed to survive another year. No pressure.

The starting point for any formula is repertoire, or the specific operas that'll be staged. Since I'm more of a foodie than a numbers person, I prefer to think of this calculation in terms of food groups. First, we have our carbohydrates: these are the canonical works that are reliably popular with audiences . . . your *Carmen*s and *La bohème*s and *Magic Flute*s. Next, we have our lesser-known canonical-ish operas from the nineteenth century or earlier, necessary protein but not quite as popular as the bread-and-pasta set. Perhaps an opera by Rossini or Donizetti or an early work by Mozart. Then we have the seventeenth- and eighteenth-century food group: operas by the likes of Handel, Gluck, and Monteverdi, which are something of an acquired taste. Finally, we have our food group of contemporary operas from the twentieth and twenty-first centuries. These are the high-risk and often-polarizing cruciferous vegetables that inevitably stick in the craw of traditionalist audiences. Dessert is musical theater—light, frothy, and generally the only way to tempt audiences who won't take a bite of actual opera.

The job of a company's executive leadership team is to decide on the proper mix from each category. And the task is not so much to provide a balanced diet. The more important goal is to ensure the season is palatable, that the audience will enjoy each show enough to buy a ticket for the next one. Program too many vegetables, too much tempeh or tofu—particularly if your audience is hankering for spaghetti—and you risk not only a financial loss but losing the favor of the board.

Opera scholars Philippe Agid and Jean-Claude Tarondeau provide a useful nutritional breakdown for any operatic dinner plate.

Fifty percent of the productions, they say, will be risk-free, that is, repertoire pulled straight from the Canon. Thirty percent will be moderate risk, that is, less popular works with limited name recognition (that's our protein). The remaining 20 percent will be split between high-risk options. This includes contemporary operas (aka brussels sprouts), those of an acquired taste (aka anchovies), and any productions that are risky due to sheer expense.

This brings us to the second part of the formula: cost. If a company decides to program a plate of pasta à la *La bohème*, they still have a decision to make. Is it going to be a luxurious truffle macaroni and cheese served with a white tablecloth and gold cutlery? Or a tub of Easy Mac from the nearest 7-Eleven? Or will it fall somewhere in the middle, somewhere between a never-ending pasta bowl from Olive Garden and a plate of penne alla vodka served at one of those Italian restaurants with candles sticking out of old Mateus bottles? In other words, there's the expensive option, the less expensive option, the inexpensive option, and the dirt cheap option.

Which leads us to the formula's next—and often most dangerous—variable. How exactly will the opera be staged? Will it be a classic production designed to appeal to opera traditionalists? Or will it be a modern interpretation, a staging that adds new layers of meaning? Will it be *La bohème* set in Paris . . . or *La bohème* set in space?

The precise what and how of an operatic formula is fluid, driven by past ticket sales, singer availability, industry trends, and a company's particular artistic proclivities. As a general rule, the more financially stable a company, the greater artistic risk it can take. Conversely, the more seats a company needs to fill, the less likely it'll take chances.

But the final calculation ultimately comes down to the Big Bosses. They choose which numbers to crunch—whether that means dedicating an entire season to canonical pasta dishes or rolling the dice with brussels sprouts. Then they cross their fingers and hope the math adds up. Unfortunately, in some cases, it doesn't. New York City Opera's slow demise over five decades can partly be attributed to programming missteps made by a series of general directors.

Darren Woods, former general director at Fort Worth Opera, strongly believes that every company formula needs to be carefully balanced to manage both artistic and financial risk. In his case, the recipe for success was always one canonical opera, one lesser-known historical work, and one contemporary opera or world premiere. This combination worked, Woods told me, because it acknowledged the need for a trade-off. If you want to program a new opera or a work that's risky, you have to counteract it with a crowd-pleaser such as *La bohème* or *Carmen*. The Canon, he said, is the "secret drug" that you give to the public. It's the only way to get away with programming riskier works—the kinds of works that advance the art form.

The Royal Danish Opera relies on a similar strategy for its programming. Artistic Director Elisabeth Linton told me that three of their eleven productions each season are always revivals. One title is always a musical. Two titles need to be popular enough to sell eighteen performances each. Another two need to sell sixteen performances each. That means those four titles generally come straight from the Canon, since it's rare for audiences to turn out in droves for works that are less familiar. With the rest of the season, Linton said, she has more artistic license and tries to program across a broad palate, which might include a contemporary opera, a romantic work from the nineteenth century, and a baroque opera.

Like Woods, Linton is keenly aware of the price that needs to be paid to program riskier works. "To be able to do those, I need to have my titles that can sell eighteen performances," she said. "To be able to do those, I have to do a new *Magic Flute*, and I have to play eighteen performances of *La bohème*." Even though Linton holds an explicitly artistic role at the company, she told me she can't ignore the commercial implications of her programming. "If you only go for your visions or art or what you want to do, the time is wasted. It will only be dreaming. You have to be pragmatic at the same time."

Even when a formula works financially, however, it may still lack an important seal of approval. It needs to be acceptable to the board of directors, many of whom have donated hundreds of thousands (or even millions) of dollars with the expectation of having an artistic say. "That's what the pressure points are," one company administrator told me. "How do you please this largely white, affluent, rich donor pool who want nothing but the classics [while also saying] something that's current and public and profound? How do you marry those two things?" In this, programming can become as much a game of politics and back-channel persuasion as a matter of juggling different repertoire options. Because if the board and the donors aren't happy—if they think the chosen formula is somehow flawed—it doesn't take much for a company leader to be deposed.

During his tenure at Fort Worth Opera, Darren Woods became something of an anomaly in the opera industry for managing to balance the budget in all but one of his sixteen years at the helm.

This was seen as particularly impressive given his penchant for programming seemingly high-risk contemporary operas. But despite the economic success of his formula, Woods was fired by his board of directors in 2017. "They came into my office and said, 'You're an artistic genius. This company would be nowhere without you. Give us your key and your credit card and get out,'" Woods told me. According to Woods, it wasn't due to financial mismanagement or any of the other reasons that are usually touted when a general or artistic director is sacked by the board. "They just flat didn't like the way I was programming," he said.

No formula is ultimately infallible or risk-free. An equation that triumphs in one season might falter in the next, just as one that brings financial stability may be deemed artistically hollow. And then we add the most uncertain variable of all: the audience. Unpredictable, argumentative, and, in some cases, shrinking. At Opera Australia, audience attendance dropped by 26 percent between 2023 and 2024 alone. In 2023, audience numbers for the largest opera companies in the United States and Canada were similarly a quarter less than they were in 2019.

In the end, if the audience doesn't buy tickets, it doesn't matter how earnestly a formula was calculated. It doesn't matter that the audience *should* have bought tickets based on their previous behavior. What matters is the snowball effect that comes from a formula that, for whatever reason, didn't get people in the door. Because no government will continue to subsidize a company that doesn't have an audience, just as no donor wants to write a check for a failing enterprise.

But this is also an audience that we know is deeply and irrevocably divided over how operas should be staged and cast—not to mention which operas should be programmed in the first place. And that's just the audience of existing operagoers, the ones that already see the value of the art form. What about the audience that isn't interested in opera yet—the audience that companies are desperate to bring into the fold but can't figure out how to reach?

"Everyone dreams of the auditorium being filled with people under the age of forty who are every color of the rainbow and not just a bunch of old white people with walkers," said one company administrator. "But no one has found the solution yet. No one knows how to develop the audience, keep the audience, develop new work, keep the new work, keep the classic work."

The challenge extends beyond disagreements over what should be presented onstage and how. It's also about what audiences are willing to attend, particularly when they're trying opera for the first time. A 2024 report from OPERA America found that most new audiences stick with the classics for their initial taste of the art form. But that doesn't mean they're hooked. According to one company administrator I heard from, a stark 80–85 percent of those first-time ticket buyers are one-and-done. They never come back.

Elisabeth Linton of the Royal Danish Opera told me that the list of operas that attract those much-needed audiences is also getting smaller. "The big audiences are most willing to see the same ten titles," she told me. "So how can opera develop? It's not the big audience that comes when we do a newly written opera or when we try to challenge the art form. So, how do we get people into opera?"

It becomes an existential question. *How do we get people into opera?* And it leads to a far more frightening follow-up for company administrators: *How do we get people into opera . . . and what happens if we can't?* How many more rows of graves will appear in the cemetery of fallen companies? What happens if, one day, it's not just a grave for a company but for the art form itself?

* * *

I managed to eke out one final season for The Figaro Project after *Camelot Requiem*. In a bit of poetic justice, the company's run culminated in a revival of our very first production: my hubris-filled, bomb-exploding version of Mozart's *The Marriage of Figaro*.

I'd been approached by a friend working at a new theater company in Virginia Beach. They were constructing a venue and hoping to build some interest from local audiences in the lead-up to their official launch. But they needed a show . . . and singers. Essentially, they had a venue, but nothing else. So we brought down the company (including a bunch of singers from the troupe) for a mini "tour."

I was more than happy to have this one last hoorah, especially since the offer included actual fees for the singers, plus a week of accommodation in Virginia Beach. For once, I wouldn't even be responsible for most of the production logistics . . . I could just be a singer.

So, in June 2014, a group of us made the trek down from Baltimore to Virginia Beach and rehearsed and performed the show. In between rehearsals, there was sunbathing and minigolf, midnight walks on the beach, and hotel pizza parties with too much cheap wine. Many of the longtime members of the troupe were involved in that final production, which felt simultaneously triumphant and bittersweet. Most of us were now closer to our early thirties than our early twenties, and a few of the troupe's original members had already moved on—some not only leaving Baltimore but leaving opera entirely.

We all knew it was the end. But as far as company deaths go, this was a gentle one. When the run of performances was over, we said our goodbyes and piled into our cars to head back to Baltimore and a future that would no longer include The Figaro Project. Except we didn't even make it that far. Just a few miles after our caravan of cars left Virginia Beach, we all pulled over at the same gas station. We loaded up on convenience-store chips and candy and sat together on the grassy shoulder of the highway, watching the cars zoom by in companionable silence. After an hour or so, slowly and with shoulders set, each of us got back into our cars and drove away.

I often think about that scene on the shoulder of the highway and wonder what it was that kept us sitting there for as long as we did. For me, it was a growing awareness of what it was we were actually losing. We were just a scrappy bunch of singers who performed together on a shoestring budget. But over five seasons, we'd built a community, a support system—a temporary oasis from toxic rehearsal rooms, imbalanced power dynamics, and the pressure that characterized so much of our careers as professional singers. In The Figaro Project, we'd somehow created a company that was about the best parts of being an opera singer—and none of the worst. Sitting there on that highway shoulder, that's what I was mourning most of all.

CHAPTER 7

The Career

— or —

A Funny Thing Happened on the Way to Exploitation

Some say it's a calling. For those who choose to dedicate their lives to a career in opera—specifically to being opera singers—there's a sense of external compulsion, even mythology about it. It's as if Zeus himself has summoned a singer to the operatic dark side. Or alternatively, as if the muses of music and poetry have personally intervened. It's not a job . . . it's a mission, a deity-approved imperative.

Except that image, ripped straight from the pages of *The Odyssey*, doesn't quite capture it either. Because the reality of "the calling" isn't so much a matter of Greek gods or even the muses. Instead, one must look elsewhere in Homer's epic, to the song of the sirens. Opera is seductive. Alluring. And—unless you have the wherewithal to tie yourself to the mast of a ship—generally fatal. Because this battleground isn't about building a career in opera, or even about keeping it. It's about trying not to drown in the process.

* * *

There's an old joke. *How do you get to Carnegie Hall? Practice, practice, practice.* No one knows exactly who came up with the bit—funny because a request for physical directions is misconstrued as a search for practical advice. But the advice is much more complicated than the punch line implies. How *do* you get to Carnegie Hall? Or the Metropolitan Opera? Or La Scala? How do you make a career as an opera singer?

The path inevitably starts with the raw material, or the Voice. Because you can't actually be a singer *without* a Voice, that is, without a physical instrument—a larynx, set of vocal folds, and breathing apparatus—that can master the musical intricacies of operatic repertoire and cut through the amassed sound of an orchestra. But a Voice also isn't a Voice until it's been cultivated and trained. That means it first needs to be identified. Someone needs to notice something's there.

I was two years old when my mother realized I had a Voice, thanks to a full-throated rendition of "The Itsy Bitsy Spider" that apparently blew my older sister's breathy performance out of the water. Clearly, I had the competitive temperament of a soprano even then. From that point on—and notably without straying into the realm of a stage parent—my mother sought out opportunities for me to develop my musical abilities. I was encouraged to join the school choir and perform in local musical theater productions. She even enrolled me in piano lessons, though there I was less than an ideal student. According to family lore, during one lesson my teacher asked me to stop fooling around with the piano keys while she was giving instructions. I gave her a glinty glare, reached under the open piano lid, and started strumming the strings on the soundboard instead—all without breaking eye contact. That was the end of piano lessons.

When I was thirteen, my mother took me to visit her former in-laws (from an earlier marriage), two opera singers who graced Broadway and West End stages in the 1940s and 1950s. John, her former father-in-law, gave me my first formal voice lesson during that trip. On his advice, as soon as we returned home, my mother found me a voice teacher. Her name was Edie Delegans, and I studied with her for an hour every week from the age of fourteen until I left for college. Under Edie's tutelage, I tackled the intricacies of vocal technique alongside Italian, German, French, and English diction. I swept all the local youth singing competitions and sang opera arias in concert with local orchestras. I had a closet full of prom dresses that doubled as performance gowns and a stack of CDs featuring my operatic role models. I knew, without a doubt, that I was going to be an opera singer. That I *was* an opera singer.

It's a similar story for many. Often a family member or an elementary-school teacher notices a potential Voice and encourages musical training: choir, musical theater, piano lessons. A few years later, a voice teacher starts digging into the more technical nitty-gritty and one day says offhandedly, "Hey, maybe you could actually be a real-life opera singer." Close on the heels of this lightbulb moment the young singer often hears a seminal recording of a famous operatic diva, someone who then serves as a North Star for their career aspirations.

Mezzo-soprano Denyce Graves told me about hearing a recording of American soprano Leontyne Price singing Puccini arias when Graves was in high school. She and her best friend started playing the album in their school's listening room at nine in the morning and listened to it on repeat until the school janitor finally kicked them out—eleven hours later. "We didn't eat. We didn't drink. We just listened to Leontyne over and over again," Graves told me. "My friend and I decided at that moment that was what we're going to do with our lives. We were going to become opera singers like Leontyne. I had no idea what that meant at all." Within ten years, Graves was on her way to an acclaimed international career, singing the role of Carmen at opera houses worldwide. Her friend? Not so much.

Few understand what being an opera singer entails when they're first starting out. Throughout high school and the early years of training, many young singers assume that "practice, practice, practice" is, indeed, all it takes to get to Carnegie Hall. So they practice and practice. And as they practice, they enjoy being the big operatic fish in the small pond of their hometown, winning local voice competitions and starring in high school musicals. They smile bashfully when their parents' friends ask when they'll be singing at the Metropolitan Opera, and in general they feel special. Because opera singers *are* special. Unique. But then our little big fish is accepted to a music conservatory and comes face-to-face with hundreds of *other* little big fishes who've been practicing this entire time and been made to feel special. And who similarly have absolutely no idea what it means—or takes—to be an opera singer.

The traditional pathway to a successful opera career is fairly simple.

Step One. Be identified as having a potential Voice, preferably at a young age. Engage in musical training throughout middle school and high school, including both voice and piano lessons.

Step Two. Go to a music conservatory for further training in vocal technique, performance, and languages. Ideally obtain both an undergraduate degree and a master's degree and perform as many operatic roles in university productions as possible. Extra points for working with a voice teacher who has industry connections.

Step Three. Attend young artist programs (aka YAPs)—ideally as many as possible, and as prestigious as possible, with the opportunity to perform as many operatic roles as possible. Alternatively (or concurrently), win as many vocal competitions as possible, both nationally and internationally. Extra points for singing in front of a panel of well-connected judges who take a shine to you.

Step Four. Get professional representation, that is, an agent (aka artist manager), who'll help you secure singing gigs in exchange for 10–15 percent of your fee. Extra points for finding an agent with high-level artists already on their roster who can leverage their availability to get you more work.

Step Five. Get hired to sing progressively larger roles with progressively larger companies, thanks to your agent and the connections you've made doing all those competitions and YAPs (see Step Three).

Step Six. Maintain a successful performance career at top opera houses worldwide. Congratulations! You've made it!

The process seems linear, even intuitive—deceptively similar to the stepwise career ladder required in professional fields such as medicine: first college, then medical school, then residency, then fellowship, and then finally getting to raise your hand unironically when a flight attendant asks for medical assistance. But the reality of moving up in the opera industry is far more challenging even than mastering a lumbar puncture.

One of the biggest hurdles looms in Step Three, what's known as the young artist stage. This arrives when opera singers are finished with their conservatory training and begin trying to break into the field. However, they're not ready to jump into opening night at the Metropolitan Opera or any of the other top international companies (known in the field as A houses). Depending on their voice type, or *Fach*, a singer might not even be vocally ready to sing certain roles until they hit their early thirties. This leaves a years-long gap between finishing a degree program and actually making a living as a full-fledged professional singer.

YAPs are designed to bridge this divide, functioning as a point of transition for singers moving from emerging to professional status. Programs come in three main tiers. The first and lowest tier is known as pay-to-sing, consisting of short-term training programs that are typically held over the summer and usually last a few weeks or a few months. In most cases, they provide an opportunity for intensive study—frequent voice lessons and coaching, plus master classes, recitals, and often in-depth language study. But, as implied by the moniker, singers have to pay. And pay-to-sings don't come cheap.

Consider the Opera Studio at the American Institute of Musical Studies (AIMS), a prestigious summer program in Graz, Austria. Over five weeks, accepted singers get twice-weekly voice lessons, daily German study, diction coaching, audition training, and acting classes, all for the not-so-low price of $7,250. This fee covers housing (a single room with a shared bathroom), daily breakfast, and weekday lunches, but notably not the cost of round-trip airfare to Austria, evening meals, textbooks, health insurance, a travel visa, or the occasional beer at the local *Schnitzelhaus*. Not to mention the $250 application fee or the cost of rent for the apartment back home that'll be left vacant for five weeks.

Pay-to-sings are generally advertised as being high impact and high reward, a critical investment for singers aspiring to level up in their career. But the actual benefit is subject to debate. More than a few pay-to-sings function primarily as revenue-making machines, using tuition dollars plucked from hopeful singers to support European holidays for the operation's administrators and faculty.

Naively, I was absolutely convinced of their value during my own young-artist stage. At twenty-three, I spent four weeks at a summer program in Salzburg, Austria, confident the crash tutorial would put me on the operatic fast track. I borrowed the cost of tuition and airfare from my parents, took daily German lessons and weekly voice lessons, saw operas at the Salzburg Festival, and subsequently returned to America with a pile of debt and a newfound appreciation for men in lederhosen. Looking back, I can't identify any tangible impact on my opera career stemming from that summer in Salzburg. All I remember is it took me four years to pay my parents back.

The next tier in the YAP track includes summer programs that don't require payment. New York's Glimmerglass Resident Artists Program and Des Moines Metro Opera's Apprentice Artist Program, for example, provide singers with a (small) stipend, plus room and board for the summer. Accepted singers perform roles in staged opera productions, work with vocal coaches, take diction and acting classes, and receive general career training.

Because singers don't pay their own way and are accepted solely on merit, these programs are significantly more prestigious than pay-to-sings, much more likely to add a gold star to a singer's CV. Many of these programs also aim to advance the careers of their singers in tangible ways, usually by creating opportunities for them to sing for agents or representatives from other companies. The summer training program at the Santa Fe Opera, for example, has an annual showcase event, where the apprentice singers perform a single aria in front of agents and other major industry players. Obviously, the pressure is intense, which is why insiders refer to the showcase as Death by Aria.

The third and highest tier of YAPs are resident artist programs. These are one- or two-year programs embedded within major companies. Singers receive lessons and coaching from company staff, participate in seminars and workshops, and receive significant performance opportunities. These might include minor roles in major productions, major roles in minor ones, and the chance to "cover"—that is, serve as an understudy who can step in if the star singer gets sick. Because of their length, resident artist programs generally pay an actual salary and also come with the expectation that singers will relocate for the entirety of their residency.

What else to say about such programs, the crème de la crème of the YAP track? Well, even bigger than the impact of the salary they dispense and the training they offer is the prestige and connections they generate. Agents and casting directors pay attention to the summer apprentice programs, but they *really* pay attention to the yearlong residencies—to the singers who've successfully battled their way past thousands of others to earn one of the few coveted spots. The most high-level resident artist programs provide an almost direct path to representation, bringing the singer one step closer to a successful operatic career.

When we spoke in 2023, Ian Stones was an associate director at HarrisonParrott, an international artist management agency that represents high-level artists such as mezzo-soprano Jamie Barton and tenor Russell Thomas. Once upon a time, Stones was part of the management teams for American opera superstar Jessye Norman and Australian soprano Joan Sutherland. Urban legend has it that the rider for Norman's contract (i.e., her specific contract demands) is still locked away in his desk, though I didn't have the nerve to ask him about the rumor during our interview.

Stones told me his roster includes singers who are working at the top of the field—he terms them Category 3 artists—as well as so-called artists in development. "These are the very young artists who you've spotted, and you take them on in order to try to get them into Category Three," he explained. High-level YAPs, he told me, can absolutely be a factor in whether he'll take a chance representing a young singer. "We're obviously inundated by people who want representation," he said. "It's almost a full-time job managing that huge number of emails. But by and large, the people who get to us are through recommendations, through our trusted channels, and through the elite training establishments. Those elite schools are very, very important."

YAPs aren't the only path to an agent, of course, or the only way to make the leap out of the young artist stage. Some singers elect to lean heavily into vocal competitions instead, which can facilitate the same professional networks and connections as YAPs, albeit in an even more stressful environment. Consider American soprano Angela Meade, who won fifty-seven out of sixty vocal competitions within the first few years of launching her career in the early 2000s. As a measure of her sheer competition dominance, in 2018 Meade launched her *own* competition at Pacific Lutheran University, appropriately named the Angela Meade Vocal Competition.

Winning competitions comes with significant visibility and usually enough cash to offset the cost of voice lessons and rent for a few months. Take the international Operalia competition, which involves singing arias with orchestra in front of a jury of judges. If a singer makes it through three different rounds of competition to nab first prize, they win bragging rights and a cool $30,000. Still, with a few exceptions, competitions rarely replace YAPs as a rung on the standard career ladder. Instead, it's usually a combination of both that provides the necessary one-two punch to break into the business. Look at most singers working at the top of the field and you'll inevitably find at least two or three YAPs on their CVs, plus a surplus of first- and second-place competitions wins.

Here's where the best-laid plans of aspiring opera singers often go awry. Only a handful of spots are available at the top YAPs each year, and competition is fierce. The Filene Artist Program, a prestigious summer training program at Virginia's Wolf Trap Opera, accepts fewer than 3 percent of singers out of an average pool of eight hundred applicants. Acceptance rates are even lower for the Vienna State Opera's Opera Studio: just twelve out of 734 singers were chosen in 2022, or a little over 1.6 percent. Competitions are even more cutthroat. Winning the top spot at Operalia means a fast track to representation, but it also means beating out a thousand other singers. And you thought Harvard was competitive.

So, what happens to the 98.4 percent of singers who *don't* get the nod from Vienna's Opera Studio? Or the 97 percent who miss out on Wolf Trap Opera? Or the 999 who don't win first prize at Operalia? For them, it's back to the drawing board, back to another spin on the merry-go-round of the audition circuit, back to hoping that, this time, the odds might be in their favor.

And so begins the hustle.

* * *

The operatic hustle is a state of existence, a go-go-go mentality that dominates nearly every waking moment for young opera singers. Practice, lessons, coaching sessions, auditions, rehearsals, performances. It's the equivalent of Sisyphus endlessly pushing that boulder up the hill, watching it roll back down, and then starting again—except, in this case, Sisyphus is a soprano in a jewel-toned wrap dress. The goal is clear: make it through the critical young-artist stage and secure the necessary combination of YAPs, competitions, and representation to have a shot at the big time.

There's a desperation to it, as if sand is sifting through the career hourglass with increasing rapidity. And this sense of time running out isn't just metaphorical—there's quite literally a ticking clock. Most YAPs have an age limit, generally around thirty, depending on the singer's gender. (More slack is traditionally cut for men, who are less in abundance than women.) Many competitions have a similar cap—Operalia, for example, is only open to singers under the age of thirty-two. This sets a tangible and ever-looming deadline for young singers, and an inescapable pressure that mounts with each passing year.

Consider: You've just graduated with your master's degree in vocal performance from a high-level music conservatory. You're twenty-four, which gives you six years to work your way through multiple YAPs, win as many competitions as possible, and land on an agent's roster. Meet these hurdles by the deadline, and you're officially on an upward trajectory. Miss the window, and you've tumbled straight off the launchpad. And while six years might seem like a long time, it's not—at least, not in opera years. That's only six audition seasons, six rounds of submitting applications and prescreening recordings, and potentially six cycles of missing out every single time.

The field is particularly tough for female singers, who are competing for a smaller number of available opportunities than men. YAPs always need good male singers, but they rarely need more than a few sopranos and mezzo-sopranos, especially if they're staging a canonical opera such as *La bohème*, which has five principal roles for men and just two for women. (Thanks, Puccini.) At the same time, women dominate the opera training pipeline, comprising roughly seven out of ten graduates from conservatory voice programs—the majority of whom are sopranos. It's not hard to see why singers from that particular *Fach* aren't known for being overly friendly to one another.

Singers can potentially audition for YAPs year after year without making any headway whatsoever. And it's not a small pool of operatic hopefuls. In her book *The 21st-Century Singer*, Susan Mohini Kane estimates that roughly thirty thousand trained opera singers are trying to progress beyond the young artist stage at any given time in the United States.

With each passing year, the financial costs of the hustle also keep adding up. In 2019, now defunct arts website *The Middleclass Artist* calculated the total cost of trying to make a career as an opera singer at roughly $1 million. So, where does all that money go? The better question is, where *doesn't* it?

First, there's the cost of weekly voice lessons and coaching sessions at roughly one hundred to two hundred dollars an hour, a necessary investment to ensure a singer can maintain their vocal technique and compete with the thousands of other singers trying to scramble up the ladder. Then there's obtaining the mandatory accoutrements of an opera singer, including buying musical scores ($), building and maintaining a professional website ($), taking professional headshots ($$), and making professional audio or video recordings ($$$). Add the cost of multiple bus rides or flights to New York City (or wherever the latest YAP audition is being held), plus application fees, audition fees, audition outfits, audition pianists, and the cost of food and accommodation for each trip. Then basic living expenses: rent, food, clothing, phone, insurance, car payments, gas, Netflix. Now add the student loan payments that just kicked in after six years of undergraduate and graduate study. You have two degrees in voice from Juilliard? Great job! And what a steal at only $55,000 a year!

Keep in mind that most singers aren't independently wealthy or sitting on trust funds dedicated to the pursuit of their operatic dreams. So, how exactly are they paying for all this? Day jobs. Usually more than one.

Some singers have administrative jobs working for opera companies or orchestras, along with church jobs, where they're paid to sing at weekly religious services. Some teach music lessons or manage elementary-school choirs or run private voice studios. Others work as substitute teachers or baristas or waiters or real estate agents. All while continuing to pursue their craft as singers and trying to make it to the next career stage before turning into a pumpkin.

Coming out of my master's degree program at the Peabody Conservatory, I immediately took a nine-to-five job as an executive assistant for an associate dean at the school. As a fellow conservatory alumnus (a composer), my boss was endlessly understanding about my career aspirations and granted me extended lunch breaks to take voice lessons, plus leave to attend opera training programs over the summer. Most bosses aren't usually this benevolent. But while it provided some security, the job barely paid minimum wage and certainly wasn't enough to cover my expenses.

So I added more jobs on top of it. I had an ongoing gig as a paid soprano soloist in the choir of a local Presbyterian church, and another stint as a paid soprano soloist at a local synagogue for the Jewish High Holidays. (As long as I could hit my high notes at 8:00 a.m., no one seemed to care that I was flirting with multiple religious denominations.) Then there was the money I brought in from my freelance singing work with local choruses and orchestras, which ranged from $200 to $1,500 a gig. On the side, I edited SAT essays, wrote online study guides for books that didn't need online study guides (Harry Potter, anyone?), and briefly worked as a hostess at the Cheesecake Factory.

More often than not, most of the money I brought in went straight back out. One year I spent $4,000 on voice lessons and coaching sessions, roughly $1,000 more than I earned from my church and synagogue jobs combined. Another year I spent $600 on application fees for thirteen different YAPs. Five invited me for in-person auditions. The other eight sent a form rejection letter and kept my money.

The financial cost of trying to make it as an opera singer can become overwhelming. One singer told me the biggest piece of advice she gives to aspiring singers is "Put a shitload of money aside beforehand." Otherwise, she said, it's almost impossible.

But the cost of the hustle isn't just financial. Many singers face years of near-constant rejection, singing audition after audition without making any progress. Meanwhile, there's the growing urgency of family life and biological clocks and aging parents. There's the cost of living combined with credit card debt and the anxiety of existing from paycheck to paycheck. There's realizing you're thirty—or thirty-five or forty—and don't have anything saved for retirement, let alone a house. For many singers, the clock simply runs out.

"Music schools tell young singers to keep chugging and stay focused, and eventually their big break will come," said Beth Stewart, a former singer and founder of classical music PR firm Verismo Communications. "But the truth is, if something big hasn't come through within a few years of graduate school, it's probably not going to happen. There are exceptions, of course. But there are many more thirty-three-year-old singers living in New York with two roommates, juggling a day job plus catering gigs and four church services every weekend, just to make rent and pay for coaching. I always encourage young singers to aim for a parallel career path outside performing. Options are good."

Out of the thirty thousand or so trained singers who hit the pavement in the United States each year—all desperately trying to level up before it's too late—only a fraction secure professional representation. According to Susan Mohini Kane in *The 21st-Century Singer*, just 6 percent. All those other singers are left with a decision to make: keep listening to the sirens' call, or cut their losses. This is when the career pipeline becomes less of a pipeline and more of a meat grinder, one through which droves of opera singers are sieved into other fields of employment.

For me, the breaking point was a combination of financial precarity and the emotional weight of the hustle, plus hitting my self-imposed deadline of thirty-two—the cutoff date for most YAPs and the age by which I figured I would have "made it" if I was actually going to. But most of all, it was because I was pregnant, approximately two years ahead of schedule according to the meticulous Life Plan I'd outlined to my husband.

Despite my best powers of delusion, I couldn't wrap my head around the logistics of practicing, auditioning, rehearsing, and performing while also having a baby. I'd seen famous opera singers do it: juggle family life with a performance career and then post adorable photos on Instagram to prove it. But I couldn't see how *I* could do it. Especially without having already "made it." Especially when the reality of my life as a singer still occasionally involved subsisting on $1 Hot Pockets.

I was six months pregnant when I sobbed through an entire voice lesson, struck by the sudden certainty that my singing career was over. At the end of the lesson, I hugged my voice teacher and took the train home. I didn't sing the next day. Or the next week. Or the next month. I packed away my scores under the excuse of Marie Kondo–ing my apartment. I dismantled my electronic piano and shoved the components under the bed, telling myself it was because my pregnant belly kept bumping into the piano's corner. And that was it. There was no fanfare. No crowd of wailing women rending their hair. I just *stopped.*

Thousands of singers turn their backs on the business long before they've made any semblance of a profit from their voice. Of the many hundreds I met during my time in the opera pipeline, only a few dozen are still pursuing opera careers. Of those who were in the original Figaro Project troupe with me, just four. The rest all pivoted to other fields.

But leaving behind such a deeply rooted calling isn't easy. The truth is, I wasn't honest with you before. Back in this book's introduction, when I mentioned I still felt a slight twinge at describing myself as a former singer. A true moment of vulnerability, right?

Except it hasn't always been a slight twinge. For many years, it was more of a monstrous gut-wrenching ache. Because even though I stopped singing, I wasn't able to suppress the accompanying feeling that I'd failed—failed not only at being an opera singer but at being *myself*, the very core of who I thought I was.

It's not unlike the personal crises we so often see among star athletes who are injured before getting their big shot. Or Marlon Brando's washed-up boxer in *On the Waterfront* (1954): "I coulda been a contender. I coulda been somebody." The sad truth is, for the majority of singers, it's not an explicit injury or external force that pushes them out of contention. It's simply the impossibility of the pipeline. In some ways, this makes the loss even harder, the grief even more difficult to bear. Because when you choose to leave an opera career behind—especially before you've "made it"—there's no escaping the niggling sense that you coulda been somebody. And now you're not.

But for all the singers who try and fail to conquer the industry's traditional pipeline—for all the thousands who grimly pack away their ball gowns and electronic keyboards and finally buy that study guide for the LSATs—there are a select few who *do* make it. A select few who master the YAP track, make it onto an agent's roster, and actually achieve what so few manage to achieve.

But that doesn't mean the hustle is over. In many ways, it's only beginning.

* * *

Singers who successfully make the leap out of the young artist stage don't have the privilege of reveling in their victory. Instead, they must now work their way up to the *next* rung of the industry ladder. The new goal is to bridge the divide between being a young professional—a singer who performs small roles with small companies—to being a singer in the top echelon of international stars. The top singers earn the highest fees, can push back against difficult conductors and directors, and can get hired on the basis of their reputation alone. But unlike in Hollywood, stars aren't catapulted to immediate fame in Opera Land. Rarely does one big job or one big competition prompt an immediate rocket launch to the top. Instead, as a rule, the only way to move up the ladder is to ascend one rung at a time.

Take the case of tenor René Barbera, who swept the top three prizes at the Operalia competition in 2011 while simultaneously landing spots in multiple high-level YAPs. Even then, it still took five years for Barbera to be offered singing contracts at the Deutsche Oper Berlin and Teatro alla Scala, two companies that operate at the top of the field. The rest of the time, Barbera was conscientiously working his way from role to role and company to company. "It seems like every new debut and every new role is one of those big moments," Barbera told me in 2024. "But the truth is, it never happens that way."

Most singers working at this level are freelancers. They hop from gig to gig, singing a combination of opera roles and short-term concert jobs (e.g., soloing with an orchestra). A successful freelance singer can potentially swing six or seven contracts with different opera companies over a year, with each lasting roughly four to eight weeks, including rehearsals and performances. Concert gigs are significantly shorter, usually involving just a few days of rehearsal plus a performance or two, which generally make them easy to squeeze in between opera contracts. But both kinds of gigs inevitably involve travel: flying from job to job, city to city, and sometimes country to country. One singer told me that one year they traveled 92 percent of the time (they literally did the math). I heard of another who was gone all but two weeks out of twelve months (that's 96.2 percent, if you're wondering). In some cases, singers travel so much they don't even bother with an apartment, instead putting all their belongings in storage and living out of a suitcase.

As freelancers, singers get paid per performance, a lump sum for each show they're contracted to sing, be it a run of four performances or fifteen. There's no pay for any of the preparation involved, for the weeks and months it takes to learn the music for a role. There's also usually no pay (or very little) for music and staging rehearsals. Instead, that performance fee is all-inclusive—and, importantly, doesn't arrive in a singer's bank account until the job is complete. This is why singers are so protective of their health: if they're too sick to sing a show, they won't get paid, not only for the performance but for all those previous months of work. As a result, it's not uncommon to see singers staggering through an opera while nursing a 101-degree fever—or at the very least, trying to hang on through the first act (the required delivery benchmark in many contracts).

For newly minted young professionals, all gigs generally start small. This includes the size of the company, often the size of the role, and particularly the size of the fee. The principle that drives every freelance opera career is that each subsequent job should be slightly bigger than the last, slightly more prestigious, slightly better paying. Over cumulative years of work, a singer should eventually reach elite status: big roles, big companies, big fees. It's one reason why many young singers will take any and every professional opportunity they're offered—even if the pay is exploitative, even if the rehearsal room is abusive, even if the conductor is a little handsy—just as long as it keeps them moving to the next job. "When you're younger, you're like a little puppy dog," one singer told me. "It's like, 'Hire me! Hire me! Do you want to hire me?' You do every trick: roll over on your back, play with the ball. You're throwing yourself at everything."

Agents have a vested interest in supporting the singers on their rosters and helping them secure bigger roles over time. Agents organize auditions, conduct back-channel chats with casting directors, and negotiate for the biggest performance fees possible. After all, the more money for the singer, the more for the agent.

Still, there's no guarantee that jobs will come. Auditions—and rejection—remain inevitable for all but the favored few who've already reached the field's highest levels. Australian soprano Helena Dix, who made her debut at the Metropolitan Opera in 2019, has sung lead roles with major companies worldwide. But she told me she's still asked to audition for some companies, even as a fully established artist—and not all auditions lead to work. "For every one gig you get hired for, there's probably twenty-two that you've sung for that you didn't get," she told me. And regardless of the artistry brought to a performance, there's still no certainty about the future. Freelance singing is highly variable from year to year. Opportunities—and income—aren't only dependent on how well a singer auditions or performs on their latest job, but on the financial ebbs and flows of the industry.

Soprano Anya Matanovic hit all the key milestones during her young artist stage in the early 2000s, including singing in the YAPs at both the Santa Fe Opera and Seattle Opera. After transitioning to the status of a young professional, Matanovic auditioned for New York City Opera and was hired to sing the role of Frasquita in their 2007 production of *Carmen*. "It felt really exciting," she told me. "I saw a future with a company where I could grow as a performer and also be paid pretty well to do so. Everyone was making good money. Fees were high everywhere." Within a year of Matanovic's signing her contract, moving to New York, and making her debut with the company, the 2008 recession hit . . . and opera felt the blow. Fees dropped, jobs dried up, and New York City Opera soon boasted a freshly chiseled headstone in the opera company graveyard. "That was my introduction to the variable nature of the business," Matanovic said.

The first years of the COVID-19 pandemic were an even more glaring reminder of the precarity of working in opera. Almost overnight, companies were forced to cancel entire performance seasons, leaving singers not only missing out on months of contracted work but also facing the loss of thousands of dollars in expected performance fees. "It is one thing when you're planning that you might get sick and lose a production or two," said René Barbera in a 2020 interview with the National Association of Teachers of Singing. "It is quite another thing when you lose 110,000 euros of income in the blink of an eye. It is just gone, completely gone. And I don't know how to recoup it."

Some companies gave singers partial pay for their canceled performances, but others abandoned them entirely, citing the force majeure contractual clause that absolved them from making financial restitution in the event of a so-called act of God. The result was a mass exodus of singers through the meat grinder of the industry pipeline in 2020 and 2021. One opera insider I interviewed guesstimated that as many as 30 percent of working singers were forced out of the field.

Acts of God notwithstanding, the freelance path can be all too precarious for some singers. That leaves only one option for an opera career: Germany. Land of pretzels, beer, and the *Festvertrag*.

A *Festvertrag*, or *Fest* (translated from the German as "firmly" or "fixed") contract, is used by companies to hire singers on a long-term basis rather than as freelancers. Companies essentially build an in-house ensemble, with each singer allocated various roles in the operas being staged that year. It's a similar model to that of Old Hollywood, when movie stars such as Clark Gable and Bette Davis had long-term and exclusive contracts with film studios such as MGM. In much the same way, the *Fest* system enables forward planning for opera companies while also providing the closest equivalent to a singing nine-to-five: typically, a two-year contract that can be renewed multiple times.

Germany isn't the only country to use *Fest* contracts: opera companies in Austria and Switzerland rely on the same system. But

Germany is where the practice most flourishes simply because it has *so* many companies: a third of all opera performances worldwide are staged in Germany. It's one reason why so many non-German opera singers consider making the move to Berlin or Hamburg when the freelance hustle starts to wear thin. After all, what could be more idyllic than wearing a dirndl while singing opera for a consistent paycheck?

When we spoke in 2024, soprano Solen Mainguené was on her second year of a *Fest* contract with Germany's Leipzig Opera. One of twenty-two singers on contract with the company (six of whom are sopranos), Mainguené sings lead roles regularly—formidable parts such as Desdemona in Verdi's *Otello* and Micaëla in Bizet's *Carmen*. She has a consistent daily rehearsal schedule (10:00 a.m. to 2:00 p.m. and 6:00 p.m. to 10:00 p.m., she told me) and also gets free vocal coaching, health care, and six weeks off in the summer.

Still, the system has its drawbacks. For one thing, *Fest* singers are essentially owned by the company for the duration of their contract. That six-week summer vacation is heavenly, but singers aren't allowed to take a vacation at any other time. Mainguené said she even needs written permission to leave the city of Leipzig, in case she's required to step in for another soprano. Any singing jobs outside her contract similarly require explicit approval: Mainguené is limited to roughly one or two external gigs each year. In a field based on networks and connections, this can be a major disadvantage for singers and also raise the ire of their agents, whose work and income is equally constrained. "You get your money every month, but you're not building any connections. You're not meeting new conductors," Mainguené told me. "You stay in your spot, and no one knows who you are."

Adding to these slightly authoritarian vibes, singers on *Fest* contracts also have limited say in what they sing and are simply earmarked for whichever roles need to be filled that year. It doesn't matter if the roles require a vocal range that's too high or too low—or even vocally dangerous. "In a sense, you're in an artistic prison," Mainguené said. "It's good if they have good plans for you, and you're in their good graces, and they want to use you well. But it depends on your status. And they come to every show. They're always there. As soon as you disappoint, you're out."

For Mainguené, accepting a *Fest* contract was strategic. She was pregnant when she signed on with Leipzig and knew the move would ensure a period of much-needed stability, not to mention a full year of paid maternity leave. But it was only ever meant to be temporary, she told me. She plans to use the remaining years on her contract to gather more performance experience and build up her arsenal of roles. Then it's right back to freelancing. To the hustle.

* * *

One of the biggest seeming benefits of "making it" is that a singer's only job is, well, singing. No more day jobs. No more multitasking. No more squeezing in practice sessions or trying to learn new roles amid a dead-end nine-to-five. Except that freedom from the grind often proves illusory. Yes, there are performances and rehearsals, there's singing beautiful music and taking bows to rapturous applause. But that's only a fraction of what being an opera singer entails. One singer told me the actual performing amounts to just 10 percent of what they do.

Outside the *Fest* system, singers are almost exclusively independent contractors: self-employed and self-sustaining. That means, in addition to singing (and practicing, auditioning, rehearsing, and performing), a working singer is also their own financial manager, their own travel agent, and their own personal assistant. Gone are the days when a diva soprano had an entourage of staff to organize her money, life, and schedule. Gone are the days when a singer could simply show up to an opera house and sing.

First, there's managing the money. As singers work their way up the industry ladder, their performance fees increase. A decent contract at a small company might pay $500 a performance. Move up in prestige and fees rise exponentially. I spoke to one singer who earned more than $10,000 per performance before COVID-19 hit in 2020. Tallying up the total fee for a hypothetical contract—$10,000 multiplied by roughly four to eight performances (if singing in the United States) up to, say, two dozen (if singing in Europe)—it's no wonder a singer's eyes light up with dollar signs. But before all you doctors and lawyers decide to swap careers, remember the age-old lesson from the Notorious B.I.G.: more money, more problems.

Depending on where a singer is working compared to where they live, they automatically lose a massive chunk of income to the government. When tenor René Barbera was working in Italy, 30 percent of his performance fees were collected as Italian taxes. Add another 10 percent wired directly to his agent, and that's 40 percent gone before any other expenses.

Then there's paying for housing and flights. A singer is expected to be on-site for the rehearsal period, as well as the run of performances. But that doesn't mean companies are necessarily paying for any of it. Some begrudgingly cover the cost of flights, but most expect singers to organize and pay for housing on their own. That means days of hunting for an appropriate Airbnb or hotel room in a local city and then paying for it—an expense that might not only exceed thousands of dollars but must also be paid before the singer has earned their performance fee.

A singer can save both money and admin by crashing on a friend's couch or renting a room in someone else's house. But it's a risk. Consider the nightmare scenario I heard from one singer who rented a room in a shared house only to have their "roommates" throw a massive rager the night before a performance. "Never again," the singer said.

Once a singer bites the bullet of paying for that quiet apartment in Amsterdam for the duration of their opera contract ($20,000 for two months, one singer told me with a grimace), there's also the administrative and financial burden of outfitting the fridge and pantry, buying basics such as salt and olive oil to ensure they can cook at home instead of paying for takeout. Add in the cost of health insurance, travel insurance, a short-term gym membership (remember, you need the right look to keep getting cast), and all the other ongoing costs of a singing career, and suddenly that $10,000 fee per performance isn't looking quite as lavish.

"When all is said and done, you take home probably between twenty and thirty percent of your entire gross income," René Barbera told me. "All those fees sound amazing until you put it in perspective. Then it just becomes, like, 'What the fuck am I doing? Where did all the money go?'"

Unfortunately, even if a singer is a whiz at thriftily organizing flights, housing, and food—and a paragon of efficiency in managing tax returns and receipts—they're *still* not back to just singing.

Because now comes the additional job of publicity. Freelance singers are entrepreneurs (or opera-preneurs, if you want to be cute about it), which means singing opportunities are often a direct result of networking and public visibility. After all, it doesn't matter how amazing you sounded in a role if no one was there to hear it.

That means a significant portion of a singer's time is focused on self-promotion, something that's essentially a full-time job in itself. Consider soprano Lisette Oropesa, who sings lead roles at opera companies such as the Paris Opéra and Spain's Teatro Real while also managing nearly 50,000 followers on Facebook and 180,000 followers on Instagram. Selfies, production photos, career advice, enticements to attend upcoming shows—it's a master class in operatic influence. But if a singer doesn't have the capacity or skill set to manage this aspect of their career themselves, they need to outsource it to a publicist, someone like Beth Stewart at Verismo Communications. (Add another $2,000 to $5,000 to that monthly expenditure.)

A publicist assumes responsibility for managing a singer's brand, generating social media content, posting reviews and videos, and securing press coverage and media spots. Stewart considers her bailiwick to be broad, involving most aspects of a singer's professional life—everything other than choosing which operas they'll sing and how much they'll get paid (that's the responsibility of the singer's agent). Instead, Stewart helps to shape a singer's "story," she told me. And an increasingly critical part of that story is social media. Opera singers are now expected to have both an active social media presence and an online fan base. More than one insider told me some companies are even now making hiring decisions based on how many followers a singer has. The thinking is, the more followers, the more free publicity for the company, and the more tickets potentially sold. While Stewart has mixed feelings about social media on a personal level, she sees it playing a crucial role in any successful singing career: "It's a way of speaking directly to the public with no intervening opinion. That's an asset that can't really be ignored."

Beyond all the annoying administrative rigmarole, financial costs, and social media hashtags, every working opera singer still faces one more challenge in "making it." The lifestyle. Look past the sequins and bouquets of flowers, past the album covers and backstage Instagram updates, and the life of a successful singer is far from glamorous. It's lonely, demanding, exhausting. As with the likes of Frank Sinatra, Elvis, the Rolling Stones, Judy Garland, and every other elite entertainer you can think of, success always comes at a cost.

Success in opera means spending months away from home and loved ones. It means packing up a semblance of your life in a suitcase and heading on the road, again and again. It means missing out on holidays, weddings, friendships, and major life milestones, all because of yet another gig. And while a singer is absent—occupied by their latest staging rehearsal or professional debut—life is going on without them. "It's very, very challenging," mezzo-soprano Denyce Graves told me. "You're gone a lot, and when you are around, you have to conserve and preserve your voice. It's not conducive to families. It's not conducive to marriage. It's not conducive to motherhood."

"You have no social life. You can never go to concerts. You can never meet up with friends. You're completely disconnected from reality," one singer told me. Another said his wife had to give up her own singing career to travel with him—"Otherwise, I would never have seen her." Another told me about missing their grandmother's funeral because of a performance. "You don't see your family. You don't see your friends. You don't get to be the best man. You're just not around," said another. And while a singer might (and usually does) make friends during rehearsals for a show, it's closer to summer camp than anything long-term. Because as soon as the curtain falls on closing night, everyone's off to their next gig.

Even the seeming perk of traveling to such places as Paris and Rome on a contract is far from an idealized fantasy. There's little time for sightseeing or a relaxed espresso at a Parisian café. "You're in your hotel room or you're in the theater. You just go back and forth and back and forth," said Denyce Graves. "You don't have a chance to actually *see* Paris or wherever you are." One singer told me they once spent three months on a job in Switzerland but never went to the Alps because they were too afraid of catching a cold and losing their performance fee. "You always imagine you'd love to travel to Spain. That's the dream," a former singer told me. "But then you're actually in your crappy Airbnb with bad Wi-Fi in Madrid, and you're wondering what the hell you're doing."

For soprano Anya Matanovic, the day-to-day reality of a successful opera career always posed the biggest hurdle. "I wanted balance in my life," she told me. "I'd seen a lot of singers go off to Europe, and their personal lives fell apart. I knew that singing made me really happy, but family and friendship and community were even more important to me."

Matanovic told me she was offered a singing contract with Lyric Opera of Chicago that conflicted with the date of her wedding. She knew the offer would likely only come once, but she nevertheless turned it down. She's aware many other singers wouldn't have made the same choice. "There's sometimes an expectation that you should just live and breathe this business. I've always rejected that." Matanovic cites the support of her longtime manager, Alex Fletcher, in making the kinds of career decisions that prioritize her personal life over her professional one. "However, the more I make these choices—and become a better artist for it, honestly—the fewer jobs come my way," she said.

Throughout the loneliness and isolation of a successful singing career, there's also still the endless pressure of the job itself—the need to deliver vocally, night after night, and repeatedly prove your value to secure the next job. "You're constantly being judged. You're constantly being examined. You're constantly being criticized," one singer told me. Reach a certain point in your career, they said, and you're no longer just competing with all the other singers in the industry: "You're also competing with yourself and the way you sang ten years ago."

At this point, you might be wondering why anyone would actually *choose* this career, let alone stick with it. It's a fair question.

None of the singers I spoke to were under any illusions about the realities of the job or the toll that "making it" had taken on them. More than one admitted they'd considered leaving the field. One said they were currently knee-deep in a midlife operatic crisis: "My body is tired. My mind is tired. My heart is aching a lot of the time when I'm gone. After years of doing this, I've been trying to identify what keeps me in this now, which is hard." Another singer told me they'd toyed with the idea of quitting every week for the past fifteen years: "I've had one foot in, one foot out the door. Always."

So then, why do they stay?

One singer was highly pragmatic, telling me they still make more money from singing than they could doing any other job. That's reason enough to persevere. But the majority of the other singers I interviewed evoked that oh-so-ephemeral calling, a sense of the art form's pulling them, even *compelling* them, to stay. "It's like a drug," said Anya Matanovic. "It speaks to the power of opera that more people don't drop out of it." One singer told me they'd once finally had enough—finally decided to leave the industry—but then an audience member came up to them after a performance and said their singing had brought them to tears. "I just thought, 'Oh, well, shoot,'" the singer said. "That's exactly what I wanted to do."

Many singers also feel grateful for the career they've made, despite the challenges. They're still getting paid to sing, paid to share their voice—their *self*—with an audience, and this feels like even more of a privilege because of how few singers actually make it. "It's so easy to be frustrated. But every day I remember I'm making a living doing what I love," one singer told me. "I'm financing my whole life just singing with my lungs and my throat. It's just a huge, huge present. I'm so thankful because I know how rare it is. I really cherish it."

* * *

The opera industry isn't designed for longevity. It's not structured for singers to be the kind of workers who get retirement parties and glass plaques commemorating fifty years of service. It's a field best suited for the young and unattached—for those who don't have family commitments or mind constant travel or being exploited for low pay—for those who'll do almost anything for the chance to sing.

I spoke to one opera insider who said COVID-19 was a good thing because it culled the herd. It forced so many singers out of the field that it created some much-needed wiggle room for the ones who were left. It's a somewhat horrifying thought—that the opera industry is only sustained through a combination of callings and cullings.

But neither opera companies nor the industry itself have a reason to make the career more manageable for singers. Why address the challenges of work-life balance for singing mothers? Why address the rising costs of housing, or the propensity for young singers to be underpaid, overworked, and abused? Why make the field better as a place of employment? All of that costs money. All of that requires an industry that's sustainable, not one that's giving constant eulogies for fallen companies.

One can almost sense Opera Land shrugging with ambivalence. *If singers can't take it, let them go.* Because for every singer who stops, for every singer who decides the costs are just too high, more are always waiting in the wings. More fresh conservatory graduates with bright eyes and unassailable confidence who long for the glory and glamour of an opera career without understanding its stark reality. All hungry, determined, and happy to endure the machinations of the industry for the slightest chance they'll make it.

CHAPTER 8

The Culture

— or —

Who's Afraid of the Big Bad Opera?

In 2023, a small nonprofit classical radio station in North Carolina took a moral stand on the question of opera's future.

For thirty-five years, station WCPE had broadcast performances from the Metropolitan Opera as part of its programming—one of more than four hundred radio stations in the United States to do so. But in 2023, the station's general manager, Deborah S. Proctor, took issue with six operas on the broadcast schedule. All six were written by living composers and librettists. All six were "new."

Proctor deemed the operas unsuitable for broadcasting due to their adult themes, which included rape, violence, and suicide, as well as offensive language and what she termed a "non-classical musical style." In a letter to station listeners, Proctor explained her decision, noting, "We strive to broadcast the classics which have earned the highest standing above all others, which are outstanding in their nature, quality and eminence. . . . Not airing modern, discordant, and difficult music is one concern." Proctor then reassured her listeners that the station would still air the "time-tested and great operas" from the rest of the Metropolitan Opera's season.

Roughly a month after the letter was distributed, news of it leaked on social media. The blowback was fierce.

Proctor was heavily criticized for the seeming hypocrisy of her decision, which overlooked the equally "adult themes" of rape, violence, and suicide in many of the canonical operas in the Met's season, including *Carmen* and *Madama Butterfly.* Proctor's complaint about offensive language was also immediately debunked, with the Metropolitan Opera confirming its radio broadcasts adhere to federal guidelines around profanity. Her criticism about a "non-classical musical style" provoked similar indignation, since several of the banned composers were particularly known for their melodic writing. And, of course, the optics of the disqualifications were hard to ignore, since three of the six banned operas had been written by people of color.

Amid national media coverage by the *New York Times* and CNN, WCPE eventually reversed its decision and committed to broadcasting the full schedule of performances. In a short public statement, station staff wrote, "The staff and volunteers of The Classical Station are dedicated to our mission to make the world a better place by providing a restful refuge from the worries of the world, and by building a community for all, brought together by the shared love of Great Classical Music." The unspoken implication: some operas are Great with a capital *G*, and some are not.

So begins the final battle of this book, one that speaks to the culture of opera—a culture that's fundamentally shaped by its audiences, performers, and companies. We know from our other battlegrounds that opera has a culture of tradition and dysfunction, of elitism and exploitation. But opera also has an underlying culture of fear. For singers, it's fear for their careers. For companies, fear for their funding. Most of all, for many in the industry, it's fear of change. Fear of the future. Fear . . . of the new.

* * *

In a 1977 television comedy sketch that appeared on *The Carol Burnett Show*, comedian Carol Burnett and her usual troupe (Vicki Lawrence, Harvey Korman, and Tim Conway) pointedly spoofed contemporary opera. Titled "A New Music Recital," the two-minute sketch begins with Burnett, Korman, and Conway solemnly entering a performance space that's outfitted with chairs, a grand piano, a harp, and a recorder. Dressed in concert black (that is, tuxedos and gown), the trio collectively bow to the audience and to one another before taking their seats—Burnett at the piano, Conway with the recorder, and Korman at the harp. Vicki Lawrence next enters in the guise of a star soprano and assumes a position at the crook of the piano, nodding for the "instrumentalists" to begin.

All four comedians then start playing and singing loud, clashing notes of music while deadpanning with a bearing of gravitas and pretension. The live television audience dissolves into hysterical laughter as each comedian makes increasingly dramatic and strident sounds with their instruments, from the random squeaks of Conway's recorder and nonsensical plucks of Korman's harp to Burnett's full-bodied piano playing and Lawrence's farcical operatic vocalizations. The lampoon is simple and effective, relying on a shared understanding from its viewers that "new music" is basically noise that no one wants to listen to.

To be fair, there's some truth to the mockery, particularly when we're talking about the avant-garde musical developments of the twentieth century. From roughly the 1890s through the 1940s, Western classical music took a decided turn toward modernism, with traditional notions of melody, rhythm, structure, and form not only examined and overhauled, but, in some cases, wholly debunked. Composers such as Arnold Schoenberg, Richard Strauss, Alban Berg, and Igor Stravinsky were among those who led the charge against opera's old guard. "Who says opera has to keep using the same kinds of notes, harmonies, and rhythms?" they declared, metaphorically tying bandannas of rebellion around their foreheads. "What if we tried something different? Something *new*?"

The innovation didn't stop with them. Subsequent twentieth-century composers such as Benjamin Britten, Morton Feldman, Philip Glass, Steve Reich, and John Adams continued to toy with operatic form and function. Computers, electronic music, and multimedia elements were newly deployed, as were nontraditional performance spaces, nontraditional performers, and even the total rejection of the basic elements of character and plot. Some of the results were so extreme that the works weren't even described as "operas"—Morton Feldman's 1977 *Neither* was, in fact, explicitly deemed an "anti-opera." Not to be outdone, fellow composer György Ligeti countered with his own "anti-anti-opera," *Le Grand Macabre*, the following year.

The result of all this wild experimentation was frequently the kind of music that a composer friend once described to me as "burp, chirp, fart" music. It's not pretty. It doesn't make obvious sense. It can be grating, ear-piercing, bizarre. Sometimes, it doesn't sound as if it was meant to be heard but, rather, muzzled.

This is precisely the type of music many still assume they'll hear at a *contemporary* opera. Or alternatively a *new* opera or a *modern* opera. All three terms are often used interchangeably, but regardless of which is invoked, the implication is always the same: there's a clear divide between Before and After, between Old and New. There's the "real" opera, written by the likes of Puccini, Mozart, Wagner, and Verdi—and then there's the new, modern, contemporary stuff. The *lesser* stuff. The kind of opera that carries a warning label to separate it from the rest of the art form. "It's not really opera," reassures a Verdi-loving operagoer to their compatriot. "It's *contemporary* opera."

As far as labels go, the very notion of *new, modern,* and *contemporary* as part of a single, all-encompassing category is chronologically problematic. Consider the death date of the last of our great canonical masters: Giacomo Puccini in 1924. That leaves more than a century of "newness," more than a century of composers and librettists actively writing new operas in different ways. It's far from a spontaneous outburst, let alone a development we can compartmentalize into a single age or epoch. Nonetheless, an opera written in the 1940s is unfailingly branded *modern* or *contemporary*, just as much as one written in the 1970s, in the 1990s, or last week. Because they're not from Before. They're not from the Canon. And they're certainly not old—or at least, not old enough.

The bigger issue with the label is that it also implies all contemporary operas are the same—all screeching clashes of recorder, piano, voice, and harp as envisioned by Carol Burnett. Over those ensuing decades in the twentieth century, however, the new operas being created were never of a single variety. Yes, some were overly cerebral and outrageously experimental. ("Intellectually masturbatory," scoffed one singer I interviewed.) Some flirted with extended musical techniques and pushed the boundaries of what an Average Joe audience member can aurally endure. But many others didn't. Many were melodic, emotionally lush, and tuneful. Many integrated opera's historical traditions with twentieth-century developments such as jazz, pop, hip-hop, and mariachi, drawing from the sounds of their time while paying homage to a time past.

The only true commonality across these myriad works is that every "new" opera is part of a shared continuum, part of a tradition that builds on the various forms of opera that preceded it—sometimes rejecting them, sometimes embracing them, but always, always aware of them. And this is a tradition that's ongoing in the twenty-first century.

Consider Missy Mazzoli, a Grammy-nominated American composer whose operas have been produced by major companies including LA Opera, Lyric Opera of Chicago, Norwegian National Opera, and Paris's Opéra Comique. In 2018, Mazzoli became one of the first two women commissioned to write an opera by the Metropolitan Opera (yes, ever).

Mazzoli recognizes her work as part of a continuing lineage. "I like the idea of being part of a long tradition," she told me in 2024. "I like the idea of studying scores that were written in the 1700s and drawing inspiration from them. I feel we tell the same stories over and over again, and, as humans, we live the same stories over and over again. So I'm drawing on the traditions of older operas as one of many tools." But at the same time, Mazzoli also frames her operas as being a reflection of modern-day influences. "I draw just as much from contemporary media, from MTV and Netflix and experimental theater and Broadway, as I do from older operas. All of that is just as much in the mix."

British composer Jonathan Dove sees his operas as a similar blend of old and new. Dove is one of the most performed living opera composers in the world, with his 1998 opera, *Flight*, produced more than forty times since its premiere.

Dove told me in 2024 that he has often felt his writing style is "a bit naughty" because he doesn't write the kind of edgy music that many expect from a living composer. Instead, he draws inspiration from a number of seemingly contradictory sources, including canonical composers Puccini and Wagner, twentieth-century composers Benjamin Britten and Philip Glass, and musical-theater maker Stephen Sondheim. "I've absolutely felt like part of a tradition and that I was learning from all those people. I certainly didn't see myself as an iconoclast, breaking with the past and doing something completely unheard of."

Indeed, most people who achieve elite status in the arts recognize that their work constitutes a form of evolution, in which each successive creation is a reaction against or attempt to pay homage to or improve upon what has come before. No work springs fully formed from a blank slate. Today's audiences might be inclined to pay greater respect to contemporary operas if they remembered that the operatic warhorses we now consider "timeless" were also once *new*—once perceived as equally modern and cutting-edge. Then as now, such future-facing music wasn't always appreciated. Consider the polite but loaded way composer Giuseppe Verdi described his operatic successor Giacomo Puccini: "He follows the modern tendencies." One can't help imagining Verdi's accompanying eye roll and unspoken follow-up: *Kids these days.*

For opera conductor Lidiya Yankovskaya, the operatic divide between old and new is inherently faulty. "There was a time where all we produced was the Canon and that created this dichotomy that never existed and shouldn't exist," she said. "All of these works were new works at one point or another. Any young composer who's writing work today has studied and admired a lot of the work on whose shoulders they stand."

Yankovskaya is an active proponent of new music and has conducted more than forty world-premiere operas in her career. During her tenure as music director of the Chicago Opera Theater, she also spearheaded the Vanguard Initiative, a two-year residency program designed to support emerging opera composers.

Regarding the dichotomy of old and new, it doesn't have to be one or the other, she said. "Both things can and should exist. Look at other art forms. Just because you include Picasso in an art museum doesn't mean all the Renaissance art needs to be thrown out. Theaters perform Shakespeare and Tennessee Williams, but then they also do new plays. Opera should be the same."

But for many audiences, traditionalist and otherwise, there remains a prejudice against contemporary opera, a common conviction that not only are new works in direct opposition to canonical masterpieces, they're also not any *good*. This was the main argument driving the decision to ban those six operas from the Metropolitan Opera's radio broadcast in North Carolina. It wasn't subject matter or language or even the music: the problem was the lack of vetting by two centuries of audiences. As the station's general manager said, the operas hadn't "earned the highest standing above all others."

Ah, you might say, but she had a point. All those canonical operas are the best of the best, right? Don't they set the benchmark of quality, a standard of comparison for all new works?

Not necessarily. Without question, they're familiar, and they've certainly been performed over and over. But no work is perfect, not even the canonical ones. Every opera has its flaws: musically, dramatically, or sometimes both.

Take Mozart's opera *The Magic Flute*, which consistently ranks in the top ten of the world's most-performed operas. The only thing more canonical than the opera itself are the enduring complaints about how terrible the story is—a convoluted tale featuring a prince, a bird catcher, a magic flute, love at first sight (via portrait, obviously), an angry mother who sings excessive high F's, and a string of Masonic rituals. "It's a bad libretto. It's garbage," said librettist Mark Campbell. "But it still gets produced, and people still see it because the composer is Mozart. And then they sit through it, thinking, 'Wow, what the hell is going on?'"

Campbell is at the forefront of twenty-first-century opera in America, having written the words for more than forty new operas since 2004. He also conceived and funded the first prize for librettists in opera history: the Campbell Opera Librettist Prize. Campbell told me he's often frustrated by the obvious double standard. "Critics and audiences are often so forgiving of bad storytelling in the classics. A different scrutiny is applied to new works—conflicting musical tastes or the smallest dramaturgical error can kill a work's chances of entering the repertoire. It's disheartening that the industry values old opera so much that it will excuse bad musical storytelling at the expense of producing new works."

As we know, the excuses so often made for old operas aren't limited to issues with music or dramatic pacing but also encompass their ethnic exoticism, racist and sexist storylines, and outdated staging practices. Here we can identify a legitimate divide between old and new.

Operas are inevitably creations of their time, which means that historical operas are forever displaced from ours. We can still connect to their stories and characters. They still hold value as musical works of art. But they'll never be a reflection of who we are in the present. Their composers and librettists will never have drawn from the contemporary experiences that have shaped us.

So, what do new, modern, and contemporary operas actually offer? For one, they give us the means to address and resolve all the battlegrounds that emerge as a direct result of the Canon. Tensions over scores, staging, and casting—these pressure points are inherently absent from newer works. But new operas also offer an opportunity for us to see our own culture reflected and interrogated onstage. They provide a glimpse into ourselves that Mozart and Puccini can never really give us. They're both for us and *of* us.

But it's still a tough sell, still a challenge to work past all the assumptions that are made about contemporary operas—assumptions that aren't based in taste but, more often, in fear.

* * *

Fear has long been a major hurdle to opera's survival. Because when people are afraid of it, they don't generally buy tickets. For first timers in particular, the art form invariably dredges up all sorts of anxieties and concerns. *What do I wear? When do I clap? What if I don't understand what's happening? What if I feel stupid?* Such intrusive thoughts can be enough to convince even the Opera Curious to stay home and binge-watch a new HBO series instead of risking Wagner for the first time. The subset of contemporary operas prompts even more trepidation, adding another uncharted layer to the already great unknown. *What if it's horrible? What if I hate it? What if I'm trapped for three hours without any way to escape?*

"Many people are still unfamiliar with new opera," said Mark Campbell. "They think of opera as *La bohème* and *La traviata* and the familiar operatic clichés." They certainly don't think of *The Shining* (2016), Mark Campbell's frightening operatic adaptation of the Stephen King novel with music by composer Paul Moravec. Nor do they think of *The Listeners* (2022), Missy Mazzoli's suspense-filled opera with librettist Royce Vavrek about the charismatic leader of a sonic cult. And they certainly don't think of *Flight* (1998), Jonathan Dove's opera with librettist April De Angelis about a refugee trapped in an airport terminal—the same story that inspired the 2004 film *The Terminal*, starring Tom Hanks.

Potential opera attendees don't generally think of *any* of the hundreds of compelling operas that've been written in the past forty years. Instead, the default is simply to see the words *new*, *modern*, and *contemporary* . . . and balk.

In part, we can blame all those avant-garde twentieth-century composers. They may have pushed the art form forward with their experimentation, but they also saddled it with a largely undeserved reputation. According to composer Missy Mazzoli, one of the goals for a majority of modern composers is to find an audience and connect with them. "No one sets out to make a work that's inaccessible," she said. "They may have done that in the past, but that was an extreme way of thinking about things. I don't know any composers who are writing today, and certainly not opera composers, who set out to create something that's alienating. As a creator, you always think that what you're writing is going to connect with people in some way."

Composer Jonathan Dove described his work as being "audience-friendly" and joked that the audience he usually starts with is himself. "I'm writing what I want to hear. I'm trying to write myself a good night out. If I'm lucky, that will also speak to other people." But Dove acknowledged that being audience-friendly isn't without its critics, particularly when the resulting work doesn't sound like the modern music that classical connoisseurs expect. There's even a certain stigma *against* opera's being accessible, a sense among some composers and critics that one has missed the mark if the work has broad appeal.

Similar high-low snobbery exists in adjacent art forms such as literature and film. Pity the writer who makes a million dollars with a novel that's all the rage on TikTok or the filmmaker whose *popcorn movie* (the critics' derisive term) sells out Cineplexes. Historically, the surest way to be denied invitations to the most exclusive salons is to create art that the unwashed masses can't get enough of.

Librettist Mark Campbell recalled being confronted by a composer collaborator after Campbell described his music as "accessible" in a public forum. "He took me aside and said, 'Don't ever use that word again. Critics will use that against me.' And I said, 'I didn't mean it was dumbed down. I meant the audience will connect with it.'"

For Campbell, it's an absurd position to take. "What's the opposite of accessibility? Alienation. Why would we want to alienate people who just spent a lot of money on tickets, who could be staying home or enjoying a nice dinner somewhere instead of going to the opera? *Accessible* only means letting the audience into the story. That shouldn't be viewed as a bad thing."

But what does it look like to let an audience into a story? What does it take to make a contemporary opera accessible instead of intimidating?

Mazzoli told me it's all about finding a "way in" for the audience. Ideally, more than one. It might be through the music or through the text or through the characters. It might even be in how the opera is publicized. Consider Mazzoli and Vavrek's opera *The Listeners*, which was inspired by the widely popular cult documentaries on Netflix. That's one way in, Mazzoli said, for the people who enjoy those documentaries to follow their interest into the opera house. Another way in (albeit an unintentional one), Mazzoli told me, was when a fifteen-second clip of the opera went viral on TikTok—a clip in which a character sings a very operatic "Fuck you!" to another character. The clip was liked nearly 140,000 times. In audience terms, that's the equivalent of thirty-seven nights of sold-out seats at the Metropolitan Opera. "I thought, 'Oh my God, this is crazy,'" Mazzoli said. "But also I knew it could be a way in for someone. I even met a student in the UK who first heard about me and the opera because of that clip."

Importantly, being accessible doesn't automatically mean an opera's music is saccharine or derivative or, heaven forbid, dumbed down. "I've seen audiences extremely engaged in new operas whose music I don't particularly like," said Jonathan Dove. "But a powerful story is being told with a very effective use of singing, and people are responding to it. Opera has many different styles. There's more than one way to skin a cat."

And, of course, audiences have long shown a capacity to handle challenging and even wildly avant-garde music *outside* the opera house. Think of science fiction movies or horror films, which often rely on experimental music to create ominous and suspenseful soundtracks. The music for sci-fi classic *2001: A Space Odyssey* (1968), for example, boasts multiple pieces by György Ligeti, that twentieth-century bogeyman of a composer who wrote the original anti-anti-opera.

Audiences simply need a way in. And sometimes they also need reassurance. "Some people may have had a bad experience or may have had a lot of bad experiences," said Dove. "There was a period where you certainly couldn't guarantee that a new opera was going to be a delightful treat. So, they need someone to say, 'We're not going to hurt you. In fact, it might even be enjoyable.'"

But here, a composer and a librettist can only do so much. They can try to ensure there's a way in to their work. But they still need the audience to come to the theater in the first place. And that comes down to the opera company.

Companies are responsible for marketing and promoting the operas they present, using every tool at their disposal to persuade a pool of potential attendees to buy an opera ticket instead of going to see a movie, attending a Taylor Swift concert, or simply staying home. And to be fair, contemporary operas do present a fundamental marketing challenge that *La bohème, Madama Butterfly,* and *Carmen* don't have: they're unfamiliar. Many contemporary operas—even the ones that have already been premiered—haven't been commercially recorded. They're not on Spotify or Apple Music and can't be *heard* anywhere. At least, not yet. This means there's no opportunity for anyone to test out the music before purchasing a ticket. That alone can convince someone to stick with a tried-and-true canonical favorite over a newer work, or even to take a pass on a night at the opera entirely.

But often a bigger challenge is that the companies themselves are hesitant about contemporary works—and aren't good at hiding it. "It's different at every company, but sometimes I do have the feeling of being shoved under a rug," said Missy Mazzoli. "A company will spend all this money advertising *The Magic Flute* or *La bohème* but then not enough to bring the most basic information about a new work to an audience. The hope just seems to be that it doesn't offend too many people or it doesn't flop or maybe they'll make their money back. There should be an actual investment in exposing possible audiences to the work."

Mark Campbell is acutely aware of how the double standard between old and new manifests in this way. "New operas are often treated differently by producers," he said. "Many companies relegate them to second, smaller spaces instead of their main stages, almost as if they're apologizing for them. A lot of companies will also program four old operas for every new one. What about adjusting that equation to half new operas and half old ones? I'd love to see new work not framed as an afterthought or something produced just to fulfill grant applications."

If you recall our operatic dinner plate from the chapter about company funding, there's no question that contemporary works are seen as high risk. These are the cruciferous vegetables, remember, the operatic kale and brussels sprouts—far less palatable than the rest of the meal. And there most assuredly *is* a risk there, particularly when an ongoing audience is used to a steady carb-heavy diet of *Carmen*s and *Tosca*s. But recent statistics suggest that contemporary operas aren't as risky as they're often perceived, particularly when a company actively promotes them.

Audience figures from the Metropolitan Opera's 2023–24 season actually showed a contemporary opera outperforming a plethora of canonical ones in business terms. Composer Anthony Davis and librettist Thulani Davis's opera *X: The Life and Times of Malcolm X* (1986) sold 78 percent of available seats for its run of performances, more than Puccini's *Madama Butterfly* and *La bohème*, and Verdi's *Nabucco*. *X* was the fourth-best-selling show in the company's entire season, ranked only behind canonical darlings *Carmen*, *The Magic Flute*, and *Turandot*. The other contemporary operas in the season also saw reasonably strong showings, each selling between 58 and 68 percent of theater capacity—not bad for a venue with nearly four thousand seats—and all notably ranking ahead of the company's least successful opera that year: Verdi's canonical *Un ballo in maschera*.

So, it's hard not to wonder whether some companies are trapped in a self-fulfilling prophecy. If they don't program contemporary operas (or alternatively market them), then their audiences will undoubtedly remain most comfortable with the Canon. But just because an audience hasn't shown interest in the past doesn't mean they don't have the potential to show interest in the future.

"Companies must have a certain amount of bravery," said Mark Campbell. "I've heard many producers say, 'Well, I'd like to program new opera, but my audience isn't ready for it.' However, I believe that persuading audiences to be excited about new work is part of a producer's job. The companies that have been successful at producing new operas are the ones that have ably demonstrated its value to their audiences."

And it shouldn't even take much convincing. After all, can you think of any other art form besides opera (and classical music) that relies so heavily on historical works? The past has always been present in literature and visual arts and theater—we have our Shakespeare and our Jane Austen and our French impressionists and all the other masterpieces from the respective canons. But they don't overdominate the way they do in opera. The old doesn't come at the expense of the new. On the contrary, new plays, new novels, and new visual artworks are not only constantly being created and produced but are accepted and embraced. As composer Jonathan Dove said to me, "Imagine being told you can only watch black-and-white movies from now on. How would you feel? We wouldn't accept this in any other medium. Why should we accept this in opera?"

* * *

Of all the battles we've trekked through, this one feels the most purposeless. Because it shouldn't matter if some people scoff at new opera while genuflecting at the altars of Wagner and Puccini. It shouldn't matter that some people gnash their teeth at the mention of *Carmen* and only buy tickets to operas written within the last five years. We should be able to have both. We deserve to have both. Both the operas that tell us who we were in the past, and the ones that tell us who we are now. And if both were equally represented and revered on opera stages—if we valued the new as much as we worship the old—no one would need to choose between one or the other. There wouldn't be any battle at all.

Too many mistakenly assume that the audience for old and new needs to be the same. It doesn't. An audience is an audience—not a Venn diagram—regardless of how or whether it overlaps. Building an audience for one form of opera doesn't by extension mean cannibalizing from another.

"We're building an audience for opera either way," Beth Morrison told me in 2024. "Whether they want to see *La bohème* or they want to see a modern work, it doesn't matter. We're still building an audience, and they're on a continuum of sorts. Maybe some of the people will cross over from *La bohème* to a new work, and other people will cross over the other way. But for the most part it's also okay if they don't."

Morrison is the founder of Beth Morrison Projects, a New York–based opera company that has supported and developed new work since 2006. For her, it comes back to the larger aim of connecting with an audience—not just any audience, let alone every audience, but rather, the right audience for each opera. "We've had so many people who are new to opera say, 'I didn't think I would like opera, but if this is opera, then I guess I like this.' It's about trying to delve more deeply into what people will connect with in the repertoire."

Morrison fully admits that she's not the right audience for some canonical operas: "A work like *Madama Butterfly* isn't interesting to me. But that doesn't mean it's not interesting to other people. It's just not for me. That distinction doesn't take anything away from the art form."

So, perhaps there's hope for some kind of truce in Opera Land, for an acknowledgment that there's room enough for the entire continuum of operatic works. But the future remains uncertain. And for advocates and creators of contemporary opera, there's still much to fear.

Many in the industry consider the last two decades a golden age for new works. But in the years since the onset of COVID-19, many opera companies have fallen into economic disarray, hemorrhaging both funding and audiences even as they're still reeling from the pandemic's initial impact. The result has been a further retrenchment into the safe arms of the Canon—and a frantic look at what else can be cut. Here, contemporary opera presents low-hanging fruit. After all, if you're in such dire financial straits that you've cut your season programming from eight operas down to just four, how many of those productions are going be contemporary works? Especially when your audience isn't presumably "ready" for them? Not many.

It's not just the productions themselves that are in danger of being sidelined. In many cases, the pipeline for developing new works is also being dismantled. Jonathan Dove told me that most of the early opportunities that helped him build his career as an opera composer are now defunct, primarily due to funding cuts. "I don't really know how companies are going to nurture and develop emerging opera makers," he said. Because it's not the big companies—the Metropolitan Operas and La Scalas—that cultivate new composers and librettists. It's the smaller ones, the companies with already-tightening budgets, that have long been the training ground for new creators and their work.

For conductor Lidiya Yankovskaya, small-scale training opportunities are critical for the development of the art form. "Composers need opportunities to hone their craft. To fail and learn and be in the theater and learn how the process works," she said. "Verdi wrote a dozen operas before any of the ones we know. So did Wagner and Puccini and Mozart. And some of those dozen operas are really bad. To learn any craft, creators need the opportunity to try and fail."

In the end, it always comes back to money and who's willing to pay. Who's willing to pull out their jingling purse to cover the training opportunities and small-scale productions and dozen or so mediocre operas that need to be written before a composer and a librettist can finally produce a "timeless" one? That, more than anything else, will be the fundamental driver of opera's future, just as it has always been. "There's no shortage of people wanting to write opera," said Beth Morrison. "There's no shortage of people wanting to perform an opera. There's no shortage of people who want to produce it. There's just a shortage of people who want to fund it."

Still, Morrison is optimistic. "Even if there are no opera companies, artists are going to create because they're driven to do it. That's what gives me hope for the form. I'm optimistic because of the people who love it and want to produce it. There's always a way."

* * *

At the beginning of this book, I tried and failed to define opera. In much the same way, I tried and failed to unpack my feelings about it. *But does the author actually like opera?*

My answer's the same. Still yes. And still no.

Because opera doesn't have to be just one thing. It doesn't have to be what we think it is, or what we've heard it is, or what we're afraid it's becoming. Opera has no personality on its own. It's nothing more than what composer Missy Mazzoli calls "a set of tools." It's whatever and however *we* choose to make it, both on and off the stage. Sometimes that means elitist, outdated, exploitative. Sometimes that means innovative, scrappy, inspiring. Sometimes transformative. Transcendent. Even life-changing.

And for those of us who'll be sitting in the audience, who might even now be weighing whether to purchase a ticket for a local production—we don't have to like every opera we see, any more than we need to like every book we read or movie we watch or song we hear. No one says we have to like the operas of Puccini or Wagner or Mozart or Dove or Mazzoli, or that something's wrong with us if we don't. But just because we *don't* like an opera doesn't mean we won't like the next one. A different one. Maybe a new one instead of an old one. Maybe a classic instead of a premiere.

From its earliest origins, opera has always been an experiment, an attempt to create something extraordinary that has both succeeded and faltered century after century. Unlike so much else in this world, that wildly chaotic, ongoing experiment still has the power to deeply move us. It's powerful enough that people love it and hate it and argue about it—and sometimes even go to war over it. And through all the metaphorical bloodshed and shrapnel and body-strewn trenches of those never-ending battles, opera is still somehow here. Somehow surviving, despite the odds.

That alone may be worth the fight.

With Thanks

To the twenty-nine opera professionals who were interviewed for this book and so generously shared their time and insights: René Barbera, Jamie Barton, Nadine Benjamin, Mary Birnbaum, Alison Buchanan, Mark Campbell, Phil Chan, Jonathan Dean, Helena Dix, Jonathan Dove, Lawrence Edelson, Cori Ellison, Denyce Graves, Claus Guth, Andrew Jorgensen, Peter Kazaras, Yunah Lee, Elisabeth Linton, Solen Mainguené, Anya Matanovic, Missy Mazzoli, Beth Morrison, Michael Solomon, Beth Stewart, Ian Stones, Evamaria Wieser, Darren Woods, Lidiya Yankovskaya, and Nina Yoshida Nelsen.

To my agent, Andy Ross, who has been a tireless advocate for my work.

To my editor, Rick Horgan, who pushed me to write a book that would speak to the opera curious as much as to the opera lovers. His thoughtful edits and incisive feedback gave me permission to swing for the fences and create something bigger and better than what I initially imagined.

To the publishing, production, and marketing teams at Scribner/Simon & Schuster, especially Sophie Guimaraes, Lauren Dooley,

Kassandra Engel, Kyle Kabel, Mark LaFlaur, Victor Hendrickson, and Laura Wise.

To the many colleagues and friends who provided advice, edits, fact checks, and hand-holding at various stages of this project: Brian Long, Laura Strickling, Kim Goodwin, Alexandra Dane, Katie Day, Paul Rae, Kirsten Stevens, Sarah Balkin, Clara Tuite, Elizabeth Kertesz, Keith Raffel, Paul Mathews, Jessica Hanel Satava, Tim Takach, and Britt Olsen-Ecker.

To the team of medical practitioners that collectively kept my hands in working (and typing) order: Melanie Cheng, Elisabeth Staunton, Isabelle Anderson, and Jeremy Nicks.

To the original troupe members of The Figaro Project and the cast and crew of SUNY Potsdam's 2024 production of *Computing Venus* for reminding me that I do actually love opera . . . most of the time.

To my sister, Jordan, for always providing a grounded perspective and a model to which to aspire.

To my parents, Larry and Sharon, for their endless cheerleading, babysitting, and in-house editing.

To Elinor and Vivien, who bring boundless love, joy, and chaos to my life.

And, most of all, to Nathan, without whom none of this would be possible.

—Melbourne, Australia
July 2025

Glossary

Aria: a song for a solo singer, typically expressing a character's thoughts or emotions during a pause in the action.

Artistic director: a chief executive of an opera company, typically responsible for artistic vision, casting, and programming.

Baritone: a male voice type, with a vocal range that falls between the tenor and bass types.

Bass: a male voice type with the lowest vocal range.

Chord: a group of three or more musical notes played at the same time.

Chorus: a group of individuals that sing together, usually with more than one singer on a vocal line. Often used to represent large groups in an opera, such as townspeople or soldiers.

Composer: an individual who writes music, typically as a profession.

Conductor: an individual who directs the musical performance of an opera, typically while standing in front of the orchestra.

Conservatory: a specialist institution or college that trains students in the study of music.

Coproduction: a production of an opera that is devised jointly with multiple companies as a way of sharing costs and resources.

Countertenor: a male voice type capable of singing in the female vocal range.

Diction: the pronunciation of words in singing.

Diva: a highly successful or talented female opera singer. Often used as a derogatory term to describe someone who is difficult or demanding.

Dress rehearsal: the final rehearsal before the first performance.

Duet: a song that involves two voices.

Dynamics: how loudly or softly a piece of music should be played.

Executive director: a chief executive of an opera company, typically responsible for financial management, operations, and strategic oversight.

Fach: literally "compartment." A German system for classifying operatic voices.

Festvertrag: a fixed-term singing contract to perform multiple roles with a company over a period of time.

Gesamtkunstwerk: literally "total work of art." A term that describes an idealized integration of multiple art forms in one.

Librettist: an individual who writes the lyrics, text, and story of an opera, typically in close collaboration with a composer.

Libretto: the text of an opera.

Mezzo-soprano: a female voice type with a medium vocal range.

Orchestra: a group of instrumentalists that accompany an opera under the direction of the conductor. Typically located in a "pit" in front of the stage.

Production: the process and organization behind a performance, including the singers, resources, and technical elements. Not to be confused with the performance itself, or the live event presented onstage.

Recitative: the equivalent of sung dialogue, or speechlike singing that advances the plot.

Regietheater: literally "director's theater." Describes a staging approach in which the director reinterprets or recontextualizes a work, often in a way that revises its traditional meaning.

Repertoire: a collection of operatic works that a company or performer is prepared to perform.

Repertory: a system for presenting operas in which a company rotates through multiple productions, often with different operas staged on consecutive nights.

Revival: a production that was designed and built in an earlier season and then "revived" with a new cast of singers.

Score: the printed music of an opera, including the notes, rhythms, and text.

Sitzprobe: literally "seated rehearsal." A rehearsal where the singers rehearse the music with the orchestra for the first time.

Soprano: a female voice type with the highest vocal range.

Stage directions: written instructions in the score that outline stage settings, actions, and technical requirements.

Stage director: an individual who oversees the theatrical performance of an opera, including the concept, setting, design, and actions of the singers.

Stagione: a system for presenting operas in which an opera company stages a production for a complete run of performances before moving on to the next production in its season.

Supertitles: also ***surtitles***. Translated lyrics that are projected above the stage during a live performance.

Tempo: the speed or pace of a piece of music.

Tenor: a male voice type with the highest vocal range (with the exception of countertenors).

Vocal coach: an instructor who trains a singer in musical expression and interpretation, often including diction and characterization.

Vocal folds: also commonly ***vocal cords***. Two folds of muscle tissue that sit within the larynx and vibrate to create sound.

Voice teacher: an instructor who trains a singer in vocal technique, including breath control, note accuracy, and vocal health.

Wandelprobe: literally "wandering rehearsal." A rehearsal in which the singers and orchestra rehearse together onstage for the first time.

Werktreue: literally "faithfulness to the work." Describes a staging approach in which the director is faithful to the intentions of the original composer and librettist.

References

CHAPTER 1 The History

1 *There'll be parades:* Tim Carter and Francesca Fantappiè, *Staging "Euridice": Theatre, Sets, and Music in Late Renaissance Florence* (Cambridge: Cambridge University Press, 2021), 9–10, 16.

2 *Based on:* Ibid., 16.

2 *One audience member:* Jacopo Peri, *Euridice: An Opera in One Act, Five Scenes*, ed. Howard Mayer Brown (Madison, WI: A-R Editions, 1981), xiv.

2 *Key to their effort:* Carolyn Abbate and Roger Parker, *A History of Opera: The Last Four Hundred Years* (New York: W. W. Norton, 2015), 43.

2 *But even centuries earlier:* Ibid., 39.

3 *Alas, all traces:* Carter and Fantappiè, *Staging "Euridice,"* 3.

3 *Written with poet:* Abbate and Parker, *History of Opera*, 41.

4 *Their venture:* Ellen Rosand, *Opera in Seventeenth-Century Venice: The Creation of a Genre* (Berkeley: University of California Press, 1991), 69.

5 *The cost of a single ticket:* Evan Baker, *From the Score to the Stage: An Illustrated History of Continental Opera Production and Staging* (Chicago: University of Chicago Press, 2013), 13.

5 *Over the next three years:* Ibid.

5 *A production of:* Beth L. Glixon and Jonathan E. Glixon, "Marco Faustini and Venetian Opera Production in the 1650s: Recent Archival Discoveries," *Journal of Musicology* 10, no. 1 (1992): 54, https://doi.org/10.2307/763560.

6 *By the 1670s:* Abbate and Parker, *History of Opera*, 63–64.

6 *But* opera seria *didn't stay . . . minimalist operas of the 1970s:* Ibid.

10 *In an ideal scenario:* Thomas Forrest Kelly, *First Nights at the Opera* (New Haven: Yale University Press, 2004), 232.

11 *Since the early 1980s:* Johan Wijnants, "Surtitles: A New Text Between Libretto, Score, Translation and Performance," in *Philology and Performing Arts: A Challenge*, eds. Mattia Cavagna and Costantino Maeder (Louvain-la-Neuve, Belgium: Presses universitaires de Louvain, 2014), 39.

13 *As opera composer John Adams:* Sophie Haigney, "The Art of the Libretto: John Adams," *Paris Review*, April 24, 2024, https://www.theparisreview.org/blog/2024/04/24/the-art-of-the-libretto-john-adams/.

13 *In a 1783 letter:* Salzburg Mozarteum Foundation, "Letters of the Viennese Years of Wolfgang Amadé Mozart," https://dme.mozarteum.at/DME/objs/raradocs/transcr/pdf_eng/0753_WAM_LM_1783.pdf.

14 *In 1889:* Mosco Carner, *Puccini: A Critical Biography* (New York: Knopf, 1959), 61.

15 *For example, Pietro Metastasio:* Richard Taruskin, *Music in the Seventeenth and Eighteenth Centuries: The Oxford History of Western Music* (Oxford: Oxford University Press, 2005), 152.

15 *For the 1637 premiere:* Rosand, *Opera in Seventeenth-Century*, 68.

15 *Instead, opera now served:* Herbert Lindenberger, *Opera in History: From Monteverdi to Cage* (Stanford, CA: Stanford University Press, 1998), 57.

15 *Nineteenth-century composer Giuseppe Verdi:* Gilles de Van, *Verdi's Theater: Creating Drama Through Music* (Chicago: University of Chicago Press, 1998), 64–65.

16 *Composer Richard Wagner:* Abbate and Parker, *History of Opera*, 311–12.

17 *The librettist would typically:* Daniel Heartz, *Mozart's Operas* (Berkeley: University of California Press, 1990), 89; and David Littlejohn, *The Ultimate Art: Essays Around and About Opera* (Berkeley: University of California Press, 1994), 57.

18 *The movement of:* Caitlin Vincent, *Digital Scenography in Opera in the Twenty-First Century* (Abingdon, UK: Routledge, 2022), 80.

18 *Here the goal:* Susan Rutherford, "Voices and Singers," in *The Cambridge Companion to Opera Studies*, ed. Nicholas Till (Cambridge: Cambridge University Press, 2012), 125.

18 *New works were:* Tim Carter, "What Is Opera?," in *The Oxford Handbook of Opera*, ed. Helen M. Greenwald (Oxford: Oxford University Press, 2014), 20–21.

19 *These were stand-alone:* Alessandra Campana, *Opera and Modern Spectatorship in Late Nineteenth-Century Italy* (Cambridge: Cambridge University Press, 2015), 3.

19 *"It is absolutely necessary":* Quoted in James Hepokoski, "Staging Verdi's Opera: The Single, 'Correct' Performance," in *Verdi in Performance*, eds. Alison Latham and Roger Parker (Oxford: Oxford University Press, 2001), 13.

19 *After first encountering:* Ibid., 12.

19 *Leading up to the premiere:* Kelly, *First Nights*, 254.

20 *New technologies:* Vincent, *Digital Scenography*, 84–85.

20 *For the premiere:* Kelly, *First Nights*, 254.

20 *From the 1890s:* Simon Williams, "Opera and Modes of Theatrical Production," in *The Cambridge Companion to Opera Studies*, ed. Nicholas Till (Cambridge: Cambridge University Press, 2012), 151–52.

22 *They're what stage director:* Quoted in Cormac Newark and William Weber, "General Introduction: Idiosyncrasies of the Operatic Canon," in *The Oxford Handbook of the Operatic Canon,* eds. Cormac Newark and William Weber (Oxford: Oxford University Press, 2020), 4.

22 *Or alternatively:* Quoted in Carlotta Sorba, "Theaters, Markets, and Canonic Implications in the Italian Opera System, 1820–1880," in *The Oxford Handbook of the Operatic Canon*, eds. Cormac Newark and William Weber (Oxford: Oxford University Press, 2020), 220.

22 *And opera scholars:* Philippe Agid and Jean-Claude Tarondeau, *The Management of Opera: An International Comparative Study* (Basingstoke, UK: Palgrave Macmillan, 2010), 21.

24 *Take the nineteenth-century view:* Lydia Goehr, *The Imaginary Museum of Musical Works: An Essay in the Philosophy of Music* (Oxford: Oxford University Press, 1992), 229.

24 *Or the same century's:* James A. Parakilas, "The Operatic Canon," in *The Oxford Handbook of Opera*, ed. Helen M. Greenwald (Oxford: Oxford University Press, 2014), 868.

24 *Between 1760 and 1770:* Christophe Charle, "The Creation of an Operatic Canon in Nineteenth-Century Europe: Towards a Quantitative Approach," *Biens Symboliques / Symbolic Goods* 8 (2021): 3, https://doi.org/10.4000/bssg.655.

24 *By the 1850s:* Abbate and Parker, *History of Opera,* 528.

25 *The success of an opera:* Sorba, "Theaters, Markets, and Canonic Implications," 218–19.

26 *Bare walls, sparse sets:* David J. Levin, *Unsettling Opera: Staging Mozart, Verdi, Wagner, and Zemlinsky* (Chicago: Chicago University Press, 2008), 42–43.

26 *Felsenstein's stagings:* Nicholas Payne, "Opera in the Marketplace," in *The Cambridge Companion to Twentieth-Century Opera*, ed. Mervyn Cooke (Cambridge: Cambridge University Press, 2005), 316.

26 *At the Bayreuth Festspielhaus:* Patrick Carnegy, *Wagner and the Art of the Theatre* (New Haven, CT: Yale University Press, 2013), 263–64.

27 *See German critic Paul Schwers:* Quoted in Tom Sutcliffe, "Technology and Interpretation: Aspects of 'Modernism,'" in *The Cambridge Companion to Twentieth-Century Opera*, ed. Mervyn Cooke (Cambridge: Cambridge University Press, 2005), 337.

27 *Consider French conductor:* Pierre Boulez, "Opera Houses?—Blow Them Up!," *Opera* 19 (1968), translated and reprinted from "Sprengt die Opernhäuser in die Luft," *Der Spiegel* 40 (September 25, 1967): 446–47.

CHAPTER 2 The Score

30 *Musicologist David Littlejohn:* David Littlejohn, *The Ultimate Art: Essays Around and About Opera* (Berkeley: University of California Press, 1994), 57.

30 *And for many:* Nicholas Till, "The Operatic Work: Texts, Performances, Receptions and Repertories," in *The Cambridge Companion to Opera Studies*, ed. Nicholas Till (Cambridge: Cambridge University Press, 2012), 227.

31 *Take the 2009 review:* Alex Ross, "The Case of the Missing Candlesticks," *New Yorker*, October 29, 2009, https://www.newyorker.com/culture/alex-ross/the-case-of-the-missing-candlesticks.

31 *Responding to the outcry:* Daniel J. Wakin, "At Library, Talk Turns to *Tosca*," *New York Times*, October 9, 2009, https://www.nytimes.com/2009/10/10/arts/10arts-ATLIBRARYTAL_BRF.html.

35 *This means that:* Philip Gossett, "Writing the History of Opera," in *The Oxford Handbook of Opera*, ed. Helen M. Greenwald (Oxford: Oxford University Press, 2014), 1035.

35 *Take the score:* Georges Bizet, *Carmen*, ed. Michael Rot (Vienna: Verlagsgruppe Hermann, 2015), xii.

36 *Two more final scores:* Mary Dibbern, *Carmen: A Performance Guide* (New York: Pendragon Press, 2001), x–xii.

36 *Ludwig van Beethoven:* Paul Robinson, *Ludwig van Beethoven, "Fidelio"* (Cambridge: Cambridge University Press, 1996), 7.

36 *Giacomo Puccini:* Dieter Schickling and Robert Vilain, "Puccini's 'Work in Progress': The So-Called Versions of *Madama Butterfly*," *Music & Letters* 79, no. 4 (1998): 527, https://www.jstor.org/stable/854624.

36 *It's a similar story:* Alan Tyson, "The 1786 Prague Version of Mozart's *Le nozze di Figaro*," *Music & Letters* 69, no. 3 (1988): 321–33.

37 *The most common strategy:* Roger Parker, *Remaking the Song: Operatic Visions and Revisions from Handel to Berio* (Berkeley: University of California Press, 2006), 8.

37 *Even the production's stage director:* Ibid., 42.

39 *Take the edition:* Dibbern, *Carmen*, xix–xx.

39 *Or, for a real Frankenstein's:* Ibid., xviii.

40 *The instability of:* Heather Mac Donald, "The Abduction of Opera," *City Journal*, Summer 2007, https://www.city-journal.org/article/the-abduction-of-opera.

40 *Companies would gleefully:* Rachel Cowgill, "Mozart Productions and the Emergence of *Werktreue* at London's Italian Opera House, 1780–1830," in *Operatic Migrations: Transforming Works and Crossing Boundaries*, eds. Roberta Montemorra Marvin and Downing A. Thomas (England: Ashgate Publishing, 2006), 147.

41 *See, for example:* Michael Christoforidis and Elizabeth Kertesz, *Carmen and the Staging of Spain: Recasting Bizet's Opera in the Belle Epoque* (Oxford: Oxford University Press, 2008), 104–6.

41 *By the turn of:* Lydia Goehr, "Being True to the Work," *Journal of Aesthetics and Art Criticism* 47, no. 1 (Winter 1989): 56.

44 *In 2022:* Mike Silverman, "New *La Bohème* Tells Story in Reverse for Happy Ending," Associated Press, March 31, 2022, https://apnews.com/article/entertainment-music-detroit-opera-27b1ef64ad1bef699795a62c24ae6f35.

45 *"It was just the last":* Quoted in James Politi, "A Happy Opera Ending Sparks a #MeToo Debate in Italy," *Financial Times*, January 17, 2018, https://www.ft.com/content/64e4c704-faac-11e7-a492-2c9be7f3120a.

45 *Stage director Leo Muscato:* Domenico Gentile, "Legendary Opera Says 'Enough' to Violence Against Women, Flips Gender Roles," SBS Italian, January 17, 2018, https://www.sbs.com.au/language/italian/en/article/legendary-opera-says-enough-to-violence-against-women-flips-gender-roles/istzmvtsl.

45 *"Bizarre Bizet":* Barbie Latza Nadeau, "Bizarre Bizet: A #MeToo Carmen Doesn't Die, and the Audience Shouts 'Kill Her!,'" *Daily Beast*, January 20, 2018, https://www.thedailybeast.com/bizarre-bizet-a-metoo-carmen-doesnt-die-and-the-audience-shouts-kill-her.

45 *"What's next?":* Ibid.

46 *"It has caused":* Quoted in Daniel Verdú, "A Feminist Twist on *Carmen* Scandalizes Italy," *El País*, January 16, 2018, https://english.elpais.com/elpais/2018/01/16/inenglish/1516100298_262837.html.

46 *In a 2018 production:* Claire Seymour, "Barrie Kosky's *Carmen* at Covent Garden," *Opera Today*, February 8, 2018, https://www.operatoday.com/content/2018/02/barrie_koskys_c.php.

46 *The version staged:* Kristin M. Turner, "Opera in English: Class and Culture in America, 1878–1910" (PhD diss., University of North Carolina, 2015), 345.

47 *Described in a review:* Melinda Bargreen, "Opera Review *Carmen* by Bizet, in Seattle Opera Production," *Seattle Times*, October 23, 1995.

47 *"Did you happen to hear":* Tamara Vallejos, "Too Much Sex & Violence at the Opera?," *Seattle Opera Blog*, September 1, 2011, https://www.seattleoperablog.com/2011/09/too-much-sex-violence-at-opera.html.

50 *"Faithful to the intentions":* Opéra Royal de Wallonie-Liège, "The Season 2019–20," accessed November 3, 2023, https://www.operaliege.be/en/the-season-2019•20/.

51 *It's "what Wagner":* Alex Ross, "Encircling the *Ring*," *New Yorker*, May 7, 2012, https://www.newyorker.com/culture/culture-desk/encircling-the-ring.

51 *"Our artistic mission":* Jay Handelman, "Sarasota Opera's DeRenzi Sticks to Tradition in His 32nd Season," *Herald-Tribune*, February 1, 2014, https://www.heraldtribune.com/story/news/2014/02/02/sarasota-operas-derenzi-sticks-to-tradition-in-his-32nd-season/29226616007/.

51 *In 1987:* Robin Pogrebin, "Donor's Estate Sues Metropolitan Opera," *New York Times*, July 24, 2003, https://www.nytimes.com/2003/07/24/nyregion/donor-s-estate-sues-metropolitan-opera.html.

51 *The case was:* "Settlement Reached in Opera Dispute," *Plainview (TX) Herald*, April 12, 2004, https://www.myplainview.com/news/article/Settlement-reached-in-opera-dispute-8757257.php.

52 *In 1988:* Richard Taruskin, "The Pastness of the Present and the Presence of the Past," in *Text and Act: Essays on Music and Performance* (Oxford: Oxford University Press, 1995), 97–98.

52 *But he dug in:* Susan McClary, *Georges Bizet: Carmen* (Cambridge: Cambridge University Press, 2012), 23.

CHAPTER 3 The Stage

55 *In 2024:* Operabase, https://www.operabase.com/statistics/en.

56 *An ominous report:* Ronald Blum, "*La bohème* in Space Returns to Paris, 6 Years After Uproar," Associated Press, May 3, 2023, https://apnews.com/article/boheme-space-guth-puccini-paris-opera-09cbbae366a312e6aae50da77b13cd59.

57 *"Claus Guth's spaceship":* Shirley Apthorp, "A Storm of Boos for *La bohème* at the Paris Opera," *Financial Times*, December 5, 2017, https://www.ft.com/content/96f740fc-d8e0-11e7-9504-59efdb70e12f.

57 *"Bizarre to the point":* Amy Donahue, "Review: Houston, *Bohème* in Space Has a Problem (Opéra de Paris)," *Twin Cities Arts Reader*, December 4, 2017, https://twincitiesarts.com/2017/12/04/review-houston-boheme-in-space-has-a-problem-opera-de-paris/.

57 *Or take this burn:* Paul Kuritz, "Paris Opera's *La bohème*: Lost in Space," *PaulKuritz.com—Theater and Film*, December 12, 2017, https://paulkuritz.com/2017/12/paris-operas-la-boheme-lost-in-space/.

57 *Boos, heckling:* Blum, "*La bohème* in Space."

60 *Video and projection:* Caitlin Vincent, *Digital Scenography in Opera in the Twenty-First Century* (Abingdon, UK: Routledge, 2022), 1–2.

61 *Consider, for example:* Ronald Blum, "Mayer's *Rigoletto*, Set in Vegas, Opens at Met," Associated Press, January 30, 2013, https://apnews.com/article/entertainment-music-arts-and-entertainment-music-reviews-eb7589d12fa24aae88dc81e66d5217ba.

61 *"It is not our responsibility":* Barbara Beyer, "Interviews with Contemporary Opera Directors, Selected from Barbara Beyer's *Warum Oper? Gespräche mit Opernregisseuren* (2005)," *Opera Quarterly* 27, no. 2–3 (2011): 310, https://doi.org/10.1093/oq/kbr027.

62 *But the bigger line:* David Littlejohn, *The Ultimate Art: Essays Around and About Opera* (Berkeley: University of California Press, 1994), 57.

62 *Depending on which:* Lynn René Bayley, "Eurotrash Revisited: The Academic Version," *Art Music Lounge: An Online Journal of Jazz and Classical Music*, February 23, 2019, https://artmusiclounge.wordpress.com/2019/02/23/eurotrash-revisited-the-academic-version/; and Olivier Keegel,

"*Regietheater*, the Ruination of Opera," *Opera Gazet*, May 26, 2022, https://operagazet.com/regietheater-the-ruination-of-opera/.

63 *After attending:* Ulrich Müller, "*Regietheater* / Director's Theater," in *The Oxford Handbook of Opera*, ed. Helen M. Greenwald (Oxford: Oxford University Press, 2014), 589.

63 *The heirs of:* Marie-Andrée Weiss, "The Paris Court of Appeals Gives Freedom of Expression the Ax in Favor of Droit Moral," Law Office of Marie-Andrée Weiss, February 10, 2016, https://www.maw-law.com/french-copyright/the-paris-court-of-appeals-gives-freedom-of-expression-the-ax-in-favor-of-droit-mor/.

63 *Normally a lighthearted comedy:* Jane Paulick, "A Violent, Drug-Addled, Hooker-Filled Opera Angers Sponsors," *DW*, June 24, 2004, https://www.dw.com/en/a-violent-drug-addled-hooker-filled-opera-angers-sponsors/a-1245750.

64 *Consider this proclamation:* Keegel, "*Regietheater.*"

66 *The so-called Orient:* Edward W. Said, *Orientalism* (Great Britain: Routledge & Kegan Paul, 1978), 17.

66 *One was the Turk:* Larry Wolff, *The Singing Turk: Ottoman Power and Operatic Emotions on the European Stage from the Siege of Vienna to the Age of Napoleon* (Stanford, CA: Stanford University Press, 2016), 1.

67 *One cookie-cutter plot:* Jama Stilwell, "A New View of the Eighteenth-Century 'Abduction' Opera: Edification and Escape at the Parisian 'Théâtres de la foire,'" *Music & Letters* 91, no. 1 (2010): 51, https://www.jstor.org/stable/40539094.

67 *Another boilerplate:* Ralph P. Locke, "Constructing the Oriental 'Other': Saint-Saëns's *Samson et Dalila*," *Cambridge Opera Journal* 3, no. 3 (1991): 263.

68 *When setting his:* Josh Stenberg, "Returning to Where She Didn't Come From: *Turandot* on the Chinese Stage," in *Opera in a Multicultural World: Coloniality, Culture, Performance*, eds. Mary I. Ingraham, Joseph So, and Roy Moodley (New York: Routledge, 2015), 153.

68 *Throughout the eighteenth:* Ralph P. Locke, *Music and the Exotic from the Renaissance to Mozart* (Cambridge: Cambridge University Press, 2015), 88.

68 *For the European premiere:* Christopher R. Gauthier and Jennifer Mcfarlane, "Nationalism, Racial Difference, and 'Egyptian' Meaning in Verdi's *Aida*," in *Blackness in Opera*, eds. Naomi André, Karen M. Bryan, and Eric Saylor (Champaign, IL: University of Chicago Press, 2012), 63.

68 *For the premiere of:* Alison Kinney, "*Otello*: Opera, Identity Politics and Blacking-Up," *Guardian*, June 15, 2017, https://www.theguardian.com/music/2017/jun/15/otello-verdi-royal-opera-race-identity-politics-black-talent.

68 *For her premiere as:* Varischi e Artico, *Rosina Storchio (1874–1945)*, photograph, Archivio Storico Ricordi, 1904, https://en.wikipedia.org/wiki/File:Rosina_Storchio_%281904%29_-_Archivio_Storico_Ricordi_FOTO000052.jpg.

68 *For his turn:* Lebrecht Music and Arts, *Gaetano Pini-Corsi—Portrait of the Italian Bass as "Goro" in Giacomo Puccini's Opera Madama Butterfly*, photograph, Alamy Stock Images, https://www.alamy.com/gaetano-pini-corsi-portrait-of-the-italian-bass-as-goro-in-giacomo-image155404650.html.

69 *The use of blackface:* Virginia Mason Vaughan, *Performing Blackness on English Stages, 1500–1800* (Cambridge: Cambridge University Press, 2005), 2.

69 *Starting in the 1820s:* Renee Lapp Norris, "Opera and the Mainstreaming of Blackface Minstrelsy," *Journal of the Society for American Music* 1, no. 3 (2007): 341, https://doi.org/10.1017/S1752196307070113.

69 *The American form:* Derek B. Scott, *Sounds of the Metropolis: The 19th-Century Popular Music Revolution in London, New York, Paris, and Vienna* (Oxford: Oxford University Press, 2008), 147.

70 *Instead, it was:* Krystyn R. Moon, *Yellowface: Creating the Chinese in American Popular Music and Performance, 1850s–1920s* (New Brunswick, NJ: Rutgers University Press, 2005), 6; and Esther Kim Lee, *Made-Up Asians: Yellowface During the Exclusion Era* (Ann Arbor: University of Michigan Press, 2022), 8.

70 *One was used:* Lee, *Made-Up Asians*, 1, 107.

70 *The other:* Ibid., 122.

70 *Incredibly, in 2014:* Nicky Woolf, "Decision to Scrap Blackface from *Otello* Not Complicated, Says Met Director," *Guardian*, September 23, 2015, https://www.theguardian.com/music/2015/sep/22/otello-metropolitan-opera-scraps-blackface.

71 *Take the 2022 production:* Kelsey Ables, "American Soprano Withdraws from Italian Festival That Used Blackface," *Washington Post*, July 16, 2022, https://www.washingtonpost.com/music/2022/07/16/angel-blue-withdraw-aida-blackface/.

71 *"Everywhere in the world":* Quoted in Sophia Alexandra Hall, "'Everywhere in the World Used to Have Blackface'—Opera Festival Defends Anna

Netrebko Controversy," Classic FM, July 13, 2022, https://www.classicfm.com/artists/anna-netrebko/soprano-blackface-accusations-verona/.

72 *Stage director Aria Umezawa:* Rocky Mountain PBS, "The Riddle of *Turandot*: A Community Conversation," YouTube, February 16, 2023, 50:10, https://www.youtube.com/watch?v=BnmKbtOlnB8.

72 *In an interview:* Oliver Mears, "Beyond Black and Yellowface: How Opera Can Address Prejudice," *Guardian*, June 14, 2022, https://www.theguardian.com/music/2022/jun/14/oliver-mears-beyond-black-and-yellowface-opera-prejudice-madama-butterfly?CMP=share_btn_url.

72 *True to Mears's word:* Craig Simpson, "Royal Opera House Defends 'Whitewashing' *Madama Butterfly*," *Telegraph*, September 10, 2022, https://www.telegraph.co.uk/news/2022/09/10/royal-opera-house-defends-whitewashing-madama-butterfly/.

73 *In a 2019 interview:* Mike Silverman, "'No Path Is Easy': Black Opera Singers Detail Struggles," Associated Press, September 20, 2019, https://apnews.com/arts-and-entertainment-music-general-news-9f4a93c655d54cfbad9cafd36c768775.

75 *"I have seen":* "Responses to *Madame Butterfly* from Members of the Asian Opera Alliance," San Francisco Opera, https://www.sfopera.com/digital/exhibit/madame-butterfly/aoa-responses/.

75 *"As I sat":* Cat-Thao Nguyen, "Ping, Pong, Pang: We Went to Enjoy the Opera but Found It Perpetuating Racism," *Sydney Morning Herald*, February 26, 2022, https://www.smh.com.au/culture/opera/ping-pong-pang-we-went-to-enjoy-the-opera-but-found-it-perpetuating-racism-20220221-p59yai.html.

77 *Currently the:* Caitlin Vincent and Amanda Coles, "Unequal Opera-tunities: Gender Inequality and Non-Standard Work in US Opera Production," *Equality, Diversity and Inclusion: An International Journal* 43, no. 2 (2024): 274, https://doi.org/10.1108/EDI-03-2023-0071.

78 *Spoiler:* Caitlin Vincent, Amanda Coles, and Jordan Beth Vincent, "Opera-ting on Inequality: Gender Representation in Creative Roles at The Royal Opera," *Cultural Trends* 31, no. 3 (2021), https://doi.org/10.1080/09548963.2021.1966295; Caitlin Vincent and Amanda Coles, "Unequal Opera-tunities: Gender Inequality and Non-Standard Work in US Opera Production," *Equality, Diversity and Inclusion: An International Journal* 43, no. 2 (2024), https://doi.org/10.1108/EDI-03-2023-0071; and Caitlin

Vincent, Katya Johanson, and Bronwyn Coate, "Risky Business: Policy Legacy and Gender Inequality in Australian Opera Production," *International Journal of Cultural Policy* 30, no. 5 (2023), https://doi.org/10.1080/10286632.2023.2239266.

78 *The rationale was:* Shuhei Hosokawa, "Nationalizing Chō-Chō-San: The Signification of '*Butterfly* Singers' in a Japanese-Brazilian Community," *Japanese Studies* 19, no. 3 (1999): 254, https://doi.org/10.1080/10371399908727681.

78 *Commenting on the production:* Rudolf Bing, *5,000 Nights at the Opera: The Memoirs of Sir Rudolf Bing* (Garden City, NY: Doubleday, 1972), 202.

78 *Consider the alternative:* Yelena Ćirić, "Icelandic Opera's *Madama Butterfly* Reinforces Racist Stereotypes, Critics Say," *Iceland Review*, March 9, 2023, https://www.icelandreview.com/news/culture/icelandic-operas-madama-butterfly-reinforces-racist-stereotypes-critics-say/.

79 *Take the Royal Ballet and Opera's:* Mears, "Beyond Black and Yellowface."

79 *The resulting staging:* Nadia Khomami, "Royal Opera Stages *Madama Butterfly* with Changes to Respect Japanese Culture," *Guardian*, June 6, 2022, https://www.theguardian.com/culture/2022/jun/05/royal-opera-madama-butterfly-japanese-culture?CMP=share_btn_url.

79 *By way of beating:* Royal Opera House, "Behind the Scenes: A Revival with Authenticity," https://www.rbo.org.uk/tickets-and-events/madama-butterfly-2022-digital#extras.

80 *"There is an expectation":* Phil Chan with Michele Chase, *Banishing Orientalism: Dancing Between Exotic and Familiar* (New York: Yellow Peril Press, 2023), 269.

81 *"I'm almost exclusively":* Rocky Mountain PBS, "Riddle of *Turandot.*"

83 *"In our staging":* "San Francisco Opera's Centennial Season Continues with New Co-Production of *Madame Butterfly* at the War Memorial Opera House, June 3–July 1," San Francisco Opera, https://www.sfopera.com/press/press-releases/Madame-Butterfly-2023/.

83 *According to Umezawa's:* "*Madame Butterfly*," New Orleans Opera Association, 2023, https://issuu.com/renaissancepublishing/docs/nooperamadamebutterfly2023.

83 *"We decided":* Javier C. Hernandez, "Reimagining *Madame Butterfly* with Asian Creators at the Helm," *New York Times*, July 24, 2023, https://www.nytimes.com/2023/07/24/arts/music/madame-butterfly-asian-creators.html.

CHAPTER 4 The Singers

89 *At the time:* Anthony Tommasini, "Deborah Voigt as a Down-to-Earth Ariadne," *New York Times*, September 26, 1997, https://www.nytimes.com/1997/09/26/movies/opera-review-deborah-voigt-as-a-down-to-earth-ariadne.html.

90 *"Get this":* Matthew Westphal, "Covent Garden's Music Director Calls Deborah Voigt's Notorious Little-Black-Dress Tale 'Rubbish' (But Evidence Suggests Otherwise)," *Playbill*, April 4, 2007, https://playbill.com/article/covent-gardens-music-director-calls-deborah-voigts-notorious-little-black-dress-tale-rubbish-but-evidence-suggests-otherwise.

90 *The drama rapidly devolved:* Ibid.

90 *"When you hire":* Ibid.

92 *Or the so-called:* Manuela Hoelterhoff, *Cinderella and Company: Backstage at the Opera with Cecilia Bartoli* (New York: Alfred A. Knopf, 1998), 235.

92 *According to reports:* Matthew Boyden, "It's Not Over till the Fat Lady Sings," in *The Rough Guide to Opera*, ed. Joe Staines (London: Rough Guides, 2002), 232.

92 *In the early 1950s:* Peter Clark, "Maria Callas at the Met," Metropolitan Opera, https://www.metopera.org/discover/archives/notes-from-the-archives/maria-callas-at-the-met/.

93 *In 2006:* Gundula Kreuzer, "Operatic Configurations in the Digital Age," *Opera Quarterly* 35, no. 1–2 (Winter-Spring 2019): 130, https://doi.org/10.1093/oq/kbz017.

105 *The more realistic:* Gabrielle Kazuko, "Opera Audition, Seen from Both Sides," *Seattle Opera Blog*, July 1, 2016, https://www.seattleoperablog.com/2016/07/opera-auditions-seen-from-both-sides.html.

107 *Singers of color:* Emma Halpern, "Race and Performance: A Brief History," in *Racial and Ethnic Diversity in the Performing Art Workforce*, ed. Tobie S. Stein (New York: Routledge, 2019), 32.

107 *In 1925:* Robin Elliott, "Blacks and Blackface at the Opera," in *Opera in a Multicultural World*, eds. Mary I. Ingraham, Joseph So, and Roy Moodley (New York: Routledge, 2015), 42.

108 *For example, soprano:* Chris Pasles, "Yoko Watanabe, 51; Japanese Soprano Known for *Butterfly*," *Los Angeles Times*, July 27, 2004, https://www.latimes.com/archives/la-xpm-2004-jul-27-me-watanabe27-story.html.

108 *As recently as 2022:* Martin Kettle, "*Otello* Review: A Truly Compelling and Long Overdue Revival," *Guardian*, July 13, 2022, https://www.theguardian.com/music/2022/jul/13/otello-review-a-truly-compelling-and-long-overdue-revival.

108 *Opera was now technically:* Maurice B. Wheeler, "An Unlikely Champion: Rudolf Bing and the Demise of Jim Crow at the Metropolitan Opera," *Notes* 75, no. 2 (December 2018): 228, https://www.jstor.org/stable/26781987.

108 *A handful:* Linda Hutcheon and Michael Hutcheon, "Jazz, Opera, and the Ideologies of Race," in *Opera in a Multicultural World*, eds. Mary I. Ingraham, Joseph So, and Roy Moodley (New York: Routledge, 2015), 25.

109 *In other words:* Nina Sun Eidsheim, *The Race of Sound: Listening, Timbre and Vocality in African American Music* (Durham: Duke University Press, 2019), 67.

109 *Meanwhile, all the other:* Jami Rogers, *British Black and Asian Shakespeareans: Integrating Shakespeare, 1966–2018* (London: Bloomsbury, 2022), 136–37.

109 *But to be fair:* Wallace McClain Cheatham, ed., *Dialogues on Opera and the African-American Experience* (Lanham, MD: Scarecrow Press, 1997), 137.

110 *The concept first:* Angela C. Pao, *No Safe Spaces: Re-Casting Race, Ethnicity, and Nationality in American Theater* (Ann Arbor: University of Michigan Press, 2011), 3–4.

110 *Pryce had previously:* Kristin Bria Hopkins, "There's No Business like Show Business: Abandoning Color-Blind Casting and Embracing Color-Conscious Casting in American Theatre," *Journal of Sports & Entertainment Law* 9, no. 2 (2018): 137–38, https://journals.law.harvard.edu/jsel/wp-content/uploads/sites/78/2018/06/HLS201.pdf.

111 *Mackintosh then:* Pao, *No Safe Spaces*, 56.

111 *A mitigating factor:* Ibid., 57.

111 *"We're committed":* Michaela Boland and Mary Lloyd, "*West Side Story* on Sydney Harbour Reignites Debate on Racial Casting," ABC News, March 22, 2019, https://www.abc.net.au/news/2019-03-22/west-side-story-revamped-at-opera-house/10924814.

111 *Or take LA Opera's:* Catherine Womack, "Demonstrators Protest L.A. Opera over Casting of White Singer as an Egyptian Pharaoh," *Los Angeles Times*, November 6, 2016, https://www.latimes.com/entertainment/arts/la-et-cm-opera-akhnaten-protest-20161106-story.html.

112 *Or Houston Grand Opera's:* Scott Cantrell, "Of Race and Opera: *Nixon in China* Provokes a Debate on Stereotypes," *Dallas Morning News*, February 5, 2017, https://www.dallasnews.com/arts-entertainment/performing-arts/2017/02/05/of-race-and-opera-nixon-in-china-provokes-a-debate-on-stereotypes/.

112 *But the bigger fallacy:* Naomi André, *Black Opera: History, Power, Engagement* (Urbana: University of Illinois Press, 2016), 14.

113 *Consider conservative writer:* Heather Mac Donald, "Can Opera Survive the Culture Wars?," *UnHerd*, July 27, 2021, https://unherd.com/2021/07/can-opera-survive-the-culture-wars/.

114 *Deciding that a singer:* Mary I. Ingraham, Joseph K. So, and Roy Moodley, eds., *Opera in a Multicultural World* (New York: Routledge, 2015), 3.

114 *Or, as arts journalist:* Anne Midgette, "In Theater and Film, We Demand That Asian Roles Be Played by Asian Actors. Why Is Opera Different?," *Washington Post*, April 29, 2017, https://www.washingtonpost.com/entertainment/music/opera-wants-more-realistic-portrayals-but-in-casting-its-all-about-the-voice/2017/04/27/3a5a46e0-29f0-11e7-b605-33413c691853_story.html.

115 *"I've often wondered":* "Responses to *Madame Butterfly* from Members of the Asian Opera Alliance," San Francisco Opera, https://www.sfopera.com/digital/exhibit/madame-butterfly/aoa-responses/.

116 *Black women are still:* Hutcheon and Hutcheon, "Jazz, Opera, and the Ideologies," 25.

116 *Meanwhile, Black male singers:* Cheatham, *Dialogues on Opera*, 115–16.

116 *Then there's the matter:* Ellen Noonan, *The Strange Career of Porgy & Bess: Race, Culture, and America's Most Famous Opera* (Chapel Hill: University of North Carolina Press, 2012), 8.

116 *In a webinar:* Long Beach Opera, "Equity and Diversity in the Arts—a Community Conversation by Long Beach Opera," June 2020, YouTube, 2:46:33, https://www.youtube.com/watch?v=L5nScHjvlno.

117 *In 1977:* Ingraham, So, and Moodley, *Opera in a Multicultural*, 3.

117 *In 2023:* "Responses to *Madame Butterfly*," San Francisco Opera.

117 *Tenor Frederick Ballentine:* Mike Silverman, "'No Path Is Easy': Black Opera Singers Detail Struggles," Associated Press, September 20, 2019, https://apnews.com/arts-and-entertainment-music-general-news-9f4a93c655d54cfbad9cafd36c768775.

CHAPTER 5 The Show

122 *But rehearsals:* Susan Letzler Cole, *Directors in Rehearsal: A Hidden World* (Abingdon, UK: Routledge, 1992), 1.

123 *Company leadership:* Paola Trevisan, *Reshaping Opera: A Critical Reflection on Arts Management* (Newcastle upon Tyne: Cambridge Scholars, 2017), 17–18.

123 *Take the revival production:* Rehearsal schedule provided by production stage director Mary Birnbaum.

124 *The culmination:* Martin Constantine, *The Opera Singer's Acting Toolkit: An Essential Guide to Creating a Role* (London: Bloomsbury, 2020), 268.

125 *A particular quirk:* Danielle Ranno, *The Beginner's Guide to Opera Stage Management: Gathering the Tools You Need to Work in Opera* (New York: Routledge, 2023), 73.

125 *The director starts:* Constantine, *Opera Singer's Acting*, 257.

125 *A key focus:* Joshua Jampol, "Robert Carsen, or Building the Bridge Between Head and Heart," in *Living Opera* (Oxford: Oxford University Press, 2010), 25.

126 *In what is known:* Ranno, *Beginner's Guide*, 127.

127 *The* Wandelprobe*:* Ibid., 140.

127 *But the Final Dress Rehearsal:* Ibid., 142.

130 *Too many missed:* Susan Bullock, Charles Edwards, Keith Warner, and Tash Siddiqui, "A Director Prepares: A Roundtable in the Rehearsal Room," *Wagner Journal* 18, no. 2 (2024): 45.

136 *American soprano:* Michael Cooper, "You're Unfired: Kathleen Battle Is Returning to the Met After 22 Years," *New York Times*, April 4, 2016, https://www.nytimes.com/2016/04/05/arts/music/youre-unfired-kathleen-battle-is-returning-to-the-met-after-22-years.html.

136 *The soprano's reputed:* "22 Years After Famous Firing, Kathleen Battle Returns to Metropolitan Opera," *All Things Considered*, April 5, 2016, https://www.npr.org/2016/04/05/473139231/22-years-after-famous-firing-kathleen-battle-returns-to-metropolitan-opera.

137 *According to reports:* Martin Kettle, "A Tantrum Too Far," *Guardian*, December 13, 2006, https://www.theguardian.com/music/2006/dec/13/classicalmusicandopera.

139 *Since 2018:* Anne Midgette, "Assaults in Dressing Rooms. Groping During Lessons. Classical Musicians Reveal a Profession Rife with Harassment,

Washington Post, July 26, 2018, https://www.washingtonpost.com/entertainment/music/assaults-in-dressing-rooms-groping-during-lessons-classical-musicians-reveal-a-profession-rife-with-harassment/2018/07/25/f47617d0-36c8-11e8-acd5-35eac230e514_story.html.

139 *The long list of alleged:* Michael Cooper, "James Levine's Final Act at the Met Ends in Disgrace," *New York Times*, March 12, 2018, https://www.nytimes.com/2018/03/12/arts/music/james-levine-metropolitan-opera.html; Jocelyn Gecker, "AP: Women Accuse Opera Legend Domingo of Sexual Harassment," Associated Press, August 14, 2019, https://apnews.com/article/c2d51d690d004992b8cfba3bad827ae9; and Tresa Baldas, "Michigan Opera Theatre Conductor Stephen Lord Resigns amid Sex Scandal," *Detroit Free Press*, June 19, 2019, https://www.freep.com/story/news/local/michigan/detroit/2019/06/19/michigan-opera-theatre-conductor-stephen-lord-resigns/1499360001/.

144 *Back in 1908:* Robert M. Yerkes and John D. Dodson, "The Relation of Strength of Stimulus to Rapidity of Habit-Formation," *Journal of Comparative Neurology & Psychology* 18 (1908): 480–82, https://doi.org/10.1002/cne.920180503.

144 *The most common:* D. Garfield Davies, Anthony F. Jahn, and Anat Keidar, "Anxiety, Artistic Temperament and the Voice," in *Care of the Professional Voice: A Guide to Voice Management for Singers, Actors and Professional Voice Users* (New York: Bloomsbury Collections, 2004), 52; and Kristina Driskill, "Symptoms, Causes, and Coping Strategies for Performance Anxiety in Singers: A Synthesis of Research" (PhD diss., West Virginia University, 2012), 13.

144 *Then there are:* Driskill, "Symptoms, Causes," 14.

145 *Operatic voices:* Maria Sandgren, "Voice, Soma, and Psyche: A Qualitative and Quantitative Study of Opera Singers," *Medical Problems of Performing Artists* 17, no. 1 (2002): 14, https://doi.org/10.21091/mppa.2002.1003.

147 *Psychologists call it:* Anja-Xiaoxing Cui et al., "The Phantoms of the Opera—Stress Offstage and Stress Onstage," *Psychology of Music* 50, no. 3 (2022): 806.

148 *In a 2003 study:* Arnold B. Bakker, "Flow Among Music Teachers and Their Students: The Crossover of Peak Experiences," *Journal of Vocational Behavior* 66, no. 1 (2005): 37–38, https://doi.org/10.1016/j.jvb.2003.11.001.

148 *If you as an:* Daniel Meyer-Dinkgräfe, *Theatre, Opera and Consciousness: History and Current Debates* (Amsterdam: Editions Rodopi, 2013), 150.

CHAPTER 6 The Company

151 *Another for the ones:* Robert D. Hume, "Handel and Opera Management in London in the 1730s," *Music & Letters* 67, no. 4 (1986): 347.

151 *Some company deaths are:* Heidi Waleson, *Mad Scenes and Exit Arias: The Death of the New York City Opera and the Future of Opera in America* (New York: Metropolitan Books, 2018), 262.

152 *Take New York's:* Michael Cooper, "Gotham Opera's Liabilities Bring Scrutiny," *New York Times*, October 16, 2015, https://www.nytimes.com/2015/10/17/arts/music/gotham-operas-liabilities-bring-scrutiny.html#:~:text=Board%20members%20at%20Gotham%2C%20which,had%20%24116%2C758%20in%20outstanding%20liabilities.

152 *Consider London's:* Curtis Price, Judith Milhous, and Robert D. Hume, "The Rebuilding of the King's Theatre, Haymarket, 1789–1791," *Theatre Journal* 43, no. 4 (1991): 422.

153 *Consider the statistics:* OPERA America, *Annual Field Report + OPERA America Year in Review 2024*, 2, https://www.operaamerica.org/industry-resources/2025/202501/2024-annual-field-report/.

153 *Different companies use:* Paola Trevisan, *Reshaping Opera: A Critical Reflection on Arts Management* (Newcastle upon Tyne, UK: Cambridge Scholars, 2017), 23.

158 *As one opera insider:* Zachary Woolfe, "Why City Opera May Bite the Dust, and What That Means for New York," *Observer*, June 14, 2011, https://observer.com/2011/06/why-city-opera-may-bite-the-dust-and-what-that-means-for-new-york/.

158 *The standard union rate:* "Information for Detroit Opera AGMA Chorus Members," *Detroit Opera*, https://detroitopera.org/app/uploads/2023/10/OP_WC_INFORMATION-FOR-DETROIT-OPERA-AGMA-CHORUS-MEMBERS.pdf.

159 *Meanwhile, a single:* "Auditions," Metropolitan Opera, https://www.metopera.org/about/auditions/orchestra/.

159 *Next comes the cost:* "How Much Are Singers, Conductors and Directors Paid?," *Gramilano*, March 11, 2015, https://www.gramilano.com/2015/03/how-much-are-singers-conductors-and-directors-paid/.

159 *According to the: Agreement Between United Scenic Artists and the Broadway League Inc., 2023–2025*, United Scenic Artists, 6–7.

160 *All in all:* Trevisan, *Reshaping Opera*, 19.

160 *Next we need:* Ibid.

160 *Timber, fabric:* Chris Harvey, "Opera Designer Charles Edwards: 'It Costs as Much to Build a Set as It Does to Build a House,'" *Telegraph*, January 20, 2023, https://www.telegraph.co.uk/opera/what-to-see/opera-designer-charles-edwards-costs-much-build-set-does-build/.

161 *According to a report:* "The True Value of Opera," LA Opera, March 14, 2023, https://www.laopera.org/discover/la-opera-content/new-blog-post-27/.

162 *While the initial cost:* Philippe Agid and Jean-Claude Tarondeau, *The Management of Opera: An International Comparative Study* (Basingstoke, UK: Palgrave Macmillan, 2010), 65.

162 *Helmed by director:* Caitlin Vincent, *Digital Scenography in Opera in the Twenty-First Century* (Abingdon, UK: Routledge, 2022), 67.

163 *The physical set:* James B. Stewart, "A Fight at the Opera," *New Yorker*, March 16, 2015, https://www.newyorker.com/magazine/2015/03/23/a-fight-at-the-opera.

163 *In a 2012 review:* Alex Ross, "Diminuendo," *New Yorker*, March 4, 2012, https://www.newyorker.com/magazine/2012/03/12/diminuendo-2.

164 *Four performances cost:* "Production Rental: *La bohème*," Sarasota Opera, https://www.sarasotaopera.org/la-boheme-set-rental.

165 *For major companies:* "2023 Financial Statement," Lyric Opera of Chicago, https://www.lyricopera.org/about/financial-statements/2023-financial-statement/.

165 *At Opera Philadelphia:* Peter Drobrin, "Opera Philadelphia's $11 Ticket Program Is a Hit. So Why Is the Financial Outlook Still Uncertain?," *Philadelphia Inquirer*, August 30, 2024, https://www.inquirer.com/arts/opera-philadelphia-tickets-sold-out-season-financial-troubles-20240830.html.

165 *"Each year":* Janos Gereben, "SF Opera Makes Big Plans in Small Numbers for 2024–2025," *San Francisco Classical Voice*, February 20, 2024, https://www.sfcv.org/articles/music-news/sf-opera-makes-big-plans-small-numbers-2024-2025.

166 *Because even as costs:* James Heilbrun, "Baumol's Cost Disease," in *A Handbook of Cultural Economics*, 2nd ed., ed. Ruth Towse (Cheltenham, UK: Edward Elgar, 2011), 67.

166 *In the world of economics:* Michael Andor Brodeur, "As Opera Companies Struggle to Survive, a Sustained Note of Alarm," *Washington Post*, February 10, 2024, https://www.washingtonpost.com/entertainment/music/2024/02/10/opera-companies-crisis-struggling-closing/.

168 *In Europe:* Trevisan, *Reshaping Opera*, 26.

168 *In 2019:* Emily Bitto, "Where's Home for Theatre and Opera Director Barrie Kosky?," *Saturday Paper*, February 2–8, 2019, https://www.thesaturdaypaper.com.au/culture/theatre/2019/02/02/wheres-home-theatre-and-opera-director-barrie-kosky/15490260007382#hrd.

169 *The national flagship:* Caitlin Vincent, Katya Johanson, and Bronwyn Coate, "Risky Business: Policy Legacy and Gender Inequality in Australian Opera Production," *International Journal of Cultural Policy* 30, no. 5 (2023): 635, https://doi.org/10.1080/10286632.2023.2239266.

169 *Since the 1990s:* Trevisan, *Reshaping Opera*, 29–30.

169 *Spanish opera company:* "News: The Teatro Real Achieves Financial Stability with 30% of Public Funding and Without Debt," Teatro Real, https://www.teatroreal.es/en/news/teatro-real-achieves-financial-stability-30-public-funding-and-without-debt.

169 *At most, a respected:* Speight Jenkins, "The Cost of Opera," *OperaSleuth*, March 31, 2014, https://www.artsjournal.com/operasleuth/2014/03/the-cost-of-opera.html.

170 *A whale such as:* Robin Pogrebin, "Metropolitan Opera Receives $30 Million Gift," *New York Times*, March 26, 2010, https://www.nytimes.com/2010/03/27/arts/music/27gift.html.

170 *Or Alberto Vilar:* Jacqueline Trescott, "Alberto Vilar, Sui Generous," *Washington Post*, April 1, 2001, https://www.washingtonpost.com/archive/lifestyle/style/2001/04/01/alberto-vilar-sui-generous/596526f9-0aed-499b-885f-f60b53d42e9b/.

171 *According to a 2015 report:* Stewart, "Fight at the Opera."

171 *"One of the scariest things":* William Burnett, "An Interview with San Francisco Opera's David Gockley, Part 1," *Opera Warhorses*, November 17, 2009, https://operawarhorses.com/2009/11/17/an-interview-with-san-francisco-operas-david-gockley-part-one/.

171 *Precarious, mind you:* Janos Gereben, "Met Deficit Way Up, S.F. Opera Looks Good," *Classical Voice San Francisco*, November 23, 2014, https://www.sfcv.org/articles/feature/met-deficit-way-sf-opera-looks-good.

174 *Critic Tim Smith:* Tim Smith, "Figaro Project Gives Admirable Premiere of *Camelot Requiem*," *Baltimore Sun*, May 15, 2013, https://www.baltimoresun.com/2013/05/15/figaro-project-gives-admirable-premiere-of-camelot-requiem/.

174 *"The Figaro Project stuns":* Megan Ihnen, "In Performance: The Figaro Project Stuns with *Camelot Requiem*," *Sybaritic Singer*, May 13, 2013, https://sybariticsinger.com/2013/05/13/camelot/.

175 *First, we have our carbohydrates:* Stoyan V. Sgourev, "The Dynamics of Risk in Innovation: A Premiere or an Encore?," *Industrial and Corporate Change* 22, no. 2 (2013): 552, https://doi.org/10.1093/icc/dts021.

175 *Opera scholars:* Agid and Tarondeau, *Management of Opera*, 20.

176 *As a general rule:* Ibid., 22.

177 *New York City Opera's slow demise:* Waleson, *Mad Scenes*, 132.

179 *At Opera Australia:* Opera Australia, *2024 Annual Report*, 11, https://opera.org.au/app/uploads/2022/08/Opera-Australia-2024-Annual-Report.pdf.

179 *In 2023, audience numbers:* OPERA America, *Annual Field Report + OPERA America Year in Review 2024*, 2, https://www.operaamerica.org/industry-resources/2025/202501/2024-annual-field-report/.

180 *A 2024 report:* OPERA America, *Understanding Opera's New Audiences*, 10, https://www.operaamerica.org/media/05flentm/understanding-opera-s-new-audiences-research-report.pdf.

CHAPTER 7 The Career

186 *The traditional pathway:* Zach Finkelstein, Dana Lynne Varga, and Hillary LaBonte, "Excluded, Penalized, Indebted, Harassed: A Study of Systemic Discrimination Against Women in Opera," *Middleclass Artist*, November 24, 2020, https://www.theempoweredmusician.com/articles/excluded-penalized-indebted-harassed-systemic-discrimination-against-women-in-opera.

188 *Consider the Opera Studio:* "Voice," AIMS Graz, https://aimsgraz.com/the-program/voice/.

189 *New York's Glimmerglass Resident Artists Program:* "Resident Artists Program," Glimmerglass Festival, https://glimmerglass.org/resident-artists-program/; and "About the Program," Des Moines Metro Opera, https://desmoinesmetroopera.org/aboutAAP/.

191 *Consider American soprano:* Vivien Schweitzer, "Review: National Council Auditions Winners Named at Grand Finals Concert," *New York Times*, March 23, 2015, https://www.nytimes.com/2015/03/24/arts/music/review-national-council-auditions-winners-named-at-grand-finals-concert.html.

192 *As a measure:* Kate Williams, "Winners of the Inaugural Angela Meade Vocal Competition," Pacific Lutheran University, January 22, 2019, https://www.plu.edu/music/news/2019/01/22/angela-meade/.

192 *If a singer makes it:* "Operalia Prizes," Operalia World Opera Competition, https://www.operaliacompetition.org/prizes/.

192 *The Filene Artist Program:* "About the Filene Artist Program," Wolf Trap Opera, https://www.wolftrap.org/opera/people/filene-artists.aspx#:~:text=Approximately%2015%2D20%20singers%20are,pool%20of%20approximately%20800%20applicants.

192 *Acceptance rates:* Francisco Salazar, "Wiener Staatsoper Announces Opernstudio Artists for 2022–23 & 2023–24 Seasons," *OperaWire*, October 24, 2022, https://operawire.com/wiener-staatsoper-announces-opernstudio-artists-for-2022-23-2023-24-seasons/#google_vignette.

194 *At the same time:* Finkelstein, Varga, and LaBonte, "Excluded, Penalized."

194 *In her book:* Susan Mohini Kane, *The 21st-Century Singer: Making the Leap from the University into the World* (Oxford: Oxford University Press, 2015), 4.

194 *In 2019, arts journalism site:* Anne Midgette, "Fleeing the Gilded Cage," NPR Classical, December 14, 2021, https://www.npr.org/sections/deceptivecadence/2021/12/14/1063035430/opera-singers-pandemic-covid-shutdown-career-freedom.

195 *And what a steal:* "Tuition, Fees, and Expenses—Student Budget for 2025–2026," Juilliard School, https://www.juilliard.edu/campus-life/tuition-financial-aid/tuition-fees-and-expenses.

197 *According to Susan Mohini Kane:* Kane, *21st-Century Singer*, 4.

203 *"It is one thing":* Timothy Bostwick, "Voices of COVID-19: René Barbera," National Association of Teachers of Singing, 2020, https://www.nats.org/Voices_of_COVID-19_-_Rene_Barbera.html.

205 *But Germany is where:* Alex Ross, "A Grand Tour of Germany's Opera Paradise," *New Yorker*, June 13, 2022, https://www.newyorker.com/magazine/2022/06/20/a-grand-tour-of-germanys-opera-paradise.

CHAPTER 8 The Culture

215 *For thirty-five years:* Devon M. Sayers and Morayo Ogunbayo, "North Carolina Radio Station Declines to Broadcast 6 Met Opera Performances over Objections to Content," CNN, October 3, 2023, https://edition.cnn.com/2023/10/03/us/nc-radio-station-wont-play-met-operas-reaj/index.html.

215 *one of more than four hundred:* "Sunday Matinee Broadcast Station Finder," Metropolitan Opera, https://www.metopera.org/user-information/articles-in-progress/radio/saturday-matinee-broadcasts/station-finder/.

215 *Proctor deemed:* Sayers and Ogunbayo, "North Carolina Radio Station."

215 *In a letter:* Deborah S. Proctor, "Opera Survey," WCPE—the Classical Station, August 31, 2023, https://theclassicalstation.org/wp-content/uploads/2023/10/Opera_Survey_scan.pdf.

216 *And, of course, the optics:* Jonathan Abrams and Javier C. Hernández, "North Carolina Radio Station Won't Ban Met Opera Broadcasts After All," *New York Times*, October 5, 2023, https://www.nytimes.com/2023/10/05/arts/music/met-opera-north-carolina-radio.html.

216 *In a short public statement:* Devon M. Sayers and Orayo Ogunbayo, "North Carolina Radio Station Will Now Air Full Season of New York's Metropolitan Opera Despite Previous Objections to Content," CNN, October 9, 2023, https://edition.cnn.com/2023/10/09/us/radio-station-reverses-met-decision-reaj/index.html.

217 *In a 1977 television comedy sketch:* "A New Music Recital," *The Carol Burnett Show*, Season 10, Episode 16, January 22, 1977, Music Lover, July 27, 2020, 1:55, https://www.youtube.com/watch?v=k20vMkklQgs.

218 *From roughly the 1890s:* Richard Begam and Matthew Wilson Smith, eds., *Modernism and Opera* (Baltimore: Johns Hopkins University Press, 2016), 5.

218 *Composers such as Arnold Schoenberg:* Carolyn Abbate and Roger Parker, *A History of Opera: The Last Four Hundred Years* (New York: W. W. Norton, 2015), 479.

218 *Subsequent twentieth-century:* Alex Ross, *The Rest Is Noise: Listening to the Twentieth Century* (New York: Farrar, Straus & Giroux, 2007).

218 *Computers, electronic music:* Caitlin Vincent, *Digital Scenography in Opera in the Twenty-First Century* (Abingdon, UK: Routledge, 2022), 114.

218 *Some of the results:* John McGrath, *Samuel Beckett, Repetition and Modern Music* (London: Routledge, 2017), 88.

218 *Not to be outdone:* Peter Edwards, *György Ligeti's "Le Grand Macabre": Postmodernism, Musico-Dramatic Form and the Grotesque* (London: Routledge, 2016), 2.

220 *In 2018, Mazzoli:* Michael Cooper, "The Met Is Creating New Operas (Including Its First by Women), *New York Times*, September 23, 2018, https://www.nytimes.com/2018/09/23/arts/music/metropolitan-opera-bam-public-theater-women.html.

221 *Consider the polite:* Harold C. Schonberg, "Always Strictly Business," *New York Times*, March 12, 1972, https://www.nytimes.com/1972/03/12/archives/letters-of-giuseppe-verdi-selected-translated-and-edited-by-charles.html.

222 *But for many:* David A. Jewell, "The Opera Is New, but Is It Good?," letter to the editor, *New York Times*, September 25, 1999, https://www.nytimes.com/1999/09/25/opinion/l-the-opera-is-new-but-is-it-good-667404.html.

223 *As the station's:* Proctor, "Opera Survey."

228 *The music for sci-fi classic:* Gillian Moore, "How György Ligeti Soundtracked *2001*, Inspired Radiohead and Composed Music like 'a Knife Through Stalin's Heart,'" *Guardian*, July 3, 2023, https://www.theguardian.com/music/2023/jul/03/how-gyorgy-ligeti-soundtracked-2001-inspired-radiohead-and-composed-music-like-a-knife-through-stalins-heart.

230 *Audience figures:* Francisco Salazar, "Contemporary Operas Average 65 Percent of Audience Attendance During Metropolitan Opera 2023–24 Season," *OperaWire*, June 14, 2024, https://operawire.com/contemporary-operas-average-65-percent-of-audience-attendance-during-metropolitan-opera-2023-24-season/#google_vignette.

Index

INDEX

INDEX